DEPORTATION *in* *the* AMERICAS

Walter Prescott Webb Memorial Lectures,
published for the University of Texas at Arlington
by Texas A&M University Press

DEPORTATION *in the* AMERICAS

Histories of Exclusion and Resistance

EDITED BY

Kenyon Zimmer and Cristina Salinas

CONTRIBUTORS

Rachel Ida Buff
Donna R. Gabaccia
David C. LaFevor
Natalia Molina
Emily Pope-Obeda
Pablo Yankelevich
Elliot Young
Kenyon Zimmer

Published for the University of Texas at Arlington
by Texas A&M University Press
College Station

Library of Congress Cataloging-in-Publication Data

Names: Zimmer, Kenyon, 1980- editor. | Salinas, Cristina, editor.
Title: Deportation in the Americas: histories of exclusion and resistance /
    edited by Kenyon Zimmer and Cristina Salinas; contributors, Rachel Ida
    Buff [and six others].
Description: First edition. | College Station: Published for the
    University of Texas at Arlington by Texas A&M University Press, [2018] |
    Series: Walter Prescott Webb memorial lectures; fifty-first | Adapted from
    the fifty-first annual Walter Prescott Webb Memorial Lecture Series. |
    Includes index.
Identifiers: LCCN 2017058029 (print) | LCCN 2018000719 (ebook) |
    ISBN 9781623496609 (ebook) | ISBN 9781623496593 |
    ISBN 9781623496593 (hardcover: alk. paper)
Subjects: LCSH: Deportation—America—History. | America—Emigration
    and immigration—Government policy—History. | Immigration
    enforcement—America—History. | Immigrants—Legal status, laws,
    etc.—America.
Classification: LCC JV6350 (ebook) | LCC JV6350 .D46 2018 (print) |
    DDC 364.6/8—dc23
LC record available at https://lccn.loc.gov/2017058029

A list of other titles in this series appears at the back of the book.

Contents

Chapter 6

Chapter 7

DEPORTATION *in* *the* AMERICAS

Introduction

From Immigration History to Deportation History

Donna R. Gabaccia

As a field of study, immigration history flourishes in part by remaining in dialogue with the many newer historiographies it has helped generate. Since 1973, when I began graduate studies at the University of Michigan, immigration historians have launched a succession of new historiographical grenades without exhausting nor destroying their field of origin. Now, the historical study of deportation has joined a group of new approaches to the study of a field that in 1973 was focused almost exclusively on the arrival, adaptation, and incorporation of immigrants to the United States.

Historical studies of the deportation of foreigners came to life rather slowly as the impact of earlier historiographical changes accumulated and as the numbers of deportees from the United States increased in the 1990s, sparking mobilizations for immigrant rights. Historiographically, in the 1970s and 1980s, my generation of scholars had first experimented with approaches that Samuel Bailey termed "village outward" to describe methods that tracked migrants in multiple directions and examined their ongoing connections to their birthplaces.[1] This was an early reminder that by no means does all human movement fit comfortably under the American umbrella of immigration history, with its attention to voluntary and permanent settlement. Next, in the 1980s and 1990s, a brilliant series of interventions peeled back the cracking veneer of the mythological American "nation of immigrants" to reveal a gatekeeping, white nation that excluded rather than welcomed people who were either not, or not quite, white.[2] More recently, border histories and histories of the expanding American empire have also encouraged studies of mobile people who were decidedly not immigrants in the traditional sense.[3] By the 1990s, many scholars trained as immigration historians proclaimed themselves to be "migration," "transnational," "global," or "world" historians of migration, or historians of "diasporas," "emigration," or "international" migration.[4]

Histories of American deportation have built on the foundation of these earlier historiographical shifts, and these influences can be seen throughout this volume. *Deportation in the Americas* contributes in four main ways to scholarly understandings of deportation as a type of coerced movement.

First, by incorporating insights from transnational and global histories, this collection offers a spatially larger and explicitly North American frame for the study of deportation. Its chapters nevertheless all acknowledge—as do the best transnational studies of migration—that the creation of immigration policy remains a national or "domestic" matter, to be determined largely by national legislatures. This is as true of Mexico or Canada as it is the United States, the three largest countries of the North American continent. Careful attention to national policies documents the diverse ways in which individual nations have repeatedly expanded their catalogs of excludable and therefore deportable human border-crossers. These catalogs of excluded categories in turn forged essential elements in the nation-building projects of all three countries—a key theme in the earlier historiography that deconstructed the American "nation of immigrants" paradigm. The excludable classes of migrants provide a key mechanism for constructing a national "us" and distinguishing it from an outsider and inadmissible "them." The resulting distinctions, like the nature of the nations being "made," differ significantly in Canada, Mexico, and the United States.

The second contribution of *Deportation in the Americas* is to show how domestically driven immigration policies nevertheless also always exist within a larger system of international (i.e., interstate or intergovernmental) relationships. Ultimately it is this international system that recognizes new states as sovereign and accepts or determines the boundaries constituting their sovereignty. This is why the writing of border histories, like transnational studies of migration, so often requires knowledge of the histories and historiographies of at least two countries, as well as their unique history of binational relations. For example, changes in US policy have often served as models to be taken up and implemented in neighboring countries and beyond; in some of the cases documented in *Deportation in the Americas*, the US government explicitly pressured its neighbors and allies to follow in the footsteps of US immigration policy. International relations, in other words, shapes nation-building projects. Furthermore, as noted by several authors throughout, deportation becomes possible only when the deporting state has a relationship to a second state that has agreed to accept the deportees.

Relationships among sovereign states have long been the special focus of international history; they have become increasingly interesting to immigration historians in the past decade.[5] The essays collected in this volume map webs of international connections that could either support or undermine the nationally determined deportation policies of any single country in North America. These webs extended not only to the smaller and larger countries of the Caribbean and Central and South America, but also to China, Russia, Australia, and the many countries of Europe. International relations define the "global" reach of *Deportation in the Americas*.

In the third main contribution of this volume, several of the chapters in *Deportation in the Americas* focus on the historical lives and experiences of deportees and immigrants themselves, thus mirroring another historiographical shift within international history toward highlighting the importance of so-called nonstate actors, including immigrants, in the international arena.[6] As nonstate actors, migrants who are deemed excludable live constantly under the threat of deportation, yet they have repeatedly chosen activism to defend or enhance their own rights to exist and to move about voluntarily. Never mere pawns of state and interstate policy, excludable migrants and deportees have fought back against deportation, detention, extradition, and stigmatization with whatever resources they could historically muster. Some of their resources emerged from within national and international law; some within communities of blood, culture, or affiliations of the like-minded, regardless of cultural identity. Ironically, perhaps, the pursuit of justice for and by deportable persons has at times worked to expand democratic practices within the very countries where border or immigration policies have aimed to instead limit the freedom of humans to move about freely in pursuit of their own agendas.[7]

Much like the earlier historians who broadened scholars' attention beyond immigration to include other kinds of movement, several of the essays in this volume push readers to think about other ways that states seek to control lives and mobility (e.g., through extradition and the removal of so-called anchor babies). Both share at least some resemblance to deportation—in the first case by forcing a person to go abroad on the request of another state, and in the second case by transforming US citizens (the American-born children of immigrant parents) into a deportable category. This fourth contribution of *Deportation in the Americas* is a reminder of other practices of exclusion and other forms of mobility control that are closely related to but not the same as deportation, and that may also spark resistance, conflict, and international diplomacy by state and nonstate actors.

As a scholarly undertaking, *Deportation in the Americas* is a product of both a very specific political moment and a long-term institutional commitment by the University of Texas at Arlington (UTA) to support scholarly collaboration on important and emerging historiographical themes. Since 1965, UTA has sponsored the Walter Prescott Webb Memorial Lecture Series. Rather than an annual stand-alone lecture, this program brings together groups of researchers to discuss, and subsequently publish, ongoing work. In March 2016, contributors David C. LaFevor, Natalia Molina, Pablo Yankelevich, Elliott Young, and Kenyon Zimmer met at UTA to discuss papers and to hear a keynote address, "'Our Badge of Infamy': The American Committee for the Protection of the Foreign Born, Multiracial Coalitions, and Repurposing of Immigrant Rights Advocacy, 1965–1980," by Rachel Ida Buff. Emily Pope-Obeda subsequently won the associated Webb-Smith Essay Competition, which solicits contributions on the Webb Lecture theme of the year. To broaden the collaboration still further, the editors of each Webb Lecture volume—in this case Cristina Salinas and Kenyon Zimmer—invite an outside scholar to prepare the introduction to the collected essays. (I was honored by their invitation.)

This collaboration on deportation was developed and the essays collected here were written, delivered, discussed, revised, and edited during the politically volatile years of 2016 and 2017. Much of the volatility of these years was sparked by ongoing controversies over how migration, international relations, and democracy have linked the United and Mexico —the two countries where all the contributors to this volume, save one, live and work.[8]

2016 was of course an election year in the United States, and the 2017 inauguration of Donald Trump as president intensified the country's ongoing debate about its borders, its relations to Mexico, its status as a nation of immigrants, and its fear of the eleven million people—roughly three-quarters of them from Mexico and Central America—who live in the United States without valid documentation. Although President Barack Obama had already been castigated as the "deporter in chief" by immigrant rights supporters, Trump followers repeatedly accused Obama of failing to control the country's border with Mexico and of being "too soft" on "illegal immigrants," for example by granting the right to work and study to "Dreamers" (immigrant children who had been brought without documentation to the United States by their parents), thus protecting them temporarily from deportation. Deportations fell rather sharply under Obama's administration—from more than twelve million during the Clinton years to ten million under the presidency of George W. Bush to only five million under Obama—largely because the number of entries across the southern border had diminished dramatically in the aftermath of the 2008 financial crisis. (Obama's main accomplishment as "deporter in chief" seems to have been what one group of specialists called "a pronounced shift in focus to the removal of recent border-crossers and criminals rather than ordinary status violators apprehended in the US interior."[9]) Trump's campaign promises to instead "build a wall" and to make Mexico pay for it produced a series of diplomatic crises but has not—as of this writing—been realized. Because Obama-era deportations had already depleted the population of "bad hombres"—Trump's code word for Mexican-born criminals—the number of deportations in early 2017 appears to be lower than in previous years. However, violent anti-immigrant public rhetoric and the decision of US Immigration and Customs Enforcement (ICE) to detain and in some cases deport activists and many long-term and well-integrated Mexican and Central American workers and community members have succeeded mainly in terrorizing immigrant communities and mixed status families around the United States.[10]

Mexico faced political turmoil of its own during these years, independent of the pressures placed on it by its northern neighbor. Efforts to build a more robust civil sphere culminated in Mexico's historic presidential election of 2000, which ended seventy years of one-party rule (the Institutional Revolutionary Party; PRI), but had the unintentional consequence of heightening opportunities for violent criminality among drug cartels and the suppression of popular political opposition, enhancing rather than ending popular distrust of the government. Struggling to control its own southern border, Mexico faced the challenge of integrating both individuals deported from the United States and those workers and family members who returned voluntarily in response to American xenophobia, the 2008 financial crisis, or the high unemployment levels that persisted during the subsequent extremely slow recovery. As Trump and his followers stigmatized undocumented Mexicans as criminals and further criminalized entry without inspection, Mexico also faced the difficult choice of either staunching or providing assistance to growing numbers of asylum-seekers from Central America, including unaccompanied minors traveling through the country in hopes of reaching the US border. There, in 2017, these Central American refugees outnumbered Mexican migrants among those apprehended by US border agents; many of the asylum-seekers, including children, languished in US detention centers, their fates uncertain as neither Mexico nor the United States showed much interest in providing asylum.[11]

It should come as no surprise that political conflict in the United States and Mexico added a measure of urgency to the work of the contributors to *Deportation in the Americas*. Historians regularly turn to analysis of the past as they seek to understand what is happening in the present. But precisely because current discussions of deportation in the United States have become so intemperate, it is important to emphasize at the outset how this UTA-based scholarly collaboration and the contributors to this volume also responded consciously to an existing and evolving historiography on deportation. This historiography is of considerable intellectual merit and worth honoring even more fully, as it allows future scholars to identify how to move beyond the essays that have been included here.

For contributors to *Deportation in the Americas*, the greatest historiographical inspiration seems to have come from publications from 2000 onward, focused almost exclusively on the United States and written from within several disciplines. Mae Ngai's 2004 study *Impossible Subjects*—which described how illegality (and thus deportability) were created in the United States[12]—and Daniel Kanstroom's 2007 historical overview *Deportation Nation: Outsiders in American History*[13] are foundational, with citations to each book included in five of this volume's seven essays. Sociologist John Torpey's 2000 book, which examines the invention of the passport, especially in Europe,[14] and political scientist Aristide R. Zolberg's 2006 survey of US immigration policy as a mechanism for selective inclusion and exclusion[15] provided other important conceptual resources (each cited in three of the essays), especially for those authors interested in how deportable categories were created by bureaucratic and administrative as well as legislative policies. Kelly Lytle Hernandez's 2010 study of American border patrols, *Migra!*[16] (also cited in three essays), encouraged contributors to consider how the implementation of policies at the border shaped transnational and binational relationships and experiences, while my own 2012 book *Foreign Relations*, cited by three contributors, encouraged greater attention to the intersection of migrant agency with the formal conduct of diplomacy.[17] Most of the historiographical shifts identified previously as foundational for historical studies of deportation are also fully acknowledged by this volume's contributors, with multiple references to whiteness studies, histories of the racialized exclusion and discrimination faced by Asian and Mexican migrants, and references to most major studies of American deportation.[18] By contrast, only the essays by David C. LaFevor and Pablo Yankelevich draw extensively on Mexican historiography, and the comparatively much sparser scholarship on Canadian exclusion and deportation is only lightly referenced.

The essay by Emily Pope-Obeda that introduces *Deportation in the Americas* clearly lays out the intersection of national immigration policy and international relations that must be central to the writing of a global history of deportation. "From its very inception," she writes, "immigration restriction was developed with one eye looking outward," suggesting that the nation cannot be the "proper and only scale at which to examine the practice of deportation." Pope-Obeda's "National Expulsions in a Transnational World" (chapter 1) culls from multiple archival examples of the confluence of national and international histories that she advocates. In doing so, she implicitly poses a number of troubling questions. For example, where exactly does the mobile, deportable person belong? The answer to that question is not always obvious, especially in a twentieth-century world of changing regimes and geopolitical borders. Even at the Canadian or Mexican borders, border-crossers deemed deportable may not be Mexican or Canadian nationals, and the course of their deportation proceedings rests ultimately on uneven networks of bilateral agreements that may or may not allow for their return to the country from which they entered the United States. Pope-Obeda's essay is particularly effective in showing how deportation practices can become an indirect tool of diplomacy and how an "outward gaze" on American deportation can reveal much about how nation-building and concepts of the nation develop from events occurring along, or beyond, the border. Ultimately Pope-Obeda concludes that deportation is "a fraught, global battlefield between competing authorities, modern methods of regulation and record-keeping, the unmanageability of the movement of peoples, and divergent discourses of nationalism."

In chapter 2, comparing how Cuba, Mexico, and other Central American and Caribbean nations have responded over time to changing US immigration policies and exclusions, Elliott Young also emphasizes the role of proliferating bi- and multilateral agreements in creating what he calls "transnational policing regimes." He documents greater resistance to America's demands for cooperation in its efforts to exclude Chinese migrants after 1880 on the part of Mexico and Cuba compared with Canada, but also shows how Cuba's Triscornia Immigration Detention Camp helped implement US policies well beyond American borders and how Mexico's revolutionary government pursued its own nation-building projects through facilitation of the repatriation of Mexican workers and families deported from the United States in the 1930s. Young includes fascinating, more recent examples of the ongoing construction of this transnational policing regime, with a focus on Ronald Reagan's interdiction policy, which pushed US borders far from its shores and had predictable consequences for Haitian asylum-seekers. In this context, more recent bilateral treaties on the suppression of smuggling among Caribbean basin nations also appear to function as mechanisms for policing human mobility. Today the consequences of more than a century of international efforts to police mobility transnationally include the extension, from Europe and the Mediterranean to the Americas, of what Aristide Zolberg termed the "remote control" of migrations. American officials train foreign consular and border officers to implement American laws and even collect biometric data on aspiring immigrants far outside American borders. The result, Young concludes, is a veritable "global lockdown" that has created a global regime of detention and deportation, shrinking options for people everywhere to move about in pursuit of their own goals and transforming many of them into criminals when they nevertheless cross borders without authorization.

In a detailed case study based on archival research in Mexico (chapter 3), David C. LaFevor explores the still poorly understood meaning of extradition and its relationship to both international deportation agreements and gendered nation-building projects. In Porfirian Mexico at the turn of the past century, the murder of the exiled ruler of Guatemala, General Barillas, by Guatemalan assassins in Mexico City raised the troubling possibility that Barillas's assassination had been masterminded in Guatemala. How could Porfirio Díaz respond to this violent expression of contempt for Mexican law, which demanded urban order? Mexico chose to pursue diplomacy but was unable to convince Guatemala's new rulers to extradite the politically well-connected witnesses Mexico wished to interrogate as possible instigators of the murderers. In a compelling and well-told story, LaFevor shows how both the inferred homosexuality of the murdered general and Mexican fears of "primitive" Guatemalan passions mattered in Mexican nation-building. Under Díaz, Mexico embraced the rule of international law and diplomacy as key markers of Mexico's civilized modernity. In this context, Guatemala's resistance posed a challenge both to national honor (symbolized as masculine, virile, and civilized) and to the authoritarian long-time president, Porfirio Díaz. Much can be learned from this incident about Mexican nationalism immediately prior to the Mexican Revolution: at one point, as the story unfolded, the Mexican press was demanding a duel, Guatemala was preparing for war, and the United States viewed Mexico as poised to conquer the rest of Central America to defend its honor and sovereignty. At issue in this dramatic case was the power of Mexican and Guatemalan states to define their own sovereignty within international law but also through their control of the mobility of their citizens across borders. Like deportation, extradition appears in LaFevor's work as a mechanism for the state control of human movement.

Pablo Yankelevich's chapter 4, "Undesirable Foreigners," also focuses on Mexico, as its postrevolutionary government sought to create a new Mexican nationalism to unite the country. In doing so, he creates the foundation for more effective future comparisons of immigration policy and nation-building across North America. In Mexico, too, immigration policy cannot be separated from nation-building; although the role of policy in distinguishing foreigners who can and cannot be included in the nation was similar in Mexico to the United States and Canada, foreigners as a group occupied a distinctive place in the Mexican revolutionary imaginary. Mexico's revolutionary nationalism was to be built on a notion of sovereignty that was expressed through explicitly wresting and protecting Mexico's resources from the control of foreigners (many of them American and Canadian). As a result, immigration policy in Mexico focused not merely on borders and entry but also on narrowing the rights of foreign residents, through, for example, limiting their ability to petition, to own property, to assemble and freely associate, and to be employed by the government. After a century of state support for the freedom of movement across its border and an overall desire to encourage immigration, after its revolution, Mexico imposed limits on entry for the first time and simultaneously granted the executive branch the right to expel foreigners from the country without any right to appeal. In Yankelevich's chapter, readers will see the invention of deportability assume rather different forms than the ones they may know from American history and historiography. Yet the reader may also identify similarities, especially in Mexico's 1926 expansion of excludable categories to encompass national and ethnic groups, including those of the "Negro race." Yankelevich's account provides a wider frame for interpreting Mexico's well-known xenophobic anti-Chinese campaigns of the 1930s. Further changes in Mexico's immigration policies in the 1930s were also implemented as Mexico sought to support and to some degree encourage the return of those being repatriated from the United States. Fear of exploitative foreigners persisted long after the Mexican Revolution, complicating Mexico's desire to attract immigrants, even as it imposed restrictions on their rights as residents.

In sharp contrast to essays focused on policy, Kenyon Zimmer's chapter 5, "Voyage of the *Buford*," uses the tools of social history to paint a rich portrait of the immigrants deported during a well-known incident of the first American red scare. Zimmer emphasizes the activism of the *Buford* deportees before, during, and after their detention and removal. To the degree possible, he traces the more than two hundred individuals who have remained rather hazy figures in accounts that focus instead on the famous (and better documented) deportees Emma Goldman and Alexander Berkman. Since many of the deportees were committed anarchists, they ultimately faced a grim future when the United States transported them to Soviet Russia. By surrounding his collective biography of the lives and travels of the *Buford* activists with demographic and international analysis, Zimmer makes important new observations. He reveals collusion between businessmen (notably Ford's sociological department) and the US Department of Justice, reminding us that many recent "*migra*" and ICE raids also have focused on immigrant workers in their workplaces, at times with the collusion of employers. The fact that the Department of Justice turned to employers reveals the considerable difficulty its agents faced in collecting sufficient intelligence to justify the deportation of largely Russian-speaking individuals. Overall, Zimmer deems the Palmer raids of 1919 a failure. He estimates that at least fifty thousand immigrants in the United States were deportable because of their political commitments, yet only a thousand or so were ultimately expelled. Latvia backed out of an initial agreement with the United States to transport the deportees across its territory, and further complicating US deportation plans, the Soviet Union declined to take additional deportees once it became clear the United States would not recognize its sovereignty. The main success of the Palmer raids, according to Zimmer, was the terrorization of immigrant communities and labor activists, introducing a period of quietude and reversals for the American labor movement and its largely immigrant workforce. He concludes that "the deportation and border enforcement regimes emerging in the United States and elsewhere were powerful, but not nearly as powerful as they imagined themselves to be." Their purpose, however, was to silence as much as to remove.

Like David C. LaFevor, Natalia Molina in "Deportable Citizens" (chapter 6) expands our understanding of the categories of people who become subject to state control of their mobility. The movement of children is almost everywhere tied to parental decision-making, but Molina's account notes that US-born infant children (who under American law are universally deemed to be citizens and therefore not deportable) have recently fallen into danger of having their citizenship denied—thereby making them deportable—if their parents cannot provide evidence of their own legal residency in the United States at the time of the child's birth. Molina traces the recent construction of the myth of the "anchor baby" in Texas and California to a longer twentieth-century discussion of American poverty, foreign birth, and the emergent American welfare state. Her analysis points toward linkages among popular understandings of a Latin "culture of poverty," disorganized black families, and so-called welfare queens with fears of racialized Latino welfare-seekers, largely children, in the run-up to the passage California's Proposition 187. Key to Molina's analysis is the observation that "anchor babies" are the products of already stigmatized mothers and of babies' unavoidable dependency. In the broadest sense, the development of an "anchor baby" discourse represents the extension to Mexican immigrant women of the "race suicide" claims of demographic

catastrophe made by Theodore Roosevelt regarding southern and eastern European immigrant women early in the twentieth century. Fears
of female and underage immigrants without male providers as "liable to
become public charges" also originated much earlier, and manifested
in some of the first immigration restrictions of the nineteenth century.
Molina offers an original examination of the little-known and ultimately
unsuccessful 1935 Kerr Act, which aimed to prevent immigrants of good
character (with no criminal offenses after ten years in the United States)
from being separated from their children during deportation proceedings,
largely by creating a stay on the parents' deportation and opening a path
to citizenship for the parents of citizen children. (She calls this a discussion of "white anchor babies," since it was largely congressmen from the
urban east, with European immigrants in mind, who supported the bill.)
The legislation found little support in California and Texas, the two sites
that became important in the later development of the anchor baby discourse. As children became one of the main beneficiaries (along with old
people) of the limited American welfare state created in the 1930s, they
also became the increasing focus of tax-cutters' passions in the 1980s and
1990s. Molina concludes that immigrant parents were deported because
they bore children who, as US citizens, qualified for government aid, rather
than children being deported as dependents of their parents. The de jure
citizenship of these American-born children, in other words, did not translate into social citizenship, at least in public discourse, and did not protect
them from deportation.

Like Kenyon Zimmer, in chapter 7 Rachel Ida Buff highlights the importance of deportable immigrants as historical actors in the United
States. As organizers of the American Committee for the Protection of the
Foreign-Born (ACPFB)—an organization founded in the 1930s and oper-
ating in scattered urban locales across the country until late in the twentieth century—immigrant Americans were vocal opponents of deportation
and other impingements on foreigners' rights to live, work, move about,
and mobilize in their new country, the United States. Borrowing from
Walter Prescott Webb (whose life is memorialized in the lecture series at
UTA), Buff repurposes Webb's concept of the "sharp edge of sovereignty"
as a tool deployed against and resisted by multiracial communities and
the immigrants affected by antiradical, antilabor, and xenophobic restrictions on immigrant rights. She focuses on key ACPFB publications
and campaigns that reveal the persistence and transformation over time

of 1930s Popular Front organizing strategies, as the ACPFB forged local, multiracial alliances to contest deportation, harassment, and attacks on the labor movement. Buff is especially interested in highlighting how the ACPFB encouraged the development of democratic resistance strategies among ever-changing groups of new immigrants and new immigrant communities. In her portrait of the ACPFB, migrants become important defenders of American democracy, determined to protect and extend human rights even as first Cold War and later neoliberal geopolitics shifted the United States from a position of advocating greater liberty to one of limiting the liberties even of its own citizens and foreign-born residents. In Buff's account, it comes as no surprise to the reader to learn that the Los Angeles ACPFB dissolved itself in order to focus its work more exclusively on defense of the Bill of Rights. Buff provides the historical background for understanding recent immigrants' rights marches and mobilizations as the latest example of newcomers' commitments to reinvigorating American democracy even as they seek to protect themselves from the American government.

Collectively, the contributors to *Deportation in the Americas* have begun to push the recent historiography on deportation into larger analytical and spatial arenas—the continental, the hemispheric, the Caribbean, the global—while remaining fully cognizant of the national dimensions, causes, and consequences of deportation for the lives of the immigrants who are subject to it. There is still a long way to go before a truly global reach can be fully attained, of course. As scholars continue to follow in the footsteps of the contributors to this volume, they may want to consider some earlier historiographical threads that were not fully exploited in the essays collected here. Some of these historiographical threads further encourage the problematization of the term "deportation" by focusing on the histories of colonization or forced mobility within individual nations, while others should encourage scholars to think cross-nationally in innovative ways as they move toward global analysis.

For example, already in the 1960s and 1970s, histories of African Americans in the United States sometimes characterized antebellum efforts to colonize Africa with former slaves and free blacks as a form of deportation, a historical precedent that needs to be brought into much more intensive dialogue with new research on the nineteenth- and twentieth-century deportations of foreigners.[19] Does deportation as part of a colonizing project differ from removal or ethnic cleansing, and if so, how? In this regard, earlier studies of "removal" of indigenous people throughout the nineteenth century in most of the countries of North and South America[20] also seem to require a broader yet simultaneously more explicitly comparative frame. Cross-national comparisons could illuminate how mobility and the control of mobility figured in nation-building and produced rather different understandings of national belonging in settler colonies, in former settler colonies that choose to become countries of immigration, and in countries with and without significant histories of coerced slave trades. Similarly, a burgeoning and exciting new scholarly literature on mass incarceration in the United States creates common ground for those interested in the expanding detention practices that accompany immigration, asylum-seeking, and deportation in the United States.[21] Comparative, cross-national studies are often particularly effective in exploring and identifying the range of practices that resemble deportation, even if they were labeled as something else at the time.[22]

Even today, most English-language scholarship on deportation focuses not on the United States or North America but on twentieth-century central Europe (especially Germany) and Asia. This emphasis may or may not be appropriate. Eventually scholars of North America will need to assess the global significance of the twenty-five million recent American deportations undertaken by the Clinton, Bush, and Obama administrations, as well as the earlier deportations from Canada, Mexico, and the United States. Do the dynamics of deportation follow or diverge from the dynamics of asylum-seeking, displacement, and other forms of coerced and forced movement? What analytical or spatial frame might best allow scholars to sort through their similarities and differences? A relatively easy step in that direction, for the early twentieth century, would be a straightforward comparison of the United States and Canada based on work done in the 1980s by Barbara Roberts and more recent studies for the United States by Daniel Kanstroom, Deirdre Moloney, and Torrie Hester.[23] More complex but even more urgent is the need for a survey of the wars of the twentieth century and the larger, changing geopolitical conflicts of the twenty-first century as they have shaped practices of deportation, extradition, ethnic cleansing, and the creation of refugees and asylum-seekers.

Kenyon Zimmer's chapter 5, which builds on a long-standing and quite rich historiography on deportation written by historians of American labor and radicalism,[24] particularly deserves emulation as scholars consider a broader spatial framing for their studies of deportation. Another modest, second step toward global analysis is Travis Tomchuk's work focusing on border-crossing anarchists as they moved back and forth between Canada and the United States.[25] Earlier work on both American immigrants involved in the Mexican Revolution[26] and Mexican revolutionaries' efforts to use the United States as a temporary place of refuge and mobilization[27] should be more widely read, acknowledged, and pursued as the foundation for eventual Atlantic- and Pacific-wide surveys of how deportation shaped the circulation and influence of radicals in an earlier age.

In chapter 1, Emily Pope-Obeda clearly outlines how future historians of deportation can productively and creatively design global research while remaining sensitive to the national causes and consequences of the phenomena they study. In a world where debates about human mobility are unlikely to cease and demands for additional restrictions on mobility are unlikely to disappear, the mobilizations of those subjected to what Rachel Ida Buff has called the "deportation terror" may very well remain one of the most important, if embattled, bastions for those who love liberty and understand mobility as essential to its pursuit.[28]

Notes

1. Samuel L. Baily, "The Village-Outward Approach to Italian Migration: A Case Study of Agnonesi Migration Abroad, 1885–1989," *Studi Emigrazione* 105 (1992): 43–68.

2. Roger Daniels, *Not Like Us: Immigrants and Minorities in America, 1890–1924* (Chicago: Ivan R. Dee, 1997); Erika Lee, *At America's Gates: Chinese Immigration During the Exclusion Era, 1882–1943* (Chapel Hill: University of North Carolina Press, 2003); Roger Daniels, *Guarding the Golden Door* (New York: Hill & Wang, 2004). The following approach produced a somewhat contentious new immigration history synthesis: Paul Spickard, *Almost All Aliens: Immigration, Race, and Colonialism in American History and Identity* (New York: Routledge, 2007).

3. Jeremy Adelman and Stephen Aron, "From Borderlands to Borders: Empires, Nation-States, and the Peoples in between in North American History," *The American Historical Review* 104, no. 3 (1999): 814–41. Border-crossers included both daily commuters and visitors from families living on both sides of borders, plus many who left their countries temporarily as tourists, students, missionaries, businessmen, investors, and in the case of US citizens, advocates and builders of American empire and international influence.

4. Donna Gabaccia, "Thoughts on the Future of Transnational History," *Yearbook of Transnational History* (forthcoming).

5. Patrick Finney, "Introduction: What Is International History?" *Palgrave Advances in International History,* ed. Patrick Finney (London: Palgrave Macmillan, 2005), 1–35; Donna Gabaccia, *Foreign Relations: American Immigration in Global Perspective* (Princeton: Princeton University Press, 2012).

6. Michael J. Hogan, "The 'Next Big Thing': The Future of Diplomatic History in a Global Age," *Diplomatic History* 28, no. 1 (2004): 1–21.

7. Rachel Ida Buff, ed., *Immigrant Rights in the Shadows of Citizenship* (New York: New York University Press, 2008).

8. With three years of residency in Toronto, I am the only nominally Canadian contributor to the group, and Canada remains a somewhat spectral presence in this volume's analysis of North America. Canada also saw a rather dramatic shift in government, from conservative to liberal leadership, in 2015, and the change from Harper's conservative to Trudeau's liberal government precipitated choices to accept more refugees from Syria and to begin repositioning Canada as the paradigmatic nation of immigrants for the twenty-first century—potentially replacing the United States as an international symbol. Although Canadians today constitute the largest national group of visa overstayers living in the United States, rendering about 100,000 of them deportable, they are infrequently deported, and Americans rarely complain about Canadians' numbers or impact on the United States. In addition, the long, porous border that the United States shares with Canada fails to produce the same level of controversy or perceived crises as the border it shares with Mexico, as several of this volume's chapters analyzing the Mexican border and deportations of Mexicans critically note.

9. Muzaffar Chishti, Sarah Pierce, and Jessica Bolter, "The Obama Record on Deportations: Deporter in Chief or Not?" *Migration Information Source,* January 26, 2017, http://www.migrationpolicy.org/article/obama-record-deportations-deporter-chief-or-not (accessed June 19, 2017).

10. Adam Goodman, "The Long History of Self-Deportation," *NACLA Report on the Americas* 49, no. 2 (2017): 152–53.

11. Jessica Bolter, "The Evolving and Diversifying Nature of Migration to the U.S.-Mexico Border," *Migration Information Source,* February 16, 2017, http://www.migrationpolicy.org/article/evolving-and-diversifying-nature-migration-us-mexico-border (accessed June 21, 2017).

12. Mae Ngai, *Impossible Subjects: Illegal Aliens and the Making of Modern America* (Princeton: Princeton University Press, 2004).

13. Daniel Kanstroom, *Deportation Nation: Outsiders in American History* (Cambridge: Harvard University Press, 2007).

14. John Torpey, *The Invention of the Passport: Surveillance, Citizenship and the State* (Cambridge: Cambridge University Press, 2000).

15. Aristide R. Zolberg, *A Nation by Design: Immigration Policy in the Fashioning of America* (New York: Harvard University Press, 2006).

16. Kelly Lytle Hernández, *Migra! A History of the US Border Patrol* (Berkeley: University of California Press, 2010).

17. Gabaccia, *Foreign Relations.*

18. Kitty Calavita, *US Immigration Law and the Control of Labor, 1820–1924* (London: Academic Press, 1984); George Sanchez, *Becoming Mexican American: Ethnicity, Culture and Identity in Mexican American Los Angeles, 1900–1945* (New York: Oxford University Press, 1993); Francisco E. Balderrama and Raymond Rodríguez, *Decade of Betrayal: Mexican Repatriation in the 1930s* (Albuquerque: University of New Mexico, 1996); Lee, *At America's Gates*; David Roediger, *Working toward Whiteness: How America's Immigrants Became White—The Strange Journey from Ellis Island to the Suburbs* (New York: Basic Books, 2005); Rachel Ida Buff, "The Deportation Terror," *American Quarterly*, 60, no. 3 (2008): 523–51; Deirdre Moloney, *National Insecurities: Immigrants and U.S. Deportation Policy Since 1882* (Chapel Hill: University of North Carolina Press, 2012); Elliott Young, *Alien Nation: Chinese Migration in the Americas from the Coolie Era through WWII* (Chapel Hill: University of North Carolina Press, 2014); Moon-Ho Jung, ed., *The Rising Tide of Color: Race, State Violence, and Radical Movements across the Pacific* (Seattle: University of Washington Press, 2014); Torrie Hester, *Deportation: The Origins of U.S. Policy* (Philadelphia: University of Pennsylvania Press, 2017).

19. To cite just one early example, see Don B. Kates, "Abolition, Deportation, Integration: Attitudes toward Slavery in the Early Republic," *Journal of Negro History* 53, no. 1 (1968): 33–47.

20. Compare, for example, the analysis of deportation by Adam Goodman, "The Long History of Self-Deportation," and Sarah H. Hill, "'To Overawe the Indians and Give Confidence to the Whites': Preparations for the Removal of the Cherokee Nation from Georgia," *Georgia Historical Quarterly* 95, no. 4 (winter 2011): 465–97.

21. Michelle Alexander, *The New Jim Crow: Mass Incarceration in the Age of Color Blindness*, revised edition (New York: The New Press, 2011).

22. See, for example, David Eltis, ed., *Coerced and Free Migration: Global Perspectives* (Stanford: Stanford University Press, 2002).

23. Barbara Ann Roberts, *Whence They Came: Deportation from Canada, 1900–1935* (Ottawa: University of Ottawa Press, 1988). See also notes 13 and 18.

24. Early studies of deportation of radicals appearing in historical journals include John H. Lindquist, "The Jerome Deportation of 1917," *Arizona and the West* 11, no. 3 (1969): 233–46; and John H. Lindquist and James Fraser, "A Sociological Interpretation of the Bisbee Deportation," *Pacific Historical Review* 37, no. 4 (1968): 401–22.

25. Travis Tomchuk, *Transnational Radicals: Italian Anarchists in Canada and the U.S., 1915–1940* (Winnipeg: University of Manitoba Press, 2015).

26. Paul Avrich, *Sacco and Vanzetti: The Anarchist Background* (Princeton: Princeton University Press, 1991). See also Michele Presutto, "The Revolution Just around the Corner: Italian American Radicals and the Mexican Revolution, 1910–1914," *Italian American Review* 7, no. 1 (2017): 8–40.

27. William Dirk Raat, *Revoltosos: Mexico's Rebels in the United States, 1903–1923* (College Station: Texas A&M University Press, 2000).

28. Buff, "The Deportation Terror."

1

National Expulsions in a Transnational World

THE GLOBAL DIMENSIONS OF AMERICAN DEPORTATION PRACTICE, 1920–1935

Emily Pope-Obeda

A 1925 *Nation* editorial entitled "Italy's Idea of Housecleaning" discussed Mussolini's political expulsions and exile of criminals, and criticized his widespread persecution and political oppression of dissenters.[1] Meanwhile, right at home in the United States, government officials were embarking on their own housekeeping mission, which was frequently compared to such projects abroad. By the following year, not only would local press in the midst of a deportation drive in Chicago argue that Mussolini's tactics ought to be lauded and emulated for the safety of the worthy citizens of that city, but, in fact, the exact same language of "housekeeping" would be used to describe raids against Italian immigrants there. "He is a poor householder who will not get rid of the rats that ravage his larder and endanger the health of his family," wrote one Chicago editorialist in February of 1926. Looking again across the ocean for a model of how to create social stability through the exile of criminals, the author proclaimed of Italian criminals: "the task of completely cleaning them up is nearly at an end." The writer argued that the immigration authorities in Chicago stood to learn from such practices.[2]

Deportation has been largely understood as the process of a single nation-state asserting and enforcing its borders through the expulsion of "undesirable" noncitizens. But as the previous example shows, from its very inception, immigration restriction was developed with one eye looking outward.[3] The deportation policies enacted in the United States during the interwar years, which provided a foundation for the rest of the twentieth century, were not shaped in national isolation. Instead, they were formed within global networks of communication, with the collaboration of officials stationed around the world and with a fundamentally global imagination. Those responsible for turning American deportation law into reality during the 1920s and early 1930s both repudiated the practices of some nations and aspired to those of others. At the same time, local officials often struggled even to identify, document, and enforce the national belonging of immigrants who were, in many cases, thoroughly transnational individuals whose lives, families, and experiences could not be compartmentalized into any single nation. The nascent American deportation regime also faced severe criticism, primarily from American radicals, which was enunciated in a language of internationalism. As the United States sought to enforce its political will and police its own borders, it gradually became clear that this could not be accomplished merely by stationing guards at the ports and patrolmen on the border—the Immigration Service would be required to send officials abroad, coordinate with foreign governments, and communicate with a wide range of global actors. Furthermore, officials on the ground soon discovered that they would not be able to enact deportation laws just as they were written on paper, but would have to develop coping mechanisms of flexibility and discretion to deal with the untidy global realities outside their borders.

This chapter delineates the wide and critical divergence between deportation as policy and deportation as practice. Deportation as a plan on paper already bore the imprint of a broader global reality, if only in the plain fact that while deportation might have begun in the United States, it required a receiving nation to be completed. However, deportation in its implementation is a much more complex terrain of transnational actors, discourses, and politics. Congressional figures, though undoubtedly informed by global conversations and the development of parallel legislation abroad, have been the most noted, and also the most unambiguously national, figures in most scholarship on deportation.[4] However, a multiplicity of other actors, both state and nongovernmental, also shaped the actual implementation of deportation as profoundly as legislators ever could: the private citizens who turned in neighbors or strangers to immigration authorities for deportation, the governments that denied the passage of deportees through their borders en route to their final destinations, weather patterns in certain regions that prevented deportation ships from traveling during some months of the year, the nongovernmental organizations conducting public opinion campaigns spanning many nations, and the deportees themselves, with their complicated, nonlinear lives.

Globalizing the History of Deportation

Because accounts of deportation are so often studies of national policy, they have tended to overemphasize federal power and to characterize deportation as a process determined solely within the borders of a single country.[5] The practice of deportation in the early twentieth century, however, presented a much more complex set of decision-making authorities, practical considerations, and ideological frameworks for expulsion. Because deportation is about placing constraints around who can belong and remain within a nation's borders, it has been easy for historians to assume that the process of marking out those constraints has been predominantly a national one. This chapter complicates that assumption and reveals the ways in which the global context, by way of policy and legislation, the exchange of ideas, the shifting imperial landscape, and transnational individuals, communities, and organizations were crucial in determining the operation of America's nascent deportation regime.

While immigration might seem to be among the most transnational aspects of American history, scholars of immigration policy have been slow to embrace the possibilities for examining the networks of communication, contact, and political engagement that have shaped its trajectory. In fact, as late as 1990, Robert Tucker argued that "the dogma that the regulation of immigration was solely the prerogative of the sovereign state went unquestioned. In consequence, the tradition of unilateralism with respect to immigration was, if anything, even more pronounced than it was in U.S. foreign policy generally."[6] In recent years, there has been a growth of scholarship engaging with migration as a complex and multidirectional process, focusing on subjects such as return migration, the global economy of remittances, and cultural continuity and hybridization across borders. This transnational shift has encompassed both topic choice and discourse. As Jorge Duany notes, "Migration studies have recently experienced a semantic explosion of key terms such as *diaspora, transnationalism, exile,* and *exodus.*"[7] In addition, there is an increased interest in the relationship between foreign policy and the ostensibly, though curiously, domestic policy of immigration. Donna R. Gabaccia's *Foreign Relations: American Immigration in a Global Perspective* performs some of the critical work of expanding knowledge about the relationship between immigration and foreign relations, thoroughly refuting the idea that the United States operated in isolation and unilaterally through most of its history. As she points out, in spite of the tendency to view US foreign policy and immigration as isolationist, immigration was always part of the expanding global economy and empires of the nineteenth century, and the domestic political struggles over restrictionism rose not because of isolationism but as a reaction to growing internationalism.[8] While scholars are increasingly recognizing the inherently transnational nature of deportation as a form of forced migration from one state to another, there is still a tendency within the field to view deportation as a unilateral set of decisions and actions by a single state entity.[9]

At a very basic level, deportation is about the physical transportation of a migrant from the state of his or her current residence to another state, most commonly that of his or her birthplace or citizenship. While exile and other forms of forced removal have existed for centuries, the late nineteenth and early twentieth century witnessed an important increase in state capacities to track the movements of individuals, and to record and trace their legal status from nation to nation. The introduction of the passport system facilitated the rise of deportations, as the capacity for tracking, surveillance, and documentation led to unprecedented possibilities for shaping the population of the national body through expulsion. Daniel Turack explains that while it is commonly accepted that a state has the "right to expel aliens through deportation," this process, which may seem like a "unilateral act" because the power to deport is in the hands of a single state, is actually a much more international quandary. Stating the obvious but remarkably overlooked point, Turack explains, "Of consequence, the deportee has to be deported somewhere.... In any case, the consent of the country to which the deportee is to be sent must be obtained before the act of deportation can be consummated."[10] Too often, scholars of immigration restriction and deportation have focused exclusively on these processes within the United States, therefore reifying the state's presentation of itself as an all-powerful determiner of who may remain in its borders.[11]

Another important development in the scholarship on deportation has been to place it within a comparative framework of various kinds of forced removal or exile. While deportation has developed as a specific form of government-ordered, involuntary removal by an administrative agency of the state, it does not exist outside of a spectrum of various forms of forced or pressured removal, expulsion, and exile. As Richard Bessel and Claudia Haake have argued, understanding deportation as part of a broader phenomenon of "forced removal" suggests "that these very same processes have often been shaped by actors and agents other than just the state."[12] Furthermore, they explain, the motivations for the involvement of non-state actors "often diverged significantly from those of governments," and were also part of a discourse in which targets of removal were more than passive victims.[13] At a moment when, across the globe, nation states were marked by a rising concern with delineating the boundaries of populations by transporting unwanted individuals and communities from their midst, removal practices took a wide variety of forms.[14]

It is a misrepresentation of deportation to think of it as a process that is primarily or exclusively rooted in the creation of stronger American borders, and the implementation of American political will regarding who could belong within the national body. At every level, from public opinion to federal law, American deportation practices were the product of an already global world. While the rise of deportation during the interwar period certainly represented a renewed desire to cordon off the boundaries of inclusion and exclusion along lines of race, class, sexuality, political orientation, and morality, this goal had to be pursued in a global reality in which American authority was internationally challenged and redirected by a range of state and nonstate actors. Elected officials themselves were divided about what immigration restriction should look like, as demonstrated by debates over exempting the Western Hemisphere from quotas under the National Origins Act of 1924 in order to maintain an open flow of low-wage labor. But even as American officials, ideologues, and nativist organizations succeeded in achieving more expansive deportation laws aimed at creating their idealized American populace—the composition of which varied heavily—they found the implementation of these laws to be its own challenge, in no small part because of global constraints.

While I will focus primarily on deportation rather than exclusion at the point of entry, it is essential to note that the struggle to properly discern national origins went beyond postentry removals. Under the National Origins Act, the nascent quota system required officials to ascertain the appropriate nationality of a given immigrant in order to know what quota they should be counted against (a process often complicated by individuals who lived outside their nations of birth for many years before immigrating to the United States). For admissions and exclusions, as well as deportations, this proved to be a challenging feat, particularly for migrants from regions where World War I had shifted national boundaries or freed migrants from sites of imperial control.[15] While the American immigration service stubbornly imagined migrants as national subjects, it continued to be plagued by the reality of transnational individuals and communities in a globalized world. These complications demonstrate the insufficiency of a national narrative in which the American government was the sole and all-powerful arbiter of its own immigration policy, and reveals how heavily constrained by global realities outside American control this policy has always been. The ineffectuality of national policy was often a frustration, or even an embarrassment, as officials regularly discovered they could not make sense of where individuals fit into geopolitical boundaries and therefore struggled to affect their expulsion from the United States.

On some occasions, immigration agents grappled with where to send residents of European imperial possessions in Africa, debating over whose responsibility it was to accept the deported individuals. In other instances, multigenerational families of migrants struggled for the right to be handled together despite the fact that members had been born in different countries as the family traveled across the globe for work opportunities. The 1922, case of a family that had arrived from Honduras reflected the complex paths taken by many migrants, and revealed the deep confusion surrounding the application of quotas and eligibility for removal. They were described as a "rather high class family of Russians," made up of two grandparents, an uncle, and two minor children born in Australia. The family's case was further complicated by the fact that the children's parents were residing in Colombia with their two youngest children. After migrating from Australia to Tegucigalpa and subsequently deciding the United States would be "a more satisfactory country to live in," the family attempted to migrate to the United States with $7,000 and a plan to buy and operate a dairy farm. However, in spite of an immigration official's note that "the aliens are far above the average European immigrant in point of education, native intelligence, and general appearance and bearing," they faced deportation. While the grandparents, Alexandria and

Nicolas Illin, and their son Romelio were considered eligible under the
Russian quota that was not yet exhausted for the year (with immigration
officials making a note that while Romelio was born in Siberia, unlike his
parents, this fell under the same categorization within the act), Romelio's
niece and nephew, Nellie and Hector McKay, had been born in Australia
and the hearing board thus ruled that they should be excluded as exceed-
ing that country's quota. Despite a testimonial from the sergeant of police
at Atherton, Australia, vowing that the family had excellent character and
"take no active part in any political matter, but they are very antagonistic
to Bolshevik ideas," officials moved forward with removal proceedings.
Ultimately, the family departed voluntarily to Honduras rather than appeal the deportation order.[16] While the case of the Illin family is unusually
complex, it demonstrates the deep challenges that immigration officials
met with in attempting to effectuate deportations during a period of great
mobility.

My work pushes against the category of the nation as the proper and
only scale at which to examine the practice of deportation. I examine the
ways that other nations constrained, inspired, contested, and communi-
cated with the United States and its process of enacting deportation legislation in the interwar decades. America strove to map its power onto the
rest of the world, and deportation policy demonstrates how imperfectly
this goal was realized. I begin by tracing the complicated global landscape
in which Americans struggled with the fact that deportees had to be sent
somewhere. Officials encountered unexpected, confounding, and often
embarrassing cases in which they either could not determine the proper
nation to which to send an individual, or, for a wide variety of reasons,
they could not solicit the international cooperation required to turn their
will into action. Beyond a practical challenge, however, the global element
of deportation was also about self-definition and national imagination.
Though seeking to define and delineate their own borders through deportation, Americans made sense of the United States as a deporting nation
through frequent engagement with a language of foreignness. One of the
most powerful discourses used by critics (both left-wing organizers and
more centrist liberal and progressive commentators) to denounce deportation was how much the practice resembled that of oppressive foreign
regimes. Furthermore, deportation was also a way of informally commen-
tating on foreign policy through discretionary implementation of national
law. While deportation was ostensibly about removing people considered

dangerous to national purity and security, this vision of controlling what was *within* the nation was both a reaction to an increasingly global world and a grasping attempt to maintain authority over the boundaries of the nation. The selective enforcement and discretionary power of the Immigration Service as an agency gave the bureaucratic officials charged with implementing deportation a significant amount of leeway to determine which nation's deportees would be handled in which ways within the system, and which claims for exemptions based on personal danger might be honored. As with the privileging of refugees fleeing Communist and Socialist regimes during the second half of the twentieth century, deportation provided an opportunity for immigration control to serve as a commentary on foreign governments.

Delineating Belonging, Enforcing Policy: The Challenges of Transnational Subjects and the Limitations of American Political Will

One of the many challenges of enforcing deportation in the early twentieth century was the geopolitical reality of a rapidly shifting world in which national borders were unclear, permeable, and often impermanent. Determining which individuals could be expelled from America's borders required ascertaining where those individuals belonged, and this process was often a formidable undertaking. As the United States sought to reiterate its borders and their exclusivity through deportation, it repeatedly ran up against immigrants whose national origin or belonging was impossible to pinpoint. In his 1921 annual report, the commissioner general of immigration bemoaned the fact that "in almost every case" foreign officials "require the presentation of documentary evidence of the citizenship of the alien before they will issue a passport to or for him. All too frequently the alien has lost his documentary evidence of citizenship, which renders it necessary to…obtain such evidence. All of this entails a vast amount of work and the results are usually quite uncertain." In that year alone, he explained, the Immigration Service had been required to communicate with foreign nations, through the State Department, in over six hundred individual cases.[17] The commissioner general noted the following year that struggles to coordinate removal with foreign consuls and their home governments, "a process which necessarily consumes many weeks time, during which the alien is being maintained at the expense of the public," had not improved. In fact, he explained, "efforts to simplify this procedure are continually being made, but so far they have borne little or no fruit."[18]

Sometimes action was blocked by an immigrant's refusal or inability to provide the necessary personal history. In the 1926 case of Eusebio Jimenez, in custody at Sing-Sing, the immigrant inspector from Ellis Island complained that the immigrant was unable to give any information about his date or place of birth, and had no known relatives or visitors to give information. All the inspector could determine, he explained, was that according to the immigrant's own testimony, "when 6 years of age, following the death of his parents, he was taken to Cuba by his uncle, who has since disappeared, and for this reason the alien is unable to state precisely the name of the locality where he was born."[19] Even in a new age of documentation, the debates over belonging continued to be messy, complex, and dependent on individual disclosure, multistep processes of migration, and unclear determinations of origins. As Turack explains, "states may intentionally frustrate the deportation through deliberate procrastination. If the deportee refuses to render sufficient information regarding his nationality, he can cause the deportation to be delayed indefinitely. The inability of a state to secure a passport to effect a deportation order against a stateless person might result in complete frustration of the deportation."[20]

In other cases, it was not the movement of migrants that complicated their legal status, but the movement of nations (or at least their borders). Particularly in the post-WWI period, immigration agents often encountered migrants from nations that no longer existed in their prewar forms, or whose borders had been significantly shifted by the outcome of the war. For example, those from certain cities, such as Danzig, faced a home that as of 1920 was no longer part of Germany, but instead an independent quasi-state under the leadership of the League of Nations with mostly Polish-controlled external affairs. Immigration authorities also debated how to make sense of immigrants from the island of Rhodes, questioning whether such individuals should be considered part of the quota for Italy or as part of "Other Asia." In 1921 the assistant secretary of labor turned to the secretary of state for assistance in sorting out the matter, explaining that while "several aliens claiming birth at Rhodes and carrying Italian passports" had demanded that they be allowed in under the higher Italian quota, the Department of Labor believed that Rhodes had not been definitively transferred to Italy under the act of May 19,

1921, therefore determining that "the classification of the island as a part of Other Asia is correct."[21] Facing a deportee from Zara, officials pondered the unconsidered question of how to handle expulsion to that city, which had gone from Dalmatian to Italian jurisdiction in 1920. However, as officials realized, the situation was even more complex, as immigrants from the District of Zara outside of the City of Zara itself actually fell under Yugoslavian jurisdiction.[22] These confusing cases were not isolated outliers, but were indicative of a fundamentally flawed deportation system unequipped to handle a world where war and empire caused such rapid shifting of borders and control.

In many instances, individuals, particularly those of European descent, protested against efforts to deport them to their lands of birth (often in Latin America) instead of to their nations of ethnic origin. At other times, immigrants pleaded for special permission to be sent to join family in other nations, or begged for access to political asylum outside their nation of birth. In the 1923 board of review report on Andrew Mazzone, who was ordered deported after a three-year imprisonment for grand larceny, the layers of global negotiation become visible. Mazzone, who had been born in France, claimed to immigration officials that he held Italian citizenship by virtue of his father, who had moved to France from Italy as a child. Mazzone then introduced an entirely new wrinkle, requesting special permission to be sent to Brazil, where his wife resided. Ultimately, unable to verify his Italian citizenship and unwilling to deport according to the immigrant's own choice, officials sent Mazzone back to France, although they allowed him to board as a foreign seaman in order to save the immigration service money and expedite the process of removal.[23]

Not infrequently, after the upheaval of the war, deported migrants faced returning to an unfamiliar homeland with a new language, a government hostile to their political orientation, and an unknown social and political environment. The seemingly simple category of "nation of origin" became blurry and called into question the meaning of "home" for immigrants in a tumultuous world order. Did it mean birthplace, regardless of which nation that place was now officially part of? Did it mean the nationality one was born into, even if that nation-state no longer encompassed the location of birth? One of the most striking examples of how geopolitical instability during the post-WWI period impacted the enforcement of American deportation law resulted from the movement of the Curzon Line, which served as the postwar boundary between the

Second Republic of Poland and Soviet Russia. As the dividing lines between nation-states shifted, American officials fumbled to deport immigrants who fell under the confusing status of no longer belonging to the nation-state in which they had been born.

Often deportees sought assistance from charitable and advocacy organizations in fighting their cases, and these agencies could be important allies in sorting out the geopolitical complexities of a particular case. In the 1922 case of Jacob Wolwelski, the Baltic America shipping line corresponded with the Hebrew Immigrant Aid Society (HIAS) about its struggle to discern a proper course of action. The HIAS representative at Ellis Island explained that the complication derived from the individual's origins as a native of Yanowa, in the county of Kobrin, which was on the eastern side of the Curzon Line (marking it as eligible for the Russian quota rather than the Polish). However, as the shipping line responded, he had been "erroneously deported" because he had initially been charged to the Polish quota, in spite of the efforts of relatives and HIAS to intervene. HIAS explained that after arriving in the United States, Wolwelski was excluded by Ellis Island authorities and deported on the S.S. *Lituania*, despite having "had little opportunity to have his rights properly defended.... [W]e strongly feel that every effort should be made to have authority obtained that this alien should be returned to the United States."[24] HIAS, a transnational organization advocating for migrants on both sides of the Atlantic, pressured the American government to adjust its policy as necessary to the rapidly shifting global terrain within which they sought to execute deportation orders. Such global shifts, so completely out of the hands of American officials, were often at the heart of the most successful efforts to fight deportation, and acted as a serious constraint on the ability of the government to enforce its will in selecting the population allowed to stay within the United States. While deportation scholarship largely leaves the category of the nation-state as an unchallenged and unchanging entity, the turbulent reality of the early twentieth century demonstrated how little control the United States had over determining the citizenship and national belonging of individuals from other parts of the globe.

Even where officials were able to successfully ascertain the national origin of an individual, they were not automatically able to transport that person, even in the not infrequent instances when the individual volunteered to depart in order to escape the prospect of indefinite detention in the United States. The challenges of passport procurement were most notable with the Soviet Union during this period, which was unrecognized by the United States diplomatically. In 1923 authorities responded to an inquiry by Judge Samuel H. Sibley, explaining that the unfortunate delays in deporting immigrants were due to the lack of passports. It was difficult to establish proof of citizenship, the official explained, because there was no treaty between the Soviet and American governments, and "[a]s a result, neither country issues passports for its nationals to travel to the other. Rare exceptions are made. Quite often, the Russian Soviet Government issues passports for deportees, upon showing that such deportee is an adherent of the Soviet Government and in harmony with its principles."[25]

However, while the lack of diplomatic relations precluded deportations to the Soviet Union except in special cases, the confusion over this policy left openings for manipulation and deceit, most commonly by immigrants, but sometimes extending to government officials. In 1924 the secretary of labor corresponded with the American Civil Liberties Union (ACLU) about the "Ukranian Diplomatic Mission," a fraudulent organization issuing false passports for the return of deportees to European nations, including the Soviet Union. The director of the ACLU explained that the organization was issuing passports to the Department of Labor, which had resulted in deportations of several individuals to Europe, at which point they either had been returned or were "in desperate straits in European countries where they do not belong." This transnational organization had offices in New York and Washington, DC, but also in Canada, where their agency office had recently been discovered and closed. The director explained that the US government's use of this agency "put the Department of Labor in a very unenviable light before the country."[26] This embarrassing instance of governmental error demonstrates that while deportation authority was consolidated on paper during this period, it remained a chaotic, uncontrolled terrain in which international criminal elements could still undermine the authority of federal officials.

Deportation at the Borders:
The Enforcement of American Boundaries
in Transnational Spaces

Where scholarship has paid attention to the international dynamics of deportation policy, it has largely focused on the border regions between the United States and adjacent nations. Although scholars have demonstrated the fluidity of American national borders, and the ways that deportation practice was carried out differently at the Mexican and Canadian borders, such scholarship has largely implied that these borders were merely the intersection point of two sets of national subjects and interests, while in reality, border disputes and policing were part of a larger global landscape. Deportees were disproportionately apprehended at the nation's land borders, but immigration proceedings there were indicative of far more than America's international relations with its nearest neighbors. Throughout the early twentieth century, as quota restrictions narrowed immigration from Europe but exempted the Western hemisphere, many immigrants crossing from Mexico and Canada came from beyond either country. Like other migrants whose paths to the United States were decidedly nonlinear, labor migrants often spent time in multiple nations before traveling to Mexico or Canada, and then struck out across a land border into the United States. Others never fully committed to a single nation, carrying on lives of seasonal labor and family relations in two nations simultaneously and making the border crossing regularly (sometimes with the assistance of deportation proceedings, which provided them with free passage back if they were able to manipulate the system to their advantage). During the 1920s, officials encountered new anxieties about the use of Mexico, and to a lesser extent Canada, as "back doors" for European and Asian migrants who would otherwise have been excluded at the nation's ports.

The process of deportation at the nation's borders caused considerable tension between the United States and both Mexican and Canadian authorities, who often expressed resentment at the practice of expelling people over the land port they had entered, even if they had no national resident status in that location. In November of 1922, the assistant commissioner of immigration in charge of appeals wrote to the commissioner general to explain that permission was often given to European deportees to go to Mexico if they did not want to go to Europe, and that "[i]n some instances the alien was refused admission to Mexico upon his arrival and not only was this office subjected to considerable work and inconvenience but the alien suffered from great inconvenience."[27] While the federal government seemed unconcerned with the inconvenience or insult to Mexican authorities, the Mexican government's anger comes through in extensive correspondence between American and Mexican officials, and they fought for a ban against the landing of any deportees except Mexican citizens. Meanwhile, US immigration officials in the 1920s increasingly revealed their stress over the permeability of the Mexican border and their inability to clamp down on border movements, which severely interfered with deportation practice. At the same time, however, as scholars have demonstrated, there was a widespread use of discretion on the part of the Immigration Service in creating that permeability and practicing nonintervention in the migration of migrant agricultural labor, particularly in points of high demand or under pressure from local business interests.[28]

In 1923 the Immigration Inspector in Charge at Tucson, Arizona, carried out extensive correspondence with the commissioner at El Paso, discussing the challenges of policing the borderlands. In one November letter, the Tucson inspector argued that Mexican criminals deported at Nogales actually used deportation to facilitate cross-border criminal activities, "slipping back and forth across the international line for that purpose."[29] Furthermore, he argued, these deportees actually sought repeated detention in the Arizona State prison, due to the high standards of clothing, food, amusement, and the lack of manual labor. He went so far as to explain of this captivity "that the environment and conditions are rather inviting compared with the conditions of aliens of this class in their native country."[30] In 1930 the district director at San Antonio echoed the same sentiment, explaining that the number of deportees who repeatedly returned from Mexico was high and stating, "[W]e are continually apprehending aliens who state they would rather be in jail in this country than free in Mexico, since an American jail at least affords them a place to eat and sleep."[31] Envisioning a world in which detention and deportation in the United States were preferable to freedom elsewhere, officials constructed a deportation rhetoric that imagined its targets as criminal, desperate, impoverished, and desperate to maintain access to the United States at any cost.

The frequency of such claims reflected both the racialization of Mexican migrants as used to subhuman conditions and criminal by nature, as well as the messiness of policing borderlands where new deportation laws meant very little against the realities of a landscape in which the border was so porous. Extensive discussions of this nature led local officials from border immigration stations, national immigration authorities, and the Mexican government to quarrel throughout the 1920s about where Mexican deportees would be sent. Local border officials and Mexican

authorities agreed that the INS should be responsible for sending deportees to wherever they originated in Mexico, rather than simply the border
town at which they crossed, in order to make repeat crossing more difficult. Mexican officials added that the tendency to return deportees from
all over the nation to a handful of border towns led to overcrowding, job-
lessness, and high crime rates in these areas.[32] Meanwhile, Arizona and
Texas immigration officials complained of how frequently such deportees
returned, often as early as the day following their deportation.[33] However,
US government officials, aligning themselves against their own local officials, argued that the practice of sending Mexican deportees in the interior
was far too expensive.

In spite of the considerably more respectful relationship between US
immigration authorities and Canadian officials, Canadian representatives
also felt the strain of unequal expectations between the nations. Reflecting frustration about the assumption that Canadian institutions would
continue to support American immigrant residents while their Canadian counterparts would be deported from the United States, the general
medical director of the hospitals for insane, reformatories, and industrial
schools in Montreal wrote to the Secretary of Labor in 1923: "Very often I
am asked by the United States authorities to receive in our Hospitals for
the Insane persons who have become insane, even after these persons
have lived twenty-five years in the United States." His complaint was a
common one among international figures who felt that it was wrong of
America to blame other nations for the deficiencies of individuals even
after they had spent most of their lives being shaped by American residence. He went on to inquire incredulously, "Do I have to understand
that any alien living in the United States, no matter what length of time,
is always deportable unless such alien has acquired citizenship through
naturalization?"[34]

Throughout 1927, the United States and Canada debated, collaborated,
and maneuvered their policies relating to mentally ill immigrants in conjunction with one another. The United States, complaining of the expense
of maintaining mentally ill Canadian migrants in American institutions,
demanded passport permission to deport numerous individuals from its
hospitals, asylums, and mental institutions. In response, Canadian officials pointed to the numerous American citizens residing in Canada and
argued that if the United States would no longer take responsibility for
the support of immigrants of Canadian birth, many of whom had lived

in the United States for decades, Canadian institutions could no longer be expected to support Americans with mental illnesses requiring public support. This led to reciprocal relations with Canada in what amounted to the swapping of deportees from Canadian and American mental institutions, with each nation agreeing to take particular lists of individuals in return for the other doing the same with their own citizens.

The commissioner of the Canadian Department of Immigration and Colonization wrote to the United States commissioner general in June of 1927 regarding the case of a man named Jolicoeur, stating that the inability of the Canadian authorities to effect the return of this US citizen and others had become "embarrassing for the Government of the province of Quebec." Indeed, he went on to threaten, "[I]f this United States citizen cannot be returned to the United States the Provincial authorities will be inclined to deal with similar cases where institutional treatment is required in the Province of Quebec on the same principle."[35] In the midst of these debates, the United States was forced to grapple with a number of complexities facing receiving nations for deportees, and a number of new questions arose. If an American citizen had lived in several states before migrating to Canada, which state bore responsibility for their institutionalization and expenses upon their return through deportation? If the American citizen under deportation proceedings from Canada was a naturalized citizen, rather than a native-born one, did the government bear the same responsibility for accepting and supporting the individual? Which government's procedures of testing and evaluating the mental fitness of individuals were to be accepted? The need to grapple with these questions demonstrates that no matter how desperately the American state wanted to view itself as only a deporting nation, in truth, it was neither as unilaterally sovereign as it hoped to be nor exempt from its own citizens being expelled from other nations.

Deportation as Foreign Policy: Selective Enforcement as a Tool of International Relations

While deportation in the early twentieth century was not officially an arm of foreign policy, or an explicit referendum on the human rights abuses of other nations, in practice it often operated as one. Through selective application of seemingly neutral immigration legislation, federal and local officials took foreign policy into their own hands and used expulsion to demonstrate their respect, disdain, or cooperation with other nations. The lenience expressed toward migrants seeking to avoid repression or state violence in Soviet Russia took on an entirely different tone, for example, than the generally rigid rejection of claims of persecution and human rights abuses in Fascist Italy. Because deportation allowed for such a great degree of discretion on the part of individual immigration officers, often low-level governmental agency employees had the power to enact their own commentary on foreign governments through their deportation decisions. As scholars have noted, officials in the early Immigration Service had a large amount of discretionary leeway.[36] In some ways, this discretion meant that the decisions of local outpost offices acted as an informal referendum on which immigrants deserved mercy, which foreign states posed true threats, and which geopolitical conflicts merited state protection of individuals.

In an extensive "Document on Deportation" prepared for the Communist-affiliated Labor Research Association, an author identified only as Honig elaborated a left-wing critique about how the United States selectively enforced its own laws as an informal commentary on global politics and through discretionary power demonstrated sympathy or disdain for foreign governments based on who they deported. Explaining that while "honest" labor activists were deported to dangerously oppressive nations, the government spared others—namely "the white guardists, enemies of the Soviet Union, the rats who ran away from Russia because they have to work for a living instead of sponge on the toiling masses."[37] In other cases, he observed of the government's uneven implementation of deportation law, "It sends them back to countries where the fiercest fascist terror holds sway, where imprisonment, torture, and death awaits the brave working-class fighters."[38]

Many opponents of the system understood that in ordering deportations, the United States was not merely protecting its own national security or interests, but was reflecting its investment in broader networks of imperialism, capitalism, and global racism and inequality. In 1919 a group called the Friends of Freedom for India published a pamphlet entitled *Doing Britain's Dirty Work*, in which they accused the United States of deporting Indian agitators for the benefit of its alliance with British colonial power.[39] Indictments of the immigration service for punishing foreign dissidents were common throughout the era, coming from immigrants themselves, political groups, immigration advocacy organizations, and at times even from self-declared conservatives who nevertheless found the deportations overreaching. As one observer commented regarding the case of Li Tao Hsuan, who was detained at Ellis Island in 1930, the immigrant was penalized with solitary confinement after joining a protest against the terrible conditions, segregation, and discrimination Chinese deportees experienced on the island.[40] In terms of the accusations levied against him by the Immigration Service, "Li refuted all these charges and declared that his persecution was only due to his propaganda against imperialism." Furthermore, his attorney argued that "deportation was a literal death sentence for the prisoner," and requested that Li be allowed to depart for the Soviet Union if he was to be deported at all.[41] An even harsher assessment of the case concluded that the interests at work were not merely those of the government, but that "Wall Street wanted to hand Li over to the Kuomintang butchers in China" for his anti-imperialist work. The observer noted the international outcry over the case, explaining that "floods of telegrams from workers and workers organizations poured in to Secretary of Labor Doak."[42]

For activists and protestors, deportation policy that endangered the lives or freedom of immigrant subjects was not merely unethical; it was a violation of the American creed. Instead, they argued, if the government was to insist on deportations—a right that some, though not all, protestors conceded—it was its duty to global standards of civilized societies to arrange for shipment to a neutral nation where the deportee's safety would not be in jeopardy. In certain instances, the United States did attempt to find ways to circumvent deportation to an individual's nation of origin, but these efforts led to their own set of complications and geopolitical maneuvering: decisions about whether to honor the deportee's own choice of nation, navigation of paperwork demands, and growing international resentment over the United States treating foreign nations as dumping grounds for their "undesirable aliens."

Most often, deported individuals who escaped repression or personal danger in their own nation of birth were sent to locations in Latin America or the Caribbean. In particular, conflicts reemerged throughout the 1920s with officials in Cuba, who resented US authorities for allowing a variety of European nationals to be deported there, where they had briefly resided before migrating to the United States. F. E. Menocal of the Cuban Department of Immigration reported in 1924 that he had been frustrated by the arrival of four more immigrants expelled from the United States, and reminded US officials that from Cuba, they would only attempt reentry. Indeed, he stated, "it is the best practice to return them to Europe."[43] In another instance, the commissioner in charge of immigration at New Orleans was severely chastised by the commissioner general of immigration for allowing a family to be sent to Cuba rather than be deported to Mexico in spite of explicit denial of permission. The 1922 letter to the commissioner at New Orleans states sternly that "the assumption indulged by you was entirely unwarranted, and has placed the Bureau in a decidedly embarrassing position," demonstrating the pressure officials were under to avoid international conflict with receiving nations.[44]

By the mid-1930s, while some cases of deportation that posed a danger to the individual's safety were still being carried out in spite of protests, officials increasingly paid attention to demands for sensitivity to the political atmosphere across the globe. This shift was facilitated in part by progressive political figures who added their voices to those of protestors and political activists in demanding that deportation consider the world outside American borders, and who insisted that the United States held a responsibility not to subject deportees to undue threats to their well-being. In response to a 1935 appeal from congressman Vito Marcantonio, Deputy Commissioner of Immigration Shaughnessy explained that in the case of Srul (a.k.a. Sol) Goldband, since it appeared that if he was deported to Poland he would indeed be subjected to persecution, the department was going to permit "his voluntary departure, without expense to the United States, to any country of his choice, except to contiguous territory or adjacent islands."[45]

Throughout the 1920s and beyond, as deportation became a common government tactic for handling political protest, challenges to authority, and ideological dissent, immigration officials and public figures were forced to reckon with the global repercussions of their acts. While deportation was ostensibly not a form of criminal punishment but merely an administrative process, many onlookers and subjects of the deportation regime were quick to argue that it was in fact a highly punitive process. In particular, many activists, potential deportees, and legal representatives argued that deportation in many cases actually served not only as punishment through removal but also as extradition. The fervor of US officials to deport political dissidents often led to the removal of people who would run up against hostile authorities in their countries of origins after return. Radicals, Communists, anarchists, free-speech advocates, and other activists were often at great risk for persecution, imprisonment, and even death in their home countries, and this created a great deal of discourse in the United States over the ethics of their return.

Though deportation was not legally deemed a punishment, lawyers of potential deportees argued that, in many cases, it could mark a sure death sentence for the deported individuals, and in some cases consisted of the return of individuals who had already fled persecution for the supposed liberty of the United States. In a 1935 novel based on the experience aboard a deportation train, one of the protagonists dramatically utters to his fellow passengers: "And in this country it is said that deportation is not a punishment. No, of course not! But for me it is a death sentence, all right."[46] This critique was a common one of the era, and many declared that deportation could endanger lives on both ends, both putting the deportee at risk for persecution abroad and, in many cases, leaving his family destitute and unable to provide for themselves in the United States. Further highlighting both the accusations of foreignness as well as the global nature of these discourses, the International Bureau against War and Reaction wrote from the Netherlands to argue: "Except in fascist countries, nowhere in the world [are] persons who belong to the class of political refugees...exiled on account of their opinions. And we do not know of any democratic country where an extradition order of political refugees to the home country, where their lives would be endangered or where they would be prosecuted, would not raise a storm of public indignation."[47]

Accusations of fascism in deportation practice were among the most powerful rhetorical attacks levied against immigration officials by activists and radicals, but they also reflected a genuine collaboration with Fascist governments to repress political activity of foreign nationals living in the United States. As scholars such have Fraser Ottanelli and Philip Cannistraro have examined, there were in fact transnational efforts to control the Italian population in the United States.[48] Ottanelli explains that "Mussolini's takeover of Italy was followed by a concerted campaign orchestrated by Fascist authorities directed toward the United States to gain the support of and establish control over the Italian American community, ensure a sympathetic public opinion, and repress antifascists and their activities."[49] These measures, Ottanelli points out, could include controlling passports of family members attempting to reunite with relatives in the United States, a set of circumstances that severely impacted

Italian radicals in the United States. As Nunzio Pernicone explains in his biography of Carlo Tresca, "There were multiple ways by which American authorities assisted Fascists against the anti-Fascists; the most effective method, of course, was deportation or the threat of it."[50] The potential danger faced by deported Italians is confirmed by Ottanelli's assessment that "[o]n specific orders from Mussolini, the Italian consulate in New York routinely provided U.S. immigration officials with names and whereabouts of any politically active illegal immigrant, who would then be arrested and held for deportation back to Italy...a practice that had tragic consequences for many."[51] Thus it is clear that the experiences of Italian American detentions and deportations were not happening within the national frame alone, as they have often been pictured, but in a context in which domestic concerns over immigration were intertwined with political developments, state authority, and transoceanic movements of ideology, political power, and people.

Sometimes attempts to convey the detrimental effects of deportation on the health and well-being of particular individuals were successful, and demonstrated the wide leeway for administrative discretion within the deportation process. In 1922 HIAS intervened on behalf of young Sora Zezombek, age fourteen, arguing that due to the "white plague" (likely tuberculosis) and the fact that she had no relatives left to care for her abroad, "deportation might possibly prove fatal."[52] In the 1922 case of sixteen-year-old Moische Zeltzer, who had a limb amputated en route to the United States, HIAS argued on his behalf that with his artificial limb and restored good health, he was sure to be employable anyway. It is hard to know what was more convincing for the immigration agents who granted his appeal: the fact that he was coming to join his "mother and grandparents as well as other near rich relatives," or the reminder of the dangers of his home country of Russia where, they explained, "social and economic conditions are at their lowest ebb."[53] As in so many other instances, expressions of sympathy for the victims of "dark Russia" amounted to a form of de facto commentary about foreign regimes through the selective enforcement of immigration policy. The struggle over how officials on the ground would implement (or decline to implement) the growing infrastructure for deportation was not merely a playing ground for local or national agendas, but international relations as well.

Understanding American Deportation through the Outward Gaze: Networks of Communication and International Discourses on Deportation

Throughout the 1920s and 1930s, activists and public figures spoke out against the damaging impact of deportation upon not only deportees and their families, but also America's image in the international arena. Speaking to the role of deportations in perceptions of America abroad, radical activist Elizabeth Gurley Flynn highlighted the injustice of the process and argued that it would shape opinion abroad, as well as at home. Addressing the case of a New Orleans deportee detained for more than six months as a Socialist and labor activist, she wrote to the commissioner general of immigration, pleading, "Mr. Caminetti, I wish you would begin to realize that American justice the world round, is being weighed through your Department and is being found wanting. I realize, of course, the flood of cases that your office has to handle. I realize that your machinery moves slowly, but it also grinds exceedingly small.... Apparently jails of America are to break the health of individuals as the wheels of old were to break their bones."[54] Protestors of deportation repeatedly reminded authorities that the world was watching (and judging) as a supposedly democratic and inclusive society stripped individuals of rights, subjected communities to invasive raids and the separation of families, and stifled dissent and free speech through expulsion. Activists such as Flynn also operated outside of national boundaries as well as within them, and organizations designed to fight deportation often stressed their international nature.

Flynn may have been approaching the issue through her experiences with global networks of radical activists, but radicals were far from the only observers to declaim the unfortunate impact of deportation on America's image in the rest of the world. A 1921 letter from the American consulate at Melbourne, Australia, to the secretary of state reported that "there has been much, [although] unorganized and friendly, criticism of the administration and effect of the provisions of the recent Immigration Act."[55] Further highlighting the tension with territories of the British Empire, the *Melbourne Age* feature an article entitled "American Exclusiveness" that same year, which proclaimed, "Much indignation has been caused by statements of the scandalous treatment accorded South African families on Ellis Island." The secretary of the YMCA of South Africa expressed rage at being treated like a common foreigner rather than a respectable traveler from the British Empire and explained that he was "herded for three days with a horde of filthy aliens."[56] Departing from the self-congratulatory narrative of America as an inclusive haven of the oppressed, it became apparent in international discourse that some foreigners looking in noted not a sanctuary but a horrifying system of uncivilized brutality.

After asserting her credentials by stating that "I am not an imperfectly assimilated alien," and explaining to the members of the congressional hearing before which she appeared that "all of my ancestors came over here at least 50 years before 1776, so I feel that I have a right to speak as an American citizen," Edith Spruance explained her perspective on the stakes of deportation proceedings by saying that it was for the protection of American values that she opposed deportation proceedings as they had been occurring.[57] A representative of the League of Women Voters, American Civil Liberties Union, and the National Society of Colonial Dames, Spruance argued that what was endangered by deportation proceedings was American respect for freedom. She stated, "The reason I have come here is less on account of the alien than on account of our own American citizens," and she proclaimed that the recent deportation drives in her eyes seemed "to shovel and generally push the country into what I can only term Prussian and Latin and general Fascisti methods of government."[58]

However, discourses around deportation sometimes focused on other nations not as negative reference points for American practices but as models for emulation. As circulation of knowledge and expertise about the policing of noncitizen populations spread during the early twentieth century, the United States joined in global conversations and analysis about the most effective mechanisms for keeping subversive elements (foreign-born and otherwise) suppressed. To build their arguments for more stringent deportation enforcement, advocates of the practice often pointed to other governments abroad who successfully eliminated threats to their own national body. For example, as the opening of this chapter suggests, when local officials and police commanders in Chicago sought to rid the city of supposed Sicilian "gangsters" and "mobsters" in 1926, they repeatedly referred to the success that Mussolini had in "cleaning up" Italy through exile of similar agents, and urged the federal government to act more quickly to emulate his tactics. In a twist in the transnational relationship between deportation in the United States and Italy, the commissioner of immigration argued that the troubles with Sicilian gangsters in Chicago were actually the result of the efficiency of the exile procedures of Mussolini's government. Commissioner Doak explained his stance in an article which argued that Chicago was populated by Italian exiles, stating, "The second factor is the widespread racketeering of the gangster type.... The Chicago racketeering game, he suspects, is peopled largely by Sicilians expelled from Italy by Mussolini."[59]

On the other side, arguing that the practice of deportation undermined the American national creed, activists and immigrant spokespeople often couched their criticism by labeling deportation as a practice typical of a more "tyrannical" nation, most often Czarist or Soviet Russia or Fascist Italy. The common language of why deportation was wrong centered on the claim that it resembled the practices of a foreign tyranny. As one journalist, who described himself as "the only newspaper man ever to be permitted to ride on one of these United States deportation trains," remarked in 1930: "Hundreds of humans gathered up as if by a gigantic continent-wide net, herded into prison cars and ridden under guard to Ellis Island and other Government stations, there to be place on ships bound for their natal-homes. How like Russia that sounded!"[60] At a 1926 "Conference in Opposition to the Registration of Aliens and Deportation Bills" held in New York, Governor Alfred Smith delivered a statement in which he argued, "This proposed law would give the kind of power to an administrative body that would inevitably lead to tyranny and abuse," and like many of his co-critics, he referred to the "tyranny of czaristic Russia" as the potential outcome of such legislation.[61] Social service and immigrant aid organizations also expressed strong consternation, viewing the excesses of American deportation practices as tarnishing their reputations abroad and as a departure from civilized modes of migration control.

Knowledge about policy and potential deportees circulated globally through both activists who tapped into international solidarity networks to raise funds and pressure public officials, and governmental officials who participated in international communication networks designed to identify and apprehend deportees. The United States therefore became part of various networks of communication regarding migrants and their dangers to the global community. Sometimes these took the form of explicit conferences and meetings among diplomats about immigration restriction.[62] At other junctures, international communication took the form of messages between nations who viewed the same individual immigrant as a threat as deportees moved across multiple borders. In October of 1920, the State Department wrote to the Bureau of Immigration to warn of a criminal, in the process of being expelled from Sweden, who it was believed would need to be apprehended next in the United States. Tovia Uusoiksa, age twenty-five, "described as a pianist, but who is really by profession a plumber, is understood to be the chief agent for the smuggling of Russian jewelry into America," the official wrote, going on to explain that "I send you this information in order that you may balk any plans which he may have to enter this country." Through the global transfer of knowledge about individual cases as well as broader potential threats, officials around the world participated in the policing of thoroughly transnational subjects, who traversed multiple borders, took part in both legal and illicit economies, and faced expulsion across a range of nation-states.[63]

Scholars of immigration history have begun to note that the migrant population that reached American ports was already a globally determined group, vetted through inspection and restriction at ports of exit, particularly in European nations. As Congress ramped up immigration restriction and deportation legislation throughout the late nineteenth and early twentieth centuries, the immigration officials responsible for turning these laws into enforceable practices were daunted by the task of policing immigration both at home and abroad, and realized that to simplify their jobs at home required taking a more active intervention in migrant departures abroad. During the early twentieth century, and particularly after the advent of stricter restriction laws in the 1910s and 1920s, a system for screening immigrants before they reached American shores became necessary.[64] For years, the United States debated in the courts who was responsible for the cost of reshipping immigrants who were marked for restriction, either for various deficiencies or, later, merely for being in excess of a quota. As a result of the turmoil caused by the return of excluded immigrants, European nations began creating their own screening procedures for would-be emigrants, often in conjunction with American officials and shipping representatives. As Donna R. Gabaccia points out, the transportation of migrants to the United States was, in addition to being a cultural and political process, an economic transaction firmly rooted in a transnational shipping industry, and immigration policy was not immune to the concerns of this industry's interests.[65]

However, what has gone largely unacknowledged is that the functioning of the growing American deportation apparatus also required contact with overseas powers for the maintenance of its success. The sheer difficulty of documenting and institutionalizing records of who had already been deported from the United States was an immense challenge, and immigration authorities found themselves creating new tactics for tracking deportees after they left the country. Indeed, by the end of the 1920s, the US Bureau of Immigration had put into limited practice a system whereby it would send out "black list cards" to European nations to ensure that they not allow these previously deported migrants to attempt to depart to the United States again. As the American Consular Office in Bremen, Germany, explained to the commissioner general in early 1930, the black list cards had "proved of great value," but required a quicker transmission of information. "From two to six months elapse between the date of an alien's deportation and receipt of his black list card by consulates," they complained, and "it is obvious that a deported alien who intends to attempt reentry is most apt to make such an attempt within that period of time."[66]

The Office of the Technical Adviser in Belfast also argued for the need for this kind of systematic global transmission of deportation records to the commissioner general in 1928. In this instance, the correspondence concerned several individuals whose status was related to the office by family members or acquaintances who exposed them as deportees. The officer wrote that while it was lucky to have informal reporting, "such an unreliable safeguard is all we have to insure [sic] our knowledge of such deportations" when they attempted to reapply for a visa. Playing into some of the worst fears of American officials regarding the types of deportees that needed to be prevented from returning, they cited an example of an immigrant deported a month earlier for having committed bigamy in the United States, whose first wife had called to inform the consul of the deportation, thus halting his chances of securing a return visa.[67] Such examples make it clear that as scholars continue to reveal the global communication and information networks required for the growth of international migration restrictions, deportation must become a more central point of focus, as its enforcement requires broad global cooperation.

Conclusion

H. T. Tsiang's 1939 "Deportation (A Poem)," written during his detention on Ellis Island, expressed the transnational realities of many of the immigrants caught up in the machinery of the deportation regime:

> Polish Passport, Portuguese visa, Italian ship, no landing at Lisbon.
> Brought here.
> No visa, no parents, no home, no country to go to.[68]

Tsiang's words encapsulate the inadequacy of a national frame for examining the lives of individuals whose experiences, alongside broader geopolitical shifts, rendered them essentially stateless under the modern deportation regime. For families and individuals facing deportation, migration often has a multistep, transnational process, and affinities do not always neatly line up with citizenship or nations of origin. For those seeking to exile such individuals from the national body, the practicalities of passports, visas, shipping permissions, and numerous other challenges impeded their ability to impose their will upon people whose statehood status was a complex and sometimes undecipherable map of experiences. More study is still required to fully understand deportation as a key site of conflict between national desires and global realities in a period of upheaval, mass migration, imperialism, and war. But it is clear that deportation has always operated as far more than a simple enforcement tool of immigration policy, and has instead been a fraught, global battlefield among competing authorities, modern methods of regulation and record-keeping, the unmanageability of the movement of peoples, and divergent discourses of nationalism.

Notes

1. "Italy's Idea of Housecleaning," *The Nation*, August 5, 1925.
2. "Drive Out the Rats," *Chicago Daily Tribune*, February 21, 1926.
3. See Marilyn Lake and Henry Reynolds, *Drawing the Global Colour Line: White Men's Countries and the International Challenge of Racial Equality* (Cambridge: Cambridge University Press, 2008); and Andreas Fahrmeir, Olivier Faron, and Patrick Weil, eds., *Migration Control in the North Atlantic World: The Evolution of State Practices in Europe and the United States from the French Revolution to the Inter-War Period* (New York: Berghahn Books, 2003).

4. Historical scholarship on deportation as its own discrete topic of study is relatively recent; see especially Kitty Calavita, *U.S. Immigration Law and the Control of Labor, 1820–1924* (London: Academic Press, 1984); Daniel Kanstroom, *Deportation Nation: Outsiders in American History* (Cambridge: Harvard University Press, 2007); Rachel Ida Buff, "The Deportation Terror," *American Quarterly* 60, no. 3 (September 2008): 523–51; Kelly Lytle-Hernandez, *Migra! A History of the U.S. Border Patrol* (Berkeley: University of California Press, 2010); Natalia Molina, "Constructing Mexicans as Deportable Immigrants: Race, Disease, and the Meaning of 'Public Charge,'" *Identities* 17, no. 6 (2010): 641–66; Torrie Hester, *Deportation: The Origins of U.S. Policy* (Philadelphia: University of Pennsylvania Press, 2017); Hidetaka Hirota, *Expelling the Poor: Atlantic Seaboard States and the Nineteenth-Century Origins of American Immigration Policy* (Oxford: Oxford University Press, 2017); Deirdre Moloney, *National Insecurities: Immigrants and U.S. Deportation Policy since 1882* (Chapel Hill: University of North Carolina Press, 2012).

5. Mae Ngai argues that deportation policy developed as part of a "new global age…marked [by] the consolidation of the international nation-state system," and immigration restriction was part of the way that modern nation-states "hardened borders" around racially imagined national communities. Mae M. Ngai, "The Strange Career of the Illegal Alien: Immigration Restriction and Deportation Policy in the United States, 1921–1965," *Law and History Review* 21, no. 1 (spring 2003): 69–107.

6. Robert W. Tucker, "Immigration and Foreign Policy: General Considerations," in *Immigration and U.S. Foreign Policy*, ed. Robert W. Tucker, Charles B. Keely, and Linda Wrigley (Boulder: Westview Press, 1990), 2.

7. See Jorge Duany, *Blurred Borders: Transnational Migration between the Hispanic Caribbean and the United States* (Chapel Hill: University of North Carolina Press, 2011).

8. Donna R. Gabaccia, *Foreign Relations: American Immigration in Global Perspective* (Princeton: Princeton University Press, 2012).

9. See Hester, *Deportation*. On some of the global dimensions of deportation, see Moloney, *National Insecurities*; Daniel Kanstroom, *Aftermath: Deportation Law and the New American Diaspora* (Oxford University Press, 2012); and David C. Brotherton and Luis Barrios, *Banished to the Homeland: Dominican Deportees and their Stories of Exile* (New York: Columbia University Press, 2011).

10. Daniel C. Turack, *The Passport in International Law* (Lexington: Lexington Books, 1972), 233.

11. John Torpey argues that passports and other controls on movement were part of the solidification of states as "'really-existing' entities." At the same time, he points out, "What is remarkable about the contemporary system of passport controls is that it bears witness to a cooperating 'international society.'" John Torpey, *The Invention of the Passport: Surveillance, Citizenship, and the State* (Cambridge: Cambridge University Press, 2000), 3.

12. Richard Bessel and Claudia B. Haake, "Introduction: Forced Removal in the Modern World," in *Removing Peoples: Forced Removal in the Modern World*,

ed. Richard Bessel and Claudia Haake (Oxford: Oxford University Press, 2009), 6.

13. Ibid., 9.

14. See also Luis Roniger, James N. Green, and Pablo Yankelevich, "Introduction," in *Exile and the Politics of Exclusion in the Americas*, ed. Luis Roniger, James N. Green, and Pablo Yankelevich (Brighton: Sussex Academic Press, 2012); Lake and Reynolds, *Drawing the Global Colour Line*.

15. See Aristide Zolberg, *A Nation by Design: Immigration Policy in the Fashioning of America* (New York: Russell Sage Foundation, 2006); and Mae Ngai, "The Architecture of Race in American Immigration Law: A Reexamination of the Immigration Act of 1924," *Journal of American History* 86, no. 1 (June 1999): 67–92.

16. File 55178/5, Records of the Immigration and Naturalization Service, Record Group 85, National Archives and Records Administration, Washington, DC (hereafter INS).

17. *Annual Report of the Commissioner General of Immigration to the Secretary of Labor*, 1921, 15.

18. *Annual Report of the Commissioner General of Immigration to the Secretary of Labor*, 1922, 17.

19. Immigrant Inspector at Ellis Island to Commissioner of Immigration at Ellis Island, June 11, 1926, File 55475/70, INS.

20. Turack, *The Passport in International Law*, 234. See also Kenyon Zimmer, "Positively Stateless: Marcus Graham, the Fererro-Sallitto Case, and Anarchist Challenges to Race and Deportation," in *The Rising Tide of Color: Race, State Violence, and Radical Movements across the Pacific*, ed. Moon-Ho Jung (Seattle: University of Washington Press, 2014), 128–58. On stateless individuals, see Linda K. Kerber, "The Stateless as the Citizen's Other: A View from the United States," *American Historical Review* 112, no. 1 (February 2007): 1–34.

21. Assistant Secretary of Labor to the Secretary of State, November 25, 1921, File 55079/338C, INS.

22. Commissioner General of Immigration to Major Lawrence Martin, Geographer, State Department, October 29, 1921, File 55079/338C, INS.

23. File 55205/739, INS.

24. HIAS Ellis Island Representative to Louis Gottlieb, Esq., February 8, 1922, Legal Briefs, 1905–1923, HIAS Archive, YIVO Institute for Jewish Research, New York City (hereafter YIVO).

25. John Kent Allison to Commissioner General of Immigration, August 23, 1923, File 54933/351B, INS.

26. Director of ACLU to Secretary of Labor, July 25, 1924, File 54933/351C, INS.

27. Assistant Commissioner in Charge of B.S.I. and Appeals to Commissioner General of Immigration, November 8, 1922, File 54933/351A, INS.

28. See, for example, Kitty Calavita, *Inside the State: The Bracero Program, Immigration, and the I.N.S.* (New York: Routledge, 1992).

29. Immigrant Inspector in Charge at Tucson to Supervisor at El Paso, November 9, 1923, File 54933/351B, INS.

30. Ibid.

31. District Director of Immigration at San Antonio to the Commissioner General of Immigration, October 21, 1930, File 55608/125, INS.

32. In late 1930, the Mexican embassy corresponded with the second assistant secretary of labor regarding the embassy's request for deportations to be discontinued along the lower California border. The Department of Labor informed the embassy that this request was found "impracticable" because "the cost of deportation proceedings would be materially increased." Mexican Embassy to Second Assistant Secretary, Department of Labor, November 13, 1930, File 55608/125, INS.

33. From even as far as Oregon, officials wrote to the commissioner general of immigration demanding his attention as to how Mexican deportees were to be handled. In a 1923 letter, the inspector in charge at Portland explained, "It is the most desirable to deport the criminal class as far away from the border as possible," and urged a return to the policy of deporting immigrants by water to Mazatlan rather than overland to points just south of the border. See Inspector in Charge at Portland, Oregon to the Commissioner General of Immigration, March 30, 1923, File 55608/125, INS.

34. General Medical Director, Montreal to US Secretary of Labor, September 24, 1923, File 54933/351B, INS.

35. Commissioner of Canadian Department of Immigration and Colonization to Commissioner General of Immigration, June 30, 1927, File 55203/177, INS.

36. As S. Deborah Kang explores in a recent study of the INS in the Mexican borderlands, local authorities utilized administrative discretion in such diverse ways that, in essence, the INS "demonstrated the breadth and depth of its ability to make the law." S. Deborah Kang, *The INS on the Line: Making Immigration Law on the U.S.-Mexico Border, 1917–1945* (New York: Oxford University Press, 2017), 4.

37. Honig, "Document on Deportation," Folder 26—Deportations (1933, ND), Box 4, Labor Research Association Records, Record Group 129, Tamiment Library and Robert F. Wagner Archives (hereafter Tamiment), New York University, New York.

38. Ibid.

39. William Marion Reedy, *Doing Britain's Dirty Work* (New York: Friends of Freedom for India, 1919), Printed Ephemera, Record Group 43—Pamphlet Collection, Reference Center for Marxist Studies, Tamiment.

40. Li Tao Hsuan was an active Chinese Communist and secretary of the Chinese Bureau Central Committee; after his detention at Ellis Island, he was deported to the Soviet Union around 1932. See Him Mark Lai, *Chinese American Transnational Politics* (Urbana: University of Illinois Press, 2010), 85.

41. Emanuel Pollack, "The Case of Li Tao Hsuan," Folder 26, Box 4, Labor Research Association Records, RG 129, Tamiment.

42. Honig, "Document on Deportations," Folder 26—Deportations, Box 4, Labor Research Association Records, RG 129, Tamiment.

43. F. E. Menocal, Cuban Department of Immigration to Daniel Trazivuk, Laredo, Texas, February 29, 1924, File 55608/123—General File Re Deportation of Aliens to Cuba, INS.

44. Assistant Commissioner General of Immigration to Commissioner of Immigration at New Orleans, April 7, 1922, File 55178/8, INS.

45. Deputy Commissioner Edw. J. Shaughnessy to Congressman Vito Marcantonio, December 4, 1935, Folder—Immigration A-B, General Correspondence, Box 3, Vito Marcantonio Papers, New York Public Library.

46. Theodore D. Irwin, *Strange Passage* (New York: H. Smith and R. Haas, 1935), 37.

47. International Bureau against War and Reaction, Holland, to Commissioner General of Immigration, June 3, 1935, File 55860/459, INS.

48. Fraser M. Ottanelli, "'If Fascism Comes to America We Will Push It Back into the Ocean': Italian American Antifascism in the 1920s and 1930s," in *Italian Workers of the World: Labor Migrations and the Formation of Multiethnic States*, ed. Donna R. Gabaccia and Fraser M. Ottanelli; Philip V. Cannistrano, *Blackshirts in Little Italy: Italian Americans and Fascism, 1921–1929* (West Lafayette: Bordighera Press, 1999).

49. Ottanelli, "'If Fascism Comes to America,'" 184.

50. Nunzio Pernicone, *Carlo Tresca: Portrait of A Rebel* (New York: Palgrave Macmillan, 2005), 149.

51. Ottanelli, "If Fascism Comes to America,'" 182–83.

52. Wm. M. Nebau, Representative at Ellis Island to Secretary of Labor, November 4, 1922, Legal Briefs, 1905–1923, HIAS Archive, YIVO.

53. Wm. M. Nebau to Secretary of Labor, December 2, 1922, Legal Briefs, 1905–1923, HIAS Archive, YIVO.

54. Elizabeth Gurley Flynn on behalf of Workers' Defense Union to Commissioner General of Immigration, Box 1, Elizabeth Gurley Flynn Papers, Record Group 118, Tamiment.

55. American Consulate General at Melbourne, Australia, to US Secretary of State, September 10, 1921, File 55079/338C, INS.

56. Quoted in Ibid.

57. *Hearings before the Committee on Immigration and Naturalization, House of Representatives, Sixty-Ninth Congress, First Session, March 25, 26, April 13, 1926* (Washington, DC: Government Printing Office, 1926), 55.

58. Ibid., 56.

59. Gardner Jackson, "Doak the Deportation Chief," *The Nation*, March 19, 1931.

60. Alan MacDonald, "A Trip on the Deportation Special: Unwanted Aliens Headed Home," *Baltimore Sun*, March 9, 1930.

61. Max J. Kohler, "Registration of Aliens a Dangerous Project: Including the Proceedings of a Luncheon Conference in Opposition to the Registration of Aliens and Deportation Bills," Box 13, Folder 32, Immigrants' Protective League Records, MSIPL_67, University of Illinois at Chicago.

62. See Lake and Reynolds, *Drawing the Global Colour Line.*

63. Department of State to Bureau of Immigration, October 20, 1920, File 54910/79, INS.

64. On the system of immigration "remote control," see Zolberg, *A Nation by Design*, 110–13, 244, 264–67.

65. Gabaccia, *Foreign Relations*, 50.

66. American Consular Office, Bremen, Germany to Commissioner General of Immigration, April 9, 1930, File 55608/210, INS.

67. Office of Technical Adviser, Belfast, Northern Ireland, to commissioner general of immigration, October 13, 1928, File 55608/210, INS.

68. H. T. Tsiang, "Deportation (A Poem)," 1939, Folder "Civil Liberties-American Committee for the Protection of Foreign Born (1 of 3)," Box 46, Vito Marcantonio Papers, New York Public Library.

2

Globalization and the Border Wall

TRANSNATIONAL POLICING REGIMES IN NORTH AMERICA, 1890S TO THE PRESENT

Elliott Young

Deportation is both a national and transnational problem. Although immigration laws and enforcement bureaucracies are national, the twentieth century saw an increasing number of international policing and migration policy agreements that made possible the regulation of millions of people seeking entry to the United States. Once the United States began enforcing restrictions against foreign immigrants, first the Chinese in the late nineteenth century and later Mexicans and others, international cooperation became key to the enforcement of immigration restrictions. The impossibility of securing thousands of miles of land borders with Mexico and Canada, as well as thousands of miles of unguarded coastline, pushed the United States to enlist private transportation companies and foreign states to help control migration. Given the hegemony of the United States in the Western hemisphere, it is hard to discern the line between US pressure and another country's voluntary cooperation. In the end, US desires to control and restrict migration won out, although the path to US hegemony was neither straight nor unchallenged.

In the late nineteenth century, Mexico refused to cooperate with US efforts to restrict migration and instead asserted the liberal right of anyone to travel unimpeded through—and out of—their country. Canada adopted a more cooperative stance, agreeing to inspect and sort migrants who arrived with the intent of crossing into the United States.[1] By the 1920s, however, as more countries in the Americas began to exclude Chinese laborers, the United States was able to garner these countries' support for enforcing migration restrictions. Ever since the 1980s, and especially after the September 11, 2001, attacks, new multilateral migration and security agreements have proliferated in Greater North America, defined as the United States, Mexico, Canada, and neighboring Caribbean island nations like Cuba. In this chapter I show how border enforcement increasingly became a matter of transnational policing, with the United States training foreign officers, establishing multilateral agreements, and collecting biometric data on migrants beyond its national boundaries. Today in the Mediterranean, where more than 46,000 migrants died between 2000 and 2016, there is a similar European effort to police the sea.[2] These efforts have culminated in the establishment of what policymakers call the "twenty-first-century border," a global lockdown that that has created a transnational detention and deportation regime.

Chinese Exclusion

Before fences, drones, remote sensors, and tens of thousands of border patrol officers, the United States relied on its neighbors to control its border. The Chinese were first group to become targets of US immigration enforcement.[3] Up until 1882, half a million Chinese migrated to the Americas, half as "coolie" labor to work on sugar plantations in Cuba and Peru, and the other half coming to the United States and Canada, mostly to work in mining and on railroads. From 1882 through the 1940s, during the period of US exclusion, 400,000 Chinese came to the United States and Canada, while fewer than 100,000 went to Latin America.[4] The increasing numbers of Chinese seeking entry to North America led the United States to engage its neighbors in its own efforts to control its borders and stop clandestine entry.

By 1890, eight years after the United States passed the Chinese Exclusion Act, it had become clear that Chinese migrants could simply enter into Canada and Mexico and then easily cross over at unguarded points along the land border. In 1893 Canada allowed US immigration officials to examine passengers who intended to cross into the United States and clear them while still on Canadian soil, and in 1903 the Canadian Pacific Railway agreed to send all Chinese passengers under guard to one of four official ports of entry.[5] Although Canada did not pass Chinese labor exclusions until 1923, it used high head taxes and other mechanisms to keep Asians out. There was domestic pressure in Canada, particularly in British Columbia, to exclude the Chinese, but in general Canada was recruiting immigrants at the time to settle vast expanses of unsettled land and build their transcontinental railroad. American efforts were aimed at preventing Chinese migrants from using Canada as a clandestine entryway into the United States. Thus it was the combination of Canadian domestic lobbying for a "white man's country" together with diplomatic efforts by the United States that led to the exclusion of Asians from Canada.[6]

Mexico was a different story. When the United States sought a similar agreement with their southern neighbor, they were soundly rebuffed. The Mexican ambassador to the United States, Matías Romero, cited a clause in Mexico's 1857 Constitution to explain why his government would not assist the United States in enforcing its immigration ban: "All men have the right of entering and leaving the Republic, of traveling through its territory, and of changing their residence without the necessity of letters of security, passports, salvo-conducto, or other similar requisite."[7] This liberal open-door policy slammed shut during the Mexican Revolution as xenophobia and revolutionary nationalism combined to reject Chinese and other "undesirable" immigrants (see chapter 4).

By the mid-1920s, Mexico had passed its own restrictions on Chinese immigration and begun to cooperate with US authorities to exclude and keep track of Chinese migrants shuttling through North America. Nonetheless, even though the United States and Mexico shared a common goal of keeping the Chinese out, there were occasional disputes over which country would be responsible for deporting them back to China. In the early 1930s xenophobic campaigns succeeded in expelling nearly the entire Chinese population from the northwestern states of Sonora and Sinaloa. Most of the Chinese population fled either to the United States or to other parts of Mexico. On one occasion in March 1932, Mexican authorities shoved Chinese migrants through a hole in the border fence in Nogales, only to have them pushed back to Mexico by a US Border Patrol agent.[8]

A year later, however, the Mexican president agreed to pay for the deportation of 297 Chinese migrants who were captured in Nogales after being expelled from Sonora. Such agreements between countries recognized that migration was a binational issue that required cooperation and incurred financial obligations. It was at this very moment that hundreds of thousands of Mexicans were being repatriated from the United States to Mexico, with employers and both governments fighting over who should pay the transportation and relocation costs.[9] The Mexican Farm Labor agreement (1942–64), known as the Bracero Program, also enlisted the Mexican government in helping the United States process, regulate, and control Mexican laborers emigrating north. Although Mexico has pushed back against the most extreme forms of US immigration restrictions, notably President Trump's proposed border wall, since the 1930s, the relationship has been marked more by cooperation than by conflict.

In Cuba, the United States used its military might to impose Chinese exclusion on the island through a 1902 military decree. However, the US law banning Chinese laborers was maintained after Cuba became an independent nation later that year, suggesting acquiescence to US interests and a neocolonial relationship between the two countries. US pressure and Cuban anti-Chinese sentiments notwithstanding, thousands of Chinese managed to sneak into the country illegally in the following decade.[10]

Throughout the first three decades of the twentieth century, the United States tried to get Cuba to shut down further Chinese immigration, but they were continually frustrated by clandestine smuggling networks and corrupt officials who provided fraudulent papers to the Chinese. In 1917 Cuba sought American aid in this endeavor when Francisco Menocal, the Cuban commissioner of immigration, asked US immigration officers to send lists of Chinese passing through the United States who claimed to be merchants. Menocal suspected that alleged Chinese merchants were in fact laborers crossing the North American continent to work on Cuban sugar plantations, and he hoped that their entry documents for the United States would prove his suspicions and allow him to exclude them. US authorities agreed to cooperate because they, in turn, worried that many of the Chinese migrants landing in Cuba would use the island as a springboard for illegal entry into the United States.[11] Sugar plantation owners, however, managed to get the ban on Chinese laborers temporarily lifted in 1917, against the wishes of Cuba's commissioner of labor. Three years later, in 1920, Daniel Trasivik, immigration inspector at Galveston, wrote to his Cuban friend Menocal to enlist his support in squelching Chinese smuggling to the United States. Menocal acknowledged that there was a large smuggling ring in Havana and ordered his detectives to investigate.[12] While the Cuban authorities were not very effective in clamping down on smuggling, both the Cuban and US governments shared a desire to control immigration and to restrict the Chinese in particular. The Menocal correspondence with US immigration officials shows that even when it was economically beneficial for Cuba to open its doors to cheap Chinese labor, Cuban authorities were willing to work with the United States to restrict Chinese entry. In the 1920s, various Cuban presidents issued decrees to stop Chinese immigration, but nonetheless tens of thousands of Chinese immigrants entered Cuba by gaining access to fraudulent papers and evading the immigration restrictions. Cuba's unsuccessful efforts to restrict Chinese laborers in the 1920s demonstrate the limits on US power, even when a friendly government wanted to accede to their demands.[13]

Triscornia Immigration Detention Camp

The United States imposed Chinese labor exclusion in Cuba was only one part of a broader effort to replicate a US immigration regime on the island. In 1900 the United States also built a processing and detention center for all immigrants across the bay from Havana in a town called Casablanca. Triscornia was a replica of Ellis Island in New York City, built to detain all immigrants until they could prove they had family members to support them or a job offer, and to quarantine those with contagious diseases. In his novel *Gallego*, the Cuban writer and folklorist Miguel Barnet described Triscornia less as an immigrant processing station and more as a prison surrounded by barbed wire with plenty of soldiers to keep the immigrants from escaping. In an explanatory footnote, Barnet wrote, "The treatment of Spanish, Asian and Jewish emigrants was particularly cruel and abusive. The administrators made great fortunes selling entry permits to the country. Triscornia is part of the black legend of Cuban immigration."[14] On reaching the immigrant camp, one of the characters in Barnet's novel exclaims, "Holy shit, this is a jail!"[15]

The Spanish immigrant press in Havana decried the horrendous conditions in Triscornia. In 1900 the Havana newspaper *El Eco de Galicia* noted, "They use forced labor which the Spanish laws only use as punishment for the worst criminals.... They demand 25 US gold cents from every immigrant (for housing)." The newspaper also blamed the occupying US authorities for preventing the immigrants from receiving letters of recommendation from merchants of Havana, letters that ostensibly would have helped them gain their release.[16] For many Spanish immigrants to Cuba,

"Triscornia Wharf. Disembarkation pier for immigrants and quarantine patients. The boat *Perey* at the service of the [immigration] department."
El Financiero hispanoamericano, December 24, 1909.

an island that a few years earlier had been their colony, being locked up like common criminals was insulting. In addition to Spaniards, Chinese and Jews were also routinely detained for periods ranging from one day to one month.

El Eco de Galicia accused the United States of trying to stem the tide of Spanish laborers to the island by using the quarantine station as a form of punishment. In October, the newspaper sent a correspondent to Triscornia to report on conditions. The writer found multitudes of immigrant men who had been held in the detention center for long periods of time. Instead of being seen as hardworking men who had come to help Cuba develop, they were being treated as "delinquents."[17] Hundreds crowded into the offices at Triscornia, pleading with authorities to release their family members. The Spanish community accused officials of being purposely slow and bureaucratic so that the detainees would grow so frustrated that they would agree to be hired by employers who paid low salaries. While Havana newspapers like the *Diario de la Marina* accused the United States of trying to "Africanize" Cuba, ostensibly by facilitating black Caribbean immigration, the Spanish immigrant press argued that the United States was using the immigration center to "delatinize" the island. *Eco de Galicia* argued that the goal of the United States was to make Cuba into another state in the union. The objective of US intervention on the island, according to this newspaper, was "to exterminate the Latin race."[18]

Accounts from Spanish immigrants themselves confirmed the negative reports in the newspapers. One Galician migrant wrote a letter describing Triscornia as "the first station of the horrible procession to Calvary...a kind of fort where people are condemned to forced labor."[19] Another Galician newspaper complained that the detention of only third-class passengers was discriminatory, creating easily exploitable laborers and extracting money from them. "Triscornia is not a residence for miserable emigrants who lack resources to wait while they look for work. Triscornia is the place where the money of the immigrants who come to these lands is indirectly deposited.... There they pay for their food, they apply fines,

"The boat *Immigración*, servicing the Port of Havana." *El Financiero hispanoamericano*, December 24, 1909.

and finally they also work under the inclement tropical sun rays, without these unhappy ones receiving anything from the Mandarins other than less than nice treatment." The article went on to argue that the detention center was not a medical facility for quarantine, but a place where bars and billiard tables drained the poor immigrants' resources.[20] Long detentions were not the norm at Triscornia; most internees remained just one day, but some were held for a whole month. Over time, the detention camp became an informal labor recruitment center. Women were recruited as domestic servants and some were also hired as prostitutes as part of the so-called white slave trade.

There is plenty of testimony condemning Triscornia, but not all immigrants who passed through the camp experienced it as a horrendous jail. Although the Spanish immigrant press regularly complained about the conditions at Triscornia, the Casino Español, representing the Spanish merchant elite in Havana, reported, "the treatment one sees [at Triscornia] is excellent; too excellent." Whether their investigatory commission was shown a true picture of the camp or not, the Casino seemed more

"Immigration Camp. Hotel for first-class quarantine patients. Passengers embarking from infested ports." *El Financiero hispanoamericano*, December 24, 1909.

concerned with preventing a flood of immigrants to the island than protecting the welfare of detained migrants. In an interview conducted in 1983 in La Coruña, Spain, one Spanish immigrant remembered the camp positively, noting that they bathed every day and the food was "not bad."[21] It is possible that not all immigrants experienced deprivation and abuse at Triscornia, but for many it was, in the words of the character in Barnet's novel, a "nightmare."[22] The US influence over Cuba is evident in the Triscornia camp, a model for immigrant processing that neither Mexico nor Canada ever followed.

Triscornia continued to be used as an immigration detention center well after the US military occupation ended. In the early 1920s, as US restrictionist legislation expanded to keep out southern and eastern Europeans and Jews, Cuba continued to collaborate to prevent unwanted migrants from using Cuba as a stepping-stone to enter the United States clandestinely. In explaining his deportation order against three Syrians and a Turk, the secretary of the interim president in Cuba explained how he was being pressured by the US consulate in Havana to reject "all Jews, Poles, Russians, Italians, Turks, Armenians, and subjects of Hungary, Croatia, Czechoslovakia, because [the consul] believed their goal was to fraudulently penetrate the US."[23] Notwithstanding the efforts of the Cuban government, historian Libby Garland has shown how Havana was a center of alien smuggling, particularly of Jews who sought entry to the United States after immigration quotas had been imposed.[24] In 1939 Cuban authorities bowed to US pressures, invalidating Cuban entry permits, and prevented the landing of more than nine hundred Jews fleeing Nazi Germany on the transatlantic liner *St. Louis*. Almost all of these Jews were returned to Europe, 254 of whom were killed during the Holocaust.[25]

While it was most often the United States pressuring Cuba to enforce restrictions and deportations, the Cubans also needed the cooperation of the United States to deport Chinese migrants. In 1927 eight Chinese migrants were deported from Havana for trafficking opium. The Chinese deportees were placed on a United Fruit ship to New Orleans, then transferred to San Francisco by rail, and finally placed on a Dollar Line ship to Hong Kong.[26] Although North American countries initially had different immigration policies regarding the Chinese, by the 1920s, Canada (1923), Mexico (1921), and Cuba (1902, 1924) had adopted the US model of Chinese exclusion. More often than not, these governments cooperated with each other to exclude and deport Chinese immigrants.

Mexican Repatriation and Central American Deportations

During the 1920s and 1930s, up to one million Mexicans living in the United States were "repatriated" to Mexico.[27] According to Mexican Migration Service reports that recorded returns at twenty-six ports along the border, there were 458,000 repatriations from 1929 to 1937.[28] Although this was clearly a program that originated in the United States, Mexico was undergoing rapid industrialization at the time and also encouraged its compatriots to return. Furthermore, Mexican consulates played a key role in facilitating the repatriations. In some cases, US state welfare societies covered the cost of transport to the Mexican border and the Mexican government paid for their travel to the interior of Mexico.[29] In the early 1930s, Mexican presidents negotiated with the US government, agreeing to exempt returnees from customs duties to encourage their return to Mexico, and even establishing a National Repatriation Board to develop colonies where the returnees could be put to work.[30]

In their book *Decade of Betrayal*, historians Franscico Balderrama and Raymond Rodríguez note the collaboration between the two governments, while also pointing out the tensions that erupted over who should bear the responsibility for the repatriations. Mexican immigrant groups like the Confederación de Sociedades Mexicanas and the Spanish language press on both sides of the border denounced repatriation as a sinister plan to get rid of all Mexicans.[31] The Mexican government generally accepted and embraced repatriation, but their efforts to fund the returns faltered in the face of financial realities. When Mexico's president Obregón helped destitute Mexicans' return to the country in the early 1920s, it rapidly depleted the country's treasury, leading the government to abandon these efforts and decide to only help in life-threatening situations.[32] Mexico's consul in Chicago wrote a scathing letter to the township trustee in Gary, Indiana, in 1932, complaining that the rapid expulsion of Mexicans with a few days notice did not permit him enough time to coordinate transportation for the returnees on the Mexican side of the border. However, the larger point the consul made was that repatriation was the responsibility of the United States and not Mexico. He wrote, "I very earnestly call again your attention to the fact that the Mexican Government is in no way obligated to take care of those people who, regardless of their nationality are members of your community.... Of course, we welcome our fellow countrymen going back to Mexico, but the Mexican Government feels that we are entitled to some attention and consideration from you in return of our willingness to take from your shoulders a problem that is not ours."[33] With employers, the US and Mexican governments, and charity organizations all shifting the blame and responsibility to one another, most returns were financed by Mexican migrants themselves, who simply picked up and left the United States under threat of forcible removal.

By the 1940s, relations between the United States and Mexico had become friendlier as a result of America's need to curry favor with its southern neighbor during WWII. In this period, Mexico expanded its cooperation with the United States to include facilitating deportations of Central Americans and others through Mexican territory. In 1943 a US immigration inspector in San Antonio approached the Mexican consul there to ask if deportees could be sent through Mexico and then back to Central America by airplane, with the United States picking up the bill for the flight.[34] It appears that the request was honored. Cooperation between the two countries broke down, however, when the United States refused to allow Mexico to send its own deported migrants through the American-controlled Panama Canal Zone during World War II, citing security concerns. Mexican officials complained that they had allowed Americans and other foreigners to pass through Mexico to help the war effort, and threatened to stop cooperating if the United States was unwilling to return the favor.[35] Such squabbles, however, represented only brief pauses in what would be increasingly intimate and intense efforts to police migrants transnationally. In the early 1950s, the US Border Patrol stepped up enforcement during Operation Wetback, removing more than three million Mexicans in five years. The Mexican government cooperated with these efforts by setting up detention camps on the Mexican side of the border with armed guards to prevent deportees from returning to the United States.[36]

Reagan and the Global Lockdown

Immigration to the United States boomed in the 1980s as a result of neoliberal policies that disrupted economies in the global south, and Mexico in particular. The 1982 debt crisis in Mexico sent shock waves through the economy, sparking an increase in migration north to escape poverty at home. Although proportionately the foreign-born population in the United States was higher in the early twentieth century, in absolute numbers the rise in immigrants was unprecedented, and most came from Mexico. More than seven million immigrants arrived legally in to the United States in the 1980s, with estimates of an undocumented population of anywhere from two to eight million.[37] In this context, President Ronald Reagan issued Proclamation 4865 on September 29, 1981, declaring, "the ongoing migration of persons to the United States in violation of our laws is a serious national problem detrimental to the interests of the United States." Among other steps, Reagan called for international cooperation to intercept sea vessels carrying "illegal migrants." Simultaneously, Reagan issued Executive Order 12324 directing the Coast Guard to interdict and repatriate migrants attempting to enter the United States illegally. The new policies pushed the enforcement of US borders well beyond the coastline and potentially into international waters.[38] On May 24, 1992, President George H. W. Bush clarified Reagan's policy in Executive Order 12807, directing the Coast Guard to interdict aliens believed to be heading to the United States without proper authorization "beyond the territorial sea of the United States."[39] Taken together, these executive orders empowered the United States to enforce its immigration restrictions on the high seas and to seek cooperative agreements with foreign governments.

Immigration and refugee advocates contended that these efforts prevented asylum seekers from reaching US waters or applying for asylum. In 1993 the Haitian Centers Council, an immigrants' rights organization, argued that Bush's executive order, which mandated that Haitian refugees found at sea be returned to Haiti or sent to the Guantanamo Bay Naval Base, violated the Immigration and Naturalization Act (INA) of 1952 and Article 33 of the United Nations' Protocol Relating to the Status of Refugees. The Supreme Court ruled in favor of the government, emphasizing that the INA and the UN protocol only referred to obligations the United States had when migrants reached the territory of the country. Since the migrants were stopped in international waters, the court decided that they were not protected.[40] In 1993 Clinton issued a presidential directive aimed at curtailing smuggling of illegal aliens, in which he reaffirmed the goal of interdicting and holding "smuggled aliens as far as possible from the U.S. border and to repatriate them when appropriate."[41] Clinton further declared that the United States would seek stiffer penalties for smugglers both at home and abroad. The policy that Reagan started, framing illegal immigration as a national security threat that should be dealt with by the Coast Guard with assistance from the Department of Defense, has been expanded by all subsequent administrations.

International cooperation is central to the mission of preventing illegal immigration and other border violations. Such cooperative agreements began more than a century ago, as described previously, but since the 1980s, the United States has entered into a series of agreements with neighboring countries to transnationalize policing on land and sea through joint training and enforcement operations. The boarding of ships flying the flags of other nations, for example, requires the consent of those nations. The Coast Guard has more than fifty agreements with other states to facilitate maritime law enforcement, the bulk of which are with Latin American countries and related, in theory, to drug enforcement. The United States also has several bilateral agreements with the Bahamas, Haiti, and the Dominican Republic to coordinate the suppression of migrant smuggling through the Caribbean basin. These agreements allow the US Coast Guard to enter the territorial waters of these countries to pursue unauthorized migrants and drug traffickers.[42] In addition, the US Department of State's Bureau of Migration, Population and Refugees sponsors programs throughout the world to increase cooperation with other countries by providing technical assistance, capacity-building, and sharing information to help strengthen their migration control efforts.[43]

In 2007 the establishment of the Mérida Initiative marked a major step toward enhancing cooperation between the United States and Mexico on security issues. As part of the program, US agencies such as ICE, the Border Patrol, and the Coast Guard trained thousands of Mexican police and military officers, provided high-tech equipment, and shared intelligence about criminal organizations, drug traffickers, and human smugglers. The initiative's stated goals are to secure the US border, disrupt drug trafficking, and prevent illegal immigration. In 2012 Mariko Silver, acting assistant secretary of international affairs for the Department of Homeland Security, testified before a House Foreign Affairs Subcommittee hearing about the importance of cooperation with Mexico. As Silver put it, "Strong partnerships with international counterparts are particularly essential when we are dealing with shared problems like the transnational drug trade, human smuggling and trafficking, and border management. We will continue to work with Mexico as a partner to address common issues and challenges along the border. As part of our partnership with Mexico, providing assistance—be it technology, training, or equipment—will and must remain central."[44] As part of the Merida Initiative, the US Congress appropriated more than $803 million between 2008 and 2014 for the

Central American Regional Security Initiative, which likewise supplied equipment and training, and facilitated information sharing about drug traffickers, criminal gangs, human smugglers, and deportees.[45] The mingling of drug enforcement and migration control activities, long a feature of border control efforts, helps solidify the idea of unauthorized migrants as dangerous criminals.

In the future, we can expect that international cooperation with neighboring countries will become increasingly important. In its strategic plan for 2012–16, the Customs and Border Patrol identified international cooperation with Canada and Mexico as a key priority. The plan states, "As the Nation's border-security efforts have expanded beyond its physical border region, cooperation through assigned liaisons with our Canadian and Mexican partners has become an integral part of daily operations." The Border Patrol's International Liaison Unit works with the Mexican government, while the International Border Enforcement Team collaborates with the Canadian government, organizing monthly meetings in addition to daily contacts between counterparts on either side of America's borders.[46] President Trump's incendiary anti-immigrant rhetoric and planned border wall might possibly lead to a break in what has been a century of cooperation over border security, but at the same time Mexico has been beefing up its own southern border enforcement at the behest of Washington, which funds these efforts through the Southern Border Plan.[47]

Cooperation and Unilateral Enforcement

Cooperation rather than conflict marked US and Mexican immigration policies for most of the twentieth century. In the 1930s, the Mexican government occasionally protested the treatment of repatriates, but presidents and foreign ministry officials mostly supported repatriation and muzzled local consuls from voicing opposition.[48] Aside from a few instances of pushback from the Mexican government, especially during the early 1950s mass deportations from the United States, Mexico worked together with the United States to control the border. By the 1990s, Mexico began to receive money from the United States to deport migrants as more and more Central Americans and others began to use Mexico as a pathway to reach the United States.

In the early 1990s, US Congress appropriated $350,000 a year to pay

Mexico to defray costs of deporting third country migrants, mostly from Central America, who were passing through Mexico on their way to the United States. In April 1993, a boat with three hundred Chinese migrants heading to San Francisco made it to Ensenada. Mexican authorities discovered the migrants locked in a smuggler's safe house and took them into custody. Mexico deported all of the Chinese migrants, except for six who were found to have legitimate claims for asylum. However, the United States refused to grant the Mexican-chartered airplane carrying the rest permission to land in Alaska, fearing that the Chinese would request asylum once they reached US soil. While awaiting deportation in a crowded hangar at Mexicali's airport, one hundred Chinese migrants escaped. In the meantime, the remaining two hundred were deported after Mexico secured permission to refuel the airplane in Europe. Although most of the escaped Chinese were later apprehended by US authorities, the lack of coordination between the governments highlighted a weakness in the deportation mechanism.[49] The initiatives undertaken in the first decade of the twenty-first century in the Caribbean, Mexico, and Central America are all designed to prevent these kinds of conflicts and ensure a smooth and efficient mechanism for deporting unwanted migrants.

The US refusal to cooperate with Mexicans by allowing an airplane carrying Chinese deportees to land in Alaska stands in stark contrast with the expectation that Mexico should be responsible for deporting Chinese caught in the open seas. A few months after the airplane incident, the United States tried to pressure Mexico to accept and deport 659 Chinese migrants who had been intercepted at sea by the US Coast Guard. A Mexican foreign ministry official protested, "I don't think it is Mexico's place, nor do I think anybody reasonably expects Mexico to become an arm of the US immigration service."[50] However, while Mexico claims not to be carrying out US immigration policy, it has received millions of dollars over the past few decades for precisely that purpose. The United States has also pressured other countries in Central America to take an active role in deporting unwanted migrants. Around the same time that these Chinese migrants were discovered near Ensenada, the US Coast Guard intercepted a boatload of Chinese migrants two hundred miles off the coast of Honduras. The United States brought the Honduran-registered boat to Honduras and sent two lawyers from the INS to interview the migrants. Even though the lawyers determined that five were political refugees and others had viable asylum claims, all of the migrants were sent back to

China, paid for by the US government. The US government therefore evaded its responsibility under international and US law to grant asylum by making Honduras deport the migrants before they even had a chance to reach US soil.

Conclusion

Controlling the flow of illegal goods and undocumented migrants into the United States has pushed enforcement outside of territorial boundaries. Efforts at what political scientist Aristide Zolberg has called "remote control" of immigration began in the late nineteenth century as the United States sought to screen prospective migrants for diseases before they even left their homelands.[51] By the 1920s, a system of passports and visas had been established around the globe that required all travelers to be documented when crossing into a different nation.[52] Since the 1980s, the United States has both sought to outsource its enforcement of migration control to neighboring countries and at times acted unilaterally beyond its territory. Although the United States has permission from some countries to board vessels registered under their flags, the US Coast Guard has taken it upon itself to board vessels even when the nationality of the ship has not been determined. As Lucas Guttentag, an immigration expert at the ACLU, put it, "This would seem to come perilously close to piracy."[53] In the cases both of US unilateral action beyond its borders and of the United States pressuring other countries to do its bidding, what we are witnessing is the expansion of state power beyond the territorial confines of the nation-state.

Scholars and journalists today often seem perplexed at the apparent contradiction between globalization and the persistence of the nation-state, asking "Should we not see the withering of the nation-state in an increasingly globalized world?"[54] The concurrent rise of the nation-state and global neoliberalism is not a paradox, however, if one looks at the symbiotic relationship between the two. Tracing the history of US migration control, one can see both the trend toward increasing international cooperation and the expansion of US imperial reach beyond its own borders. Controlling migration is both an act of national sovereignty and an expression of global empire.

President Donald Trump's outlandish proposal to build a big wall between the United States and Mexico and make Mexico pay for it is only a more extreme version of the kind of cooperative policing of borders that has existed for more than a century. While this great wall will not likely ever be built, and Mexico is certainly not going to pay for it, Mexico continues to help the United States by blocking the flow of migrants through its own territory. In 2014 Mexico's President Enrique Peña Nieto announced his Southern Border Plan to help create a twenty-first-century border and stem the tide of Central American refugees. As a result of this plan, deportations doubled in two years, reaching more than 180,000 in 2015, 98 percent involving Central Americans.[55] So while it is unlikely that Mexico will build a wall on its northern border, it is busy erecting a virtual wall on its southern border through heightened policing and enforcement actions.

Borders, migration control, and deportations proliferate in this age of globalization. President Trump's ill-conceived and unconstitutional executive orders on immigration and his calls to deport upward of three million undocumented immigrants from the United States illustrate that we are in an age of increased border control. Perhaps Trump and the worldwide resurgence of populist nationalism represents the last gasp of an earlier era of nation-state supremacy before the world gets homogenized into a happy-meal global supermarket, as the neoliberal apologist Thomas Friedman imagined at the end of the last century.[56] But it is just as likely that this new age of globalization will result in the kind of anti-immigrant xenophobia that we are witnessing from the United States to Europe and beyond. Globalization and the border wall are not antithetical; they are two sides of our dystopia.

Notes

1. David Scott Fitzgerald and David Cook-Martin, *Culling the Masses: The Democratic Origins of Racist Immigration Policy in the Americas* (Cambridge: Harvard University Press, 2014).

2. Missing Migrants Project, "Latest Global Figures," http://missingmigrants.iom.int/latest-global-figures (accessed February 14, 2016).

3. Erika Lee, *At America's Gates: Chinese Immigration during the Exclusion Era, 1882–1943* (Chapel Hill: University of North Carolina Press, 2003); Kornel Chang, *Pacific Connections: The Making of the U.S.-Canadian Borderlands* (Berkeley: University of California Press, 2012).

4. Elliott Young, *Alien Nation: Chinese Migration in the Americas from the Coolie Era through WWII* (Chapel Hill: University of North Carolina Press, 2014), 32–33.

5. Ibid., 165–67.

6. Chang, *Pacific Connections.*

7. Young, *Alien Nation*, 100.

8. Ibid., 245; Kelly Lytle Hernández, *Migra! A History of the Border Patrol* (Berkeley: University of California Press, 2010), 78–79.

9. Francisco E. Balderrama and Raymond Rodríguez, *Decade of Betrayal: Mexican Repatriation in the 1930s* (Albuquerque: University of New Mexico, 1996), 130.

10. Kathleen López, *Chinese Cubans: A Transnational History* (Chapel Hill: University of North Carolina Press, 2013), 145–46.

11. Inspector, Buffalo, to Commissioner General of Immigration, Washington, DC, March 14, 1917, Records of the Immigration and Naturalization Service (hereafter INS), Record Group 85, National Archives and Records Administration, Washington, DC, Box 3, Folder 309/10.

12. Francisco E. Menocal, Immigration Commissioner, Havana, to Daniel Trasivuk, Immigration Service, Galveston, March 17, 1920, ibid.

13. López, *Chinese Cubans*, 158–61.

14. "Particularmente cruel y abusivo fue el trato que siempre se le dio allí a los emigrantes españoles, asiíaticos y judíos. Triscornia fue un antro de delincuencia y corupción. Sus administradores hicieron fortunas con el negocio de los permisos de entrada al pais. Trisocornia es parte de la leyenda negra de la inmigración a Cuba." Miguel Barnet, *Gallego* (Madrid: Alianza Editorial, 1987), 41.

15. "Pa su madre, esto es una cárcel!" Ibid., 42.

16. "Se les obliga a trabajos forzados que las leyes españolas aplican solamente como castigo a los mayores criminales [...] Se les exige 25 céntimos de oro americano a cada emigrante (por el alojamiento)." *El Eco de Galicia*, October 14, 1900, quoted in José Antonio Vidal Rodríguez, "La inmigración española en Cuba durante la primera ocupación militar norteamericana (1899–1902): El control del mercado laboral," *Migraciones y Exilios* 4 (2004): 47.

17. *El Eco de Galicia*, October 10, 1900, quoted in ibid.

18. *El Eco de Galicia*, December 15, 1900, quoted in ibid., 48.

19. "La primera estación del horrible calvario es Triscornia, una especie de presidio donde se le condena a trabajos forzados." Letter from a Galician emigrant, *La Habana*, January 25, 1903, quoted in ibid.

20. "La Triscornia no es un alojamiento donde los infelices emigrantes, faltos de recursos, encuentren albergue mientras no hallan trabajo. Triscornia es el lugar donde indirectamente va a parar el dinero del inmigrante que llega a estas tierras [...]. Allí pagan su comida, allí se les ponen multas, allí, en fin, también penosamente trabajan bajo los inclementes rayos del sol tropical, sin que el trabajo de aquellos desgraciados merezca otra recompensa de los mandarines que un trato poco delicado." Galicia, *La Habana*, January 31, 1904, quoted in ibid., 49.

21. "El trato, como se ve, es excelente; demasiado excelente." Consuelo Naranjo Orovio, *Del campo a la bodega: recuerdos de gallegos en Cuba (siglo xx)* (Coruña: Ediciós do Castro, 1988), 86.

22. Barnet, *Gallego*, 43.

23. "Al llegar a Cuba a todos aquellos Judios, Polacos, Rusos, Italianos, Turcos, Armenios, y subditos o ciudadanos de Hungria, Croacia, Checoslovakia puesto que tenia la conviccion de que su objeto era penetrar fraudulentamente en los Estados Unidos." Secretary of the Interim President to Mr. Kadi Aly, January 15, 1924, Archivo Nacional de Cube (hereafter ANC), Secretaria de la Presidencia, Leg. 121, Exp. 22.

24. Libby Garland, *After They Closed the Gates: Jewish Illegal Immigration to the United States, 1921–1965* (Chicago: University of Chicago, 2014), 89–91.

25. John Mendelsohn, *Jewish Emigration: The St. Louis Affair and Other Cases* (New York: Garland Publishing, 1982).

26. Deportados (Chinos), December 30, 1926, ANC, Secretaria de la Presidencia, Leg. 108, Exp. 68.

27. Balderrama and Rodríguez, *Decade of Betrayal*, 122.

28. Abraham Hoffman, "Mexican Repatriation Statistics: Some Suggested Alternatives to Carey McWilliams," *Western Historical Quarterly* 3, no. 4 (1972): 397–99.

29. Silvano Barba González to Sec. de Gobernación, October 20, 1931, Archivo de la Secretaría de Ralaciones Exteriores, Mexico City (hereafter SRE), IV-355-5.

30. Balderrama and Rodríguez, *Decade of Betrayal*, 133, 142–43.

31. Ibid., 118–19.

32. Ibid., 130.

33. Rafael Aveleyra, Consul, Chicago, to Mary Grace Wells, Township Trustee, Gary, Indiana, July 22, 1932, SRE, IV-354-12, in ibid., 152.

34. Manuel Tello to Sec. de Gobernación, October 14, 1943, Archivo Histórico del Instituto Nacional de Migración, Instituto Nacional de Migración, Mexico, 4-353-1943-2948.

35. Hector Perez Martinez, Servicio de Inspección, to Gobernación, April 17, 1945, SRE, III-2489-9.

36. Hernández, *Migra!*, 156–57, 172–73.

37. Mae Ngai, *Impossible Subjects: Illegal Aliens and the Making of Modern America* (Princeton: Princeton University Press, 2004), 266, 273.

38. Brian W. Robinson, "Smuggled Masses: The Need for a Maritime Alien Smuggling Law Enforcement," *The Army Lawyer* 447 (August 2010): 30–31.

39. George H. W. Bush, Executive Order 12807, May 14, 1992, 57 Fed. Reg. 23, 133 (1992), http://www.presidency.ucsb.edu/ws/?pid=23627 (accessed February 14, 2017).

40. Sale, Acting Commissioner, Immigration and Naturalization Service, v. Haitian Centers Council Inc., 509 U.S. 155 (1993), https://www.oyez.org/cases/1992/92-344 (accessed February 14, 2017).

41. William J. Clinton, PDD 9: Alien Smuggling, June 18, 1993, partial text available at http://fas.org/irp/offdocs/pdd9.txt (accessed August 19, 2014).

42. Robinson, "Smuggled Masses," 27, n. 61.

43. US Department of States, Bureau of Population, Refugees and Migration, http://www.state.gov/j/prm/migration/index.htm (accessed February 14, 2017).

44. "Statement of Assistant Secretary of International Affairs (Acting) Mariko Silver before the House Foreign Affairs Subcommittee on the Western Hemisphere and the House Homeland Security Subcommittee on Oversight, Investigations, and Management: Assessing the Mérida Initiative: The Evolution of Drug Cartels and the Threat to Mexico's Governance, Part 2," October 3, 2011, http://www.dhs.gov/news/2011/10/03/statement-asst-sec-international-affairs-acting-mariko-silver-house-foreign-affairs (accessed February 14, 2017).

45. Peter J. Meyer, "Central American Regional Security Initiative: Background and Policy Issues for Congress," *Congressional Research Service*, May 6, 2014, 36, http://fas.org/sgp/crs/row/R41731.pdf (accessed February 14, 2017).

46. US Customs and Border Patrol, "2012–2016: Border Patrol Strategic Plan," 11, http://www.cbp.gov/sites/default/files/documents/bp_strategic_plan.pdf (accessed February 14, 2017).

47. Julian Borger and David Agren, "Mexico Will Not Accept Trump's Immigration Plans, Says Foreign Minister," *Guardian*, February 22, 2017, https://www.theguardian.com/world/2017/feb/22/mexico-trump-immigration-foreign-minister-luis-videgaray (accessed April 19, 2017).

48. Balderrama and Rodríguez, *Decade of Betrayal*, 138.

49. Deborah Sontag, "Mexico's Position on Aliens Contradicted by Past Deeds," *New York Times*, July 15, 1993.

50. Ibid.

51. Aristide R. Zolberg, *A Nation by Design: Immigration Policy in the Fashioning of America* (New York: Harvard University Press, 2006), 9.

52. John Torpey, *The Invention of the Passport: Surveillance, Citizenship and the State* (Cambridge: Cambridge University Press, 2000).

53. Sontag, "Mexico's Position on Aliens."

54. Parag Khanna, "The End of the Nation State?" *New York Times*, October 12, 2013, http://www.nytimes.com/2013/10/13/opinion/sunday/the-end-of-the-nation-state.html (accessed February 14, 2017); William I. Robinson, "Beyond Nation-State Paradigms: Globalization, Sociology and the Challenge of Transnational Studies," in *Globalization, the Nation-State and International Relations*, ed. Roland Robertson and Kathleen E. White (London: Routledge, 2003), 211.

55. Secretaria de Gobernación, "Extranjeros presentados y devueltos: Cuadro 3.2.1," http://www.politicamigratoria.gob.mx/es_mx/SEGOB/Extranjeros_alojados_y_devueltos_2015 (accessed February 14, 2017); Stephanie Nolan, "Southern Exposure: The Costly Border Plan Mexico Won't Discuss," *Globe and Mail*, January 5, 2017, http://www.theglobeandmail.com/news/world/the-costly-border-mexico-wont-discuss-migration/article30397720/ (accessed February 14, 2017).

56. Thomas L. Friedman, *The Lexus and the Olive Tree: Understanding Globalization* (New York: Picador, 1999).

3

Assassination, Extradition, and the Public Sphere

THE CABRERA-BARILLAS AFFAIR
IN PORFIRIAN MEXICO

David C. LaFevor

At a little past seven o'clock in the evening of April 7, 1907, the aging General Lisandro Barillas walked through the *zócalo* (central plaza) of Mexico City toward his home in exile on Calle Reloj, two blocks from the center of the nation's political and cultural life.[1] It was growing dark, and though this was not the first attempt to assassinate him, the former president of Guatemala likely did not suspect that one of his compatriots waited for him with an unsheathed dagger in the Plaza del Seminario.[2] After all, the general had political asylum in Mexico and was under the protection of Mexican President Porfirio Díaz. As Barillas crossed the street toward a used bookstore and drink stand, without warning the eighteen-year-old Florencio Morales approached him from behind. Seconds later, Barillas stumbled forward and fell facedown across the streetcar tracks, immobile, with a pool of blood extending from his well-dressed corpse.[3] This version of the stabbing was one the most consistent among several later told by witnesses to the police and the press.

This chapter examines the international crisis that opened with this assassination and quickly escalated into a challenge for the geopolitical objectives of the United States, Guatemala, Mexico, and Nicaragua. Throughout the nineteenth century, Central Americans battled over the question of regional unity under one state, or whether national interests would be best served under a system of small independent republics.

President Theodore Roosevelt, in the same month as the Barillas assassination, had brokered a Central American peace deal in Washington that was designed to protect the Panama Canal Zone from the instability that might be brought on by a regional war.[4] The murder of Barillas put into motion a succession of bombings and assassination attempts in Guatemala that culminated in the massing of troops on both sides of the contested Mexican-Guatemalan border and threatened to alter the tenuous balance of power in the region. The impasse arose not over the murder itself, but due to conflicting interpretations of the ambiguous legal doctrine of extradition and the tension between cosmopolitanism and nationalism: international law versus perceptions of national honor. The juridical principle that a sovereign nation would voluntarily deport a suspected criminal had evolved over the nineteenth century. Extraditions were highly choreographed affairs that resulted from international cooperation and compromise. The treaties that legalized and bound these actions reversed the previous "sacred" doctrine of asylum, by which national governments often refused to render political refugees or accused criminals without a compelling establishment of habeas corpus. These agreements most often stemmed from legally binding bilateral treaties whose enactment conferred international political legitimacy on both signatories. Adherence to the standards of international law—in this case a limitation of pure sovereignty—provided a claim to modernity. Problems arose, as in this case, in the execution of the details. In the Barillas case, the Guatemalan government refused to deliver the accused instigators of the murder to Mexico. Older concepts of national honor, at least rhetorically, replaced the dictates of treaty obligations in the expression of sovereignty. These events provide a counterpoint to most studies in this volume—a refusal to deport or extradite. It also focuses attention away from the US-Mexico border, to trace how unequal power relations manifested over extradition and deportation when Mexico was the more powerful side of the international equation.

As this chapter will show, the stakes involved in this single case of extradition were extremely high, especially when it intertwined with deeply embedded perceptions of honor, civilization, and modernity. The Cabrera-Barillas Affair threatened to tip Central America back into a cycle of revolutionary violence. In Mexico, the assassination endangered the celebrated Porfirian peace: a symbol of President Díaz's long dictatorship and his fundamental claim to political legitimacy. The march to war also endangered US objectives of stability and control over the Panama Canal, then under construction. It threatened to render the Roosevelt Corollary, which self-defined the United States as a hemispheric police force, into an unworkable proposition that would draw a reluctant Roosevelt administration further into the complex and volatile relations among Central American nations.[5] The Guatemalan dictator, President Estrada Cabrera, was likely responsible for ordering the assassination that was at the root of this crisis, but he used his close relationship with the United States as a check on retaliation by Mexico.[6]

The examination of coded diplomatic correspondence from the Mexican novelist Federico Gamboa (then the head of the Mexican legation in Guatemala City) and Secretary of State Ignacio Mariscal shows the extreme measures the Mexican government underwent to avoid war. It pursued peace amid appeals in the transnational public sphere for Mexico to invade and colonize Central America. The Mexican press, citing editorials from the United States and Europe, sought to shame the Mexican government into military action. The diplomatic finesse of Mexican inaction shows how the Porfirian regime worked behind the scenes to avoid becoming an imperial power in Central America. This preference was often at odds with nationalist public opinion as expressed in a number of widely distributed newspapers and *revistas* (periodical reviews). Imperial expansion was an aspirational expression of belle époque nationalism, but despite Díaz's program to raise Mexico to an imagined par with Western Europe and the United States, he resisted these incitements to take territory in Central America.[7] His anxieties were based on the historical precedent of US empire at Mexican expense, and specifically on growing US political and economic collusion with the Estrada-Cabrera regime that endangered national security on Mexico's southern border.[8]

The Mexican press's portrayal of their southern neighbors as barbaric racial others illustrated how the regime of Porfirio Díaz circumvented the racial determinist trap of positing that all Latin Americans were congenitally incapable of civilized modern nationhood by distancing Mexican people from those of Central America.[9] Mexicans, by implication, were modern because they were not Guatemalans. The Mexican dictator was enlightened, while the US press generally agreed that Estrada Cabrera was an atavistic "Nero" who presided over an army of "submissive and ignorant" peons.[10] The denigration of Central American nations was also an indicator of Porfirian success in distancing Mexicans from their own violent nineteenth-century past.

Alongside the salacious details of the assassination, attempted reprisals, espionage, and executions, Mexican writers used a lexicon of outrage to define themselves against Central Americans and to delineate the
nature of nationhood by celebrating what it was not. The moderate and
diplomatic response of the Mexican government was designed to maintain the approval of international public opinion while repressing domestic jingoism. It ended up exacerbating a national pride wounded by the
assassination, and increased discontent with the Díaz regime that would
contribute to revolution three years later.

The popular Mexican illustrator José Guadalupe Posada seized on the
mundane and humanistic dimensions of the assassination. He featured
Barillas's Guatemalan killers, the seventeen-year-old Florencio Morales

"Las Bravisimas Calveras Guatemaltecas de Mora y Morales."
Jose Guadalupe Posada, 1907. Courtesy of the University of
New Mexico, Fernando Gamboa Collection.

and his handler, the taciturn Bernardo Mora, as mediums of political intrigue they did not fully comprehend. Their actions nearly led to war before they were executed in the courtyard of a seventeenth-century convent, Mexico City's infamous Belen Prison. Like so many people parodied by Guadalupe Posada, Mora and Morales were portrayed as *calaveras* (satirical skulls and skeletons), and their story was written as a *corrido* (popular ballad).[11]

The Barillas affair resulted from what one journalist called the most dramatic crime in living memory.[12] The fallout from the murder and the subsequent diplomatic crisis nearly pushed Mexico and Guatemala into a war that likely would have engrossed all of Central America, as well as the United States. These events have been obscured by better known crises, such as the Cananea Massacre in 1906, when US militia members, acting in complicity with the Mexican government, quelled a nationalistic labor dispute at an American-owned mine by murdering labor leaders on Mexican soil. Historians often portray the massacre at Cananea and the Rio Blanco textile strike as precursors to the Mexican Revolution.[13] Both events ultimately resulted from the liberal developmentalist aspirations of Porfirio Díaz and the necessity to attract and protect foreign capital as a precondition for the modernizing project—railroads, mines, diplomacy, export agriculture, and an enhanced perception in the eyes of the nations of the "civilized world." The tension between this official xenophilia and the growing nationalism that, ironically, resulted in part from Mexico's international stature under the Díaz dictatorship was clearly on display in the fallout from Cananea. It contributed to the galvanizing of Mexican nationalism that increasingly found Díaz to be a traitor to the nation. The Cananea massacre, along with the case examined here, evoked a central tension of the Porfirian era: cosmopolitanism versus nationalism. Díaz's pursuit of international legitimacy, manifest in his ultimate inaction over extradition, exposed what many Mexican nationalists in the public sphere labeled his debilitating embrace of cosmopolitanism.

Porfirian Perceptions and International Public Opinion

During the Porfiran Era (1876–1910), domestic political legitimacy derived in part from the international veneration and backing of President Díaz's authoritarian government. The diplomatic corps, carefully managed from Mexico City via an emergent network of telegraphs and steamship mail service, portrayed Mexico as a "secure, sanitary, free, sovereign, liberal, republican and democratic country."[14] This disciplined and technocratic self-promotion hinged on the provision of stability, and it cultivated international acclaim for Mexico's economic dynamism. This selling of Porfirian Mexico led to increased foreign investment, migration, and technological transfers that assured a continued trajectory toward the Porfirian ideal of first-tier modern nationhood. Despite this carefully executed plan, courting of international opinion in this case ran counter to the vital defense of concepts and practices of honor, both in everyday interactions among Mexicans and in the conduct of foreign affairs. Masculine honor, as historian Pablo Piccato has written, was understood and expressed in a language that closely paralleled notions of violence and aggression.[15] Diplomats and journalists who cleaved to these notions of Porfirian progress articulated national honor embodied by Díaz as the patriarchal *retired* warrior who acted with studied restraint; his violent days, like Mexico's, were in his past. But as Mexico entered the twentieth century, the nationalistic defense of honor against foreign aggression clashed with Díaz's central governing project: the provision and defense of predictability and stability and the avoidance of large-scale armed conflict.[16]

While the vindication of perceived slights to national honor in this period often ended in violent action in neighboring Central America, the Díaz regime stressed moderate responses constrained by treaties and the evocation of its civilized status among an imagined group of peer nations that excluded most of its southern neighbors. Civilization, in this formulation, was fragile and required constant vigilance. The Porfirian imagination of honor and masculinity was antithetical to aggression and violence—characteristics it imputed to the Mexican working class.[17] This aversion to the being perceived as violent, however, did not constrain the murderous suppression of Mayan rebellions and the massive deportations of the Yaqui from Sonora to work on the henequen plantations of Yucatan, among other systematic acts of murder and oppression in the name of the modernizing project.[18]

Díaz and his technocratic bureaucrats saw threats to their civilized creation in both the mundane and the abstract. Porfirian men, cognizant of the value of order and progress, were to be sedate, reflective, and restrained, and it was this vision of the nation that the diplomatic corps honed so carefully.[19] The "taming" of public opinion was among the most important functions of diplomacy.[20] The image of a cosmopolitan

Mexico was carefully promoted in the international public sphere. The Mexico City press, especially the subsidized dailies *El Imparcial* and the English-language *Mexican Herald*, served as de facto government information sheets domestically and internationally. Due to the high cost of lengthy telegraph messages, the Mexican government kept its foreign diplomatic representatives informed of the official interpretation of events by sending copies of these newspapers in diplomatic pouches. Mexican embassies and consulates conducted official business informed not by direct communication with their government but through the detailed reasoning of a supposedly independent press.[21] *The Mexican Herald* also served the US State Department as an unofficial but purportedly reliable source for facts on the ground.[22]

The idea of a "virile" and benevolent dictatorship was central to the public image of Díaz, and his diplomatic corps dutifully transmitted press clippings from the United States that lauded the president as a man of "extraordinary virility" who had "recreated Mexico."[23] His supporters, domestically and abroad, argued that dictatorial tactics were necessary to maintain order and promote progress at home and to meet international obligations such as debt repayments and adhesion to a growing number of treaties. Regularity and predictability, whether real or imagined, allowed the diplomatic corps to promote Mexico as the best governed country in Latin America, and it had made Díaz into a political celebrity. By the early twentieth century, Díaz had succeeded, in the minds of laudatory observers, in taming the Mexican "race" and detaching it from its increasingly distant and troubled cousins, the violent and "passionate" Central Americans. While Mexico was stable and prosperous, bloodthirsty tyrants such as Estrada Cabrera ruled Central Americans amid their never-ending blood feuds. The US press, in particular, called on Díaz to invade Central America and to forcibly civilize and Mexicanize the territories and people all the way to Panama. Mexico, in this vision, would take on the burden that resulted from its superior civilization.[24] Díaz, through his diplomatic service, worked behind the scenes to dissuade international observers from publically encouraging such an action, likely knowing that it threatened the peace and stability that were increasingly tenuous as the Díaz regime reached its final years.[25]

The Porfirian government funded the publication of sycophantic biographies and entire volumes that reprinted glowing press accounts of his rule that had appeared in newspapers and political speeches in Europe and the United States.[26] The diplomatic corps carefully monitored any mention of Mexico in the foreign press. They obediently reported back to Mexico City, mailing press clippings that showed their aggressive rectification of negative remarks on Mexico that had appeared in newspapers from China to the United States.[27] By the end of his nearly forty years in power, however, Mexican nationalists increasingly viewed this xenophilia as a sign of Díaz's weakness and inability to protect Mexican sovereignty and honor at home and abroad.[28] The preferential treatment of outside opinions had more concrete effects on Mexican soil. Foreign companies and individuals, especially from the United States, enjoyed a variety of privileges denied most Mexicans. Surveying this crucial imbalance, historian John Hart writes, "The resultant political instability led to a revolution that was decided by a compromise between Mexican nationalism and American intervention." Radicals such as the Flores Magón brothers and the Zapatistas objected to the massive foreign ownership of Mexican land and industry, while a "spontaneous working-class anti-Americanism" challenged the regime's domestic legitimacy.[29] Díaz's egoistic valuation of foreign approbation and his desire to please the United States made him downplay slights on Mexican honor and the negative effect this had on his earlier image as a nationalist hero. The defensive nationalism of the Mexican Revolution can be explained in part by this tension.

Extradition agreements were a principal symbol of Díaz's international statesmanship, but they constituted a double-edged sword.[30] While these treaties provided juridical proof of Mexican civilizational parity with the most advanced nations and the latest trends in international law, they also constrained the sphere of executive action within often ambiguous parameters. As the outside world showered Mexico with praise for its advances toward modernity and other Latin American leaders sought to emulate Díaz, Mexican nationalism outgrew the grasp of the aging general. Domestic legitimacy based on international acclaim was inherently unstable. It defined Mexican civilization and nationalism as emanating from the consent and esteem of non-Mexicans. The fact that Theodore Roosevelt revered Díaz so highly that he offered to aid him in incorporating almost all of Central America into Mexico likely meant little to the majority of Mexicans living under authoritarian rule. If Díaz was unable to defend Mexican sovereignty, even against relatively weaker nations such as Guatemala, how could he be trusted to navigate the relationship with the aggressively expansionist United States?

While Díaz called for peace and diplomacy, writers in the public sphere created meanings of the Cabrera-Barillas Affair that impugned Guatemala as a barbaric and flagrantly aggressive assailant that threatened to drag Mexico back into the Middle Ages.[31] Díaz could not control public opinion at home despite his cooptation of important newspapers, the existence of press juries, and the calculated publication of confidential diplomatic correspondence that portrayed Mexican restraint in the face of Guatemalan provocation and insult. The public sphere, as represented by the press, was far from a propaganda branch of the Porfirian government, despite the oft-cited restrictions placed upon it.[32] Nor could the regime force the Guatemalan dictator, Manuel Estrada Cabrera, to extradite one of his own generals, José María Lima, who was clearly complicit in the assassination just steps from the Mexican national palace. The affair illustrated the regime's inability to pursue satisfaction for a major injury to national pride precisely because Díaz had legally constrained the autonomy of his government. Extradition treaties had previously been touted by Díaz and his foreign minister as proof of Mexican modernity as a central cog in the modernizing machine, but in this instance they impeded executive authority to satisfy a variant of popular nationalism predicated upon violent retribution for insult.

From the mid-nineteenth century onward, the technological revolutions in transportation (steam and rail) and communication (telegraph and telephone) had made the pursuit of international criminals easier, and the older philosophies of asylum had been eroded by the transnational pursuit of what one historian has called the "empire of justice."[33] Díaz's pursuit of acclaim and the approbation of foreigners, including direct investment in industry and infrastructure, damaged his self-promotion as a nationalist hero at home, even though the Mexican government tried to spin this diplomatic defeat against a much weaker Guatemala as a triumph of Mexican law and civilization based on the masculine virtue of restraint. These events contributed to the nationalist and xenophobic sentiment that led to the outbreak of the Mexican Revolution. By the end of the revolutionary decade (1910–20), nearly two million Mexicans would die in a political and, later, social revolution that enshrined Mexican sovereignty and the attempt to exclude foreigners from cultural, political, and economic power as a renewed basis of political legitimacy.

Looking south to Guatemala complicates the traditional focus on the unequal relationship between the United States and Mexico, to reveal the complexity and creativity of diplomatic actions on the part of Secretary of State Ignacio Mariscal and Mexican minister to Guatemala Federico Gamboa. The dramatic narrative of these events also invigorated the Mexican public sphere. In both cases, dozens of editorialists and critics from across the political spectrum used these transnational events to define Mexican civilization in opposition to their Central American neighbors and, in a few cases, to subtly critique the authoritarian political culture of Mexico. The ultimate meanings of these diplomatic events were transfigured and humanized as they entered Mexican popular culture.

Morales and Mora and the Transnational Criminal Justice System: Murder by the Cathedral

After the teenaged Florencio Morales stabbed General Barillas in the street at dusk, eyewitness reports of the event varied. Some claimed that the assailant had screamed, "Now, finally, for my revenge!"[34] Others were certain that Morales had said, "Now you have to pay me!" to which Barillas had responded, "Don't bother me anymore.… I don't have to pay you."[35] The assailant then turned and walked quickly away toward the pedestrian traffic on the Zócalo. He dropped the double-edged dagger into the gutter and tried to blend into the crowd.[36] Despite these efforts, two beat officers nearby heard Barillas cry out as he was stabbed and immediately pursued Morales—picking up the knife and tracking the killer in the crowd—aided by the unusual bright yellow pants the assailant was wearing.[37] Blowing his whistle, one of the officers attracted the attention of two military police officers who happened to be passing by on their bicycles.[38] Together they overcame Morales and held him at gunpoint as a shocked crowd gathered at the general's body. Morales offered no resistance and immediately confessed, claiming that he killed Barillas to avenge his parents, whose cantina and home were burned on Barillas's orders fifteen years earlier in the Guatemalan coastal town of Ocos.[39] Morales, even though he had confessed, soon backtracked and claimed his name was José Estrada. It was clear to police that Morales was a bad liar.[40]

Morales was marched to the police station to undergo interrogation. His explanation of the murder quickly disintegrated and simultaneously broadened the scope of his crime. The evidence alarmed the police. Investigators learned that he had lived in Mexico City for several months without seeking any type of employment.[41] When the police searched his lodging, a few blocks from the home of General Barillas, they encountered a second Guatemalan when they forced their way into what they described as a one-room pigsty on an interior patio of a large building that had been subdivided into cheap apartments. Bernardo Mora, who they would discover was Morales's more seasoned accomplice, was ill and in bed.[42] In the apartment the police uncovered passports and letters bearing the real names of the suspects.[43] Most importantly, the older Mora was in possession of a sheath that fit the murder weapon. He was arrested on the spot and taken to the police station where he was interrogated, and likely tortured, separate from Morales. Dozens of reporters gathered on the street in front of the station, but few details emerged other than those leaked by members of the Guatemalan expatriate community, several of whom had rushed to the station, hoping to catch a glimpse of the killer.[44] Within hours, news had spread to every corner of the metropolis.[45]

As police canvassed the neighborhood where Morales and Mora lived, a picture of the two men emerged. The officers, under the command of Félix Díaz, the president's nephew, gathered testimony from a range of people who had known them, including a bullfighter from Seville, Spain, who had accompanied them on the ship from San José, Guatemala, to the port of Salina Cruz, in the state of Oaxaca, several months earlier.[46] Morales had been an avid card player and gambler, and though they were not of the class of exile that was flush with cash, they always paid their rent and other debts in gold coins.[47] Morales was known to be the more outgoing of the two, and was given to drinking, while Mora was a brooding presence who seldom spoke to his neighbors. Morales was only seventeen years old, and his time in Mexico City had introduced him to the urban demimonde. He frequented brothels, court testimony later revealed, and often bought drinks, flashed a gold pocket watch, and spent enough to hire the services of his favorite lover for nights on end.[48] A reporter for the leading English-language newspaper in Mexico City, *The Mexican Herald*, described Morales by using the criminal anthropology designations that all but proved his embodiment of the usual suspect: "The assassin gave his name as Jose Estrada, and his home as Ocos, Guatemala. He is a youth of about 20 years, very dark, and with tight, kinky hair. The low brow recedes rapidly from the prominent eyebrows, and last night at the comisaria, the dull conscious ignominy of the born criminal lurked over his features."[49]

Adding to the suspicion of a wider conspiracy, both men's passports had been issued at the Presidential Palace in Guatemala City, and their serial numbers were sequential.[50] Onofre Bone, the political chief of the Guatemalan port city of San Jose where they had embarked on the German steamship *Amasis* for Mexico on January 18, had allowed them to board without all of the proper papers. Bone broke the usual protocol after receiving secret instructions from Guatemala City.[51] That Morales, an illiterate youth with no known profession, had been granted a passport at all fed the growing consensus that high-ranking Guatemalans had enabled his travel to Mexico. Individuals such as Morales, in most cases, were unlikely to be granted a passport by the Guatemalan government, much less have the available funds to live abroad for months at a time. That both men had freely spent gold coins and yet been shoeless had made them suspicious—even leading to Mora's arrest for that reason in the town of Tierra Blanca (state of Veracruz), as they had made their way overland from the Pacific coast to Mexico City.[52]

Most members of the Guatemalan expatriate community who came to the police station did not know Morales, but one prominent woman claimed that she had seen him working as the doorman for the head of the secret police in Guatemala City, General José Lima.[53] Mora, however, had in fact been an officer in the secret police and death squads of President Estrada Cabrera. This police force had been responsible for the extrajudicial killing and torture of thousands of political opponents in Guatemala and are perhaps best described in the novel *El Señor Presidente* (1946), by the Nobel Prize-winning Guatemalan writer Miguel Ángel Asturias.[54] Estrada Cabrera's domestic terror had spread to Mexico.

Patrons at Morales's favorite bar added that he had bragged about using a razor to slice the face of a woman in Guatemala and gotten away with it. Other witnesses further associated the men with violence and intrigue. The room they had rented in Mexico, the press claimed, had been occupied several months before by a Belgian man named Josephs, who was a well-known spy in the service of Guatemalan President Estrada Cabrera. Josephs had been sent to Mexico to report back on the actions of the exile community.[55]

As the guilt of Mora and Morales was presumed and then broadly disseminated in the Mexico City press, the details of the interrogation were leaked. The biography of General Barillas and the complexity of his relationship with Mexico stoked the rage of the public sphere. In 1892 Barillas had been the only leader in Guatemalan history to voluntarily leave office at the end of his presidential term. This detail of Barillas's adhesion to constitutional term limits was used as a tacit criticism of the Díaz regime's hold on power—though it would have been unwise to state this directly in the Mexican press.[56] Outraged at this attack on a guest of Mexico, one of the most widely read newspapers openly and "categorically" demanded war to end what it deemed the atavism of the Estrada Cabrera regime. *El Tiempo* combined this jingoist call with a nationalistic defense of Mexican independence from the foreign policy preferences of the United States—worrying what Theodore Roosevelt might think of an invasion should not hold Mexico back.[57] General Barillas had received de facto asylum in Mexico. When Estrada Cabrera took office in 1898, Barillas had quickly found himself in danger, as Cabrera sought to kill or imprison any potential alternatives to his rule. Fleeing north with his son and entourage on horseback, he had forded the river separating Mexico from Guatemala and reached the state of Chiapas.[58] Mexico was a haven for political refugees, and the violation of this protection while Barillas was under de facto house arrest just blocks from the national palace was a clear and egregious violation of Mexican sovereignty and honor.[59]

The government presses in Guatemala, catering to the tastes of Estrada Cabrera, had published a scathing pamphlet on General Barillas shortly before his assassination that attempted to discredit him as a genetically inferior homosexual. The author of the pamphlet claimed that any anthropometric and Lombrosian analysis of Barillas would clearly show his criminal and subhuman nature, evinced by his "misshapen head, low and backwards brow ridge, twisted and deformed nose, asymmetric face, misaligned eyes, wide ears with enormous lobes…the cheek bones that give him such a stupid and ugly face…. Education could not smooth or counteract these physiological signs."[60] The character assassination intensified, moving beyond his appearance and calling into question his manhood. The author claimed to know that Barillas had been a serial masturbator (*onanismo*) as a youth, and that this likely led to his imputed homosexuality.[61] As the Cabrera-Barillas affair intensified, government newspapers in Guatemala struck a telling contrast, vaunting Cabrera as the "virile" hero of the nation, the bringer of progress "sewing elements and promises for the future."[62] In Mexico, the press continued calling for regime change in Guatemala and the swift enactment of justice for the assassination.

The details of the crime, as they appeared in court documents, further outraged the Mexican press. They also provide insight into the class-based definitions of criminality and barbarism that guided explanations and degrees of guilt. The official aggravating factors revealed that the crime was classified as a cowardly attack on social class.[63] Three factors were important and demanded the ultimate punishment: the assailant had acted at night, without warning, and without taking into account the victim's social rank and age. The press portrayed Barillas as the antithesis of his attacker. He was a robust man who surely would have been able to defend himself against such a degenerate criminal had his murderer given him fair warning. That a short, dark-skinned, and illiterate outcast had the effrontery to commit this crime against position and respectability led to clear conclusions: a crime was more criminal when crossing the class barrier.[64] A writer for the semiofficial newspaper *El Imparcial* argued that Mexicans were too civilized to commit such a barbaric political act.[65] Political killings of this sort were a thing of the past in Mexico—a past that, thanks to President Díaz, was quickly receding. Adding to these troubling conclusions, the assailant was perhaps too young to receive the death penalty—a diabolical calculation on the part of his handlers meant to further prevent the enactment of justice. Despite this fact, a writer for *El País* argued that justice must be swift in order to salvage Mexican respectability in the eyes of the civilized world. This was the worst crime in living memory, he bemoaned.[66]

What troubled observers more acutely was that Central American barbarism had bled over the border and into the political center of Mexico. Order and progress and the nation as a whole had been attacked. The act had detracted from hard-won civilization and clearly constituted a foreign import of atavism in the person of a criminal and pernicious foreigner. A writer for the *Voz de México* summed up public reaction: "We very sincerely lament that the politicians and malcontents of the neighboring country choose our nation as the theater to play out their passions. They seek out our streets and plazas as a place to wield the homicidal dagger, and to cut short the life of a man who, at the sundown of his life, came to seek asylum and to enjoy the hospitality that is offered to all born on American soil and who speak the same language as us."[67]

El Tiempo Ilustrado, a Conservative Catholic newspaper, contributed its judgment on the state of civilization in Central America:

Once again it is demonstrated that the character of the Central-Americans is rebellious in the extreme, restless, untamable, and that politicians in those countries are dominated by their passions to such an extent that nothing can satiate them. It matters little to them to show the world spectacle of anarchy and war, it is undignified how revolutions happen there one after the other, and Presidents and ex-Presidents find death...on the square, under an assassin's dagger...just as happened to Barillas in our capital. When will this shameful spectacle that the Central American Republics offer to the world end?[68]

A writer for *El País* internalized the crime as an attack on the Mexican race. Though Guatemalan politics were a remnant of the Middle Ages, "It aggravates us that a country linked to us by true fraternity...still has such horrors and political hatred and thus contributes to the discredit of our common race."[69] These denunciations resembled descriptions by writers from the United States when they imagined Latin America as a whole.[70]

As these attacks on Guatemala reverberated across Mexico, the Guatemalan Minister in Mexico City, Manuel Girón, issued an official protest over what he argued were false and libelous accusations in the press.[71] Girón had recently arrived in Mexico City and was seldom seen in public. President Díaz and Mariscal had secretly confided to the American ambassador David Thompson in Mexico City that they believed Girón had been the "fountainhead" of the killing.[72] Díaz also confided in Thompson that he had ordered the dispatch of Mexican troops to the Guatemalan border "to keep matters there well in hand."[73]

As part of his protest, Girón had impugned the professionalism of the entire Mexican press. For a Guatemalan to label these writers as "passionate" made them nearly apoplectic. Their calls for war intensified. The official government response came from Secretary of State Mariscal a few days after Girón's demands. The Mexican government would not order an apology or a retraction. Mariscal would merely admonish the reporters from *El Imparcial* to follow the laws on diplomatic privilege (*fueros*) and refrain from gathering outside the minister's residence.[74] An unofficial government response, unrestrained by Mariscal's careful diplomatic language, came a few weeks later from a member of the Mexican Senate.[75]

On April 30, Melesio Parra wrote an open letter to Guatemala. Senator Parra was a logical person to pen such a defense of the free press and public opinion in Mexico. Seven years earlier, he had compiled and published a book with translations of hundreds of pages of foreign articles in praise of Porfirio Díaz and his civilizing project.[76] That volume promoted the cult of Díaz, helping manufacture domestic political legitimacy, and praised his strong authoritarianism. For Parra, the free press abroad and, he contended, the unanimity of praise for Díaz in the civilized world proved that Díaz had created a country beyond the comprehension or critique of lesser peoples such as Guatemalans. The fact that Díaz was called upon to arbitrate international disputes was further proof of his, and Mexico's, global credibility.

In responding to the minister from Guatemala's complaints about the Mexican press, Parra made it clear that he and likeminded Mexicans viewed this attack on civil liberties as an attack on the nation and an attack on God. The press was the reflection of the voice of the people, and the voice of the people was the utterance of the divine. A society like Guatemala, which groped forward, looking for progress on "twisted paths in the darkness," could not understand the enlightened and transparent role of the press in Mexico. Mexicans, he argued, were devoid of passion, by which he meant animal rage and irrationality. Guatemalans were citizens of a disturbed nation, tilting toward ruin. Mexico—both civilized and civilizer—looked with paternal pity on the disgrace of a fellow Spanish-speaking nation. The lack of patriotism in Guatemala was due to the fact that Guatemalans "haven't had the luck to find an energetic, valiant, and prestigious man who knows how to bridle the diverse passions and point them toward love of country."[77] What separated Guatemalans from Mexicans, in his final analysis, was not race or language; it was that they had no Díaz.

Echoing Parra, editorialist Samuel Ávila scoffed at the Guatemalan attempt to "suffocate" the Mexican press.[78] He phrased his polemical response to the protest as a didactic lesson for Girón: this was how the press operated within and helped countries to reach civilized status. Avila defined Mexico by delineating how it was not like Guatemala—a country, in his words, "on a level of degradation and moral debasement led by malevolent and cynical tyrants." Another editorialist writing for *El Popular* further stoked the nationalist response: "This protest is really against the entire nation."[79] This enraged reaction by the Mexican press to efforts by a resident foreigner to limit freedom of expression shows how central writing in the public sphere was to Mexican claims for cultural and political modernity. As historian Pablo Piccato argues, "Free speech was a greater concern for Mexican politicians, legislators, and intellectuals during the 19th century than electoral democracy."[80]

The message from the Mexican press was clear and decisive. It was delivered in the format of a public call for a duel. Guatemala would do well to acknowledge Mexico and to respect the "distinguished seat in the concert of enlightened and civilized peoples that Mexico owed to the personal virtues of the eminent statesmen who governs its destiny."[81] Echoing the general consensus of those writing in the Mexican public sphere, the answer for small nations in Latin America was capable and benevolent dictatorship. Authoritarianism was not objectionable if it yielded railroads, telegraphs, stability, and international esteem. The calculation was simple: "[We have] peace in the interior and confidence abroad.... And rapid communication…that carries the standard of civilization and progress."[82] Clearly a country this concentrated on development and civilization would have little time to plan and execute political assassinations. Parra's long and ornate prose, contained in five entire newsprint columns and disseminated in hundreds of thousands of copies, ended with a thinly disguised threat. If Guatemalans did not rise to the level of Mexican civilization, they risked war. Mexico would be a reluctant civilizer, a carrier of the Mexican burden to Central America.

On May 14, President Díaz responded to the growing popular consensus that Mexico should bestow its civilization, by force, on Guatemala. Since the assassination on April 7, Secretary of State Mariscal had received secret coded messages from a network of informers in Guatemala that told of massive movements of troops and artillery, the dispatch of other assassins to kill Mexican ambassador to Guatemala Federico Gamboa, and the rounding up of political opponents by the forces of Estrada Cabrera.[83] Despite these provocations, the Mexican consulates from China to Chile to the United States had been ordered to place news in the press that Mexico was not in danger of going to war. Díaz explained to an American interviewer that Mexico was still too deeply entrenched in the work of national development to attempt an intervention in Guatemala to remove Estrada Cabrera.[84] He was, however, willing to act in concert with the United States to oversee the creation of a union of all of Central American nations under one leader, presumably himself.

US newspapers seized the news that Díaz might finally take over Central America. Several prominent papers, such as the *New York Herald*, supported these actions. Mexican consuls across the United States and Europe dutifully reported what they presented as an international consensus: the civilized world as ready to support Díaz.[85] The following day, April 15, newspapers printed a hasty retraction, blaming the discordant portrayal of Díaz's interventionist stance on an inexperienced translator.[86] Díaz stressed he would act in concert with the United States only for the protection and respect of national sovereignty in Central America and to maintain the present international boundaries. This was clever diplomatic maneuvering on his part. He was loath to be drawn into a potential regional war, but more importantly, he feared instability in Central America would be an excuse for further US occupation of Latin American countries.[87] With protectorates in Cuba and the Dominican Republic, growing economic interests in every country in Central America, and the paramount necessity of protecting the ongoing construction project in the Canal Zone, Díaz understood that US action threatened to completely surround Mexico. Theodore Roosevelt had previously offered Díaz and Mexico all the Central American countries down to Panama. On multiple occasions, Roosevelt implored Díaz to allow "natural growth" to expand Mexican borders to encompass virtually all of the former dominions of New Spain (excepting Texas, of course), but including Cuba, Puerto Rico, and the Dominican Republic. Because Mexico was the best country in Latin America, it could be trusted to act "by Uncle Sam's grace" as the watchman envisioned by the Roosevelt Corollary to the Monroe Doctrine.[88] Díaz consistently demurred, knowing that this would be an enormously expensive endeavor that would stretch his thin military resources while yielding little benefit. He also knew that territorial aggrandizement by US concession would permanently tie Mexico to US supervision and intervention. He politely declined, refusing the pseudo-imperialist mantle offered by the Roosevelt. Finally, Díaz knew that the US was playing both sides: they also supported Estrada Cabrera, who had become exceedingly wealthy from concessions given to American railroads, construction companies, and the United Fruit Company. If Mexico were to invade Guatemala, they might actually meet US marines and end up losing territory. Mexican diplomats complained to Mariscal that their US counterparts were actively thwarting an otherwise unified response against Estrada Cabrera by the diplomatic corps of almost every country with representatives in Guatemala.[89]

While the Mexican public sphere radiated heat from calls for war, the slow process of international law and the doctrine of extradition moved forward. Under what might be called "enhanced interrogation," Morales and Mora revealed that they had been commissioned to commit the assassination by one of the highest-ranking Guatemalan military officers, General José María Lima, the right-hand man of President Estrada Cabrera.[90] They had been paid in gold coins and American dollars, and assisted by the political chief Onofre Bone, head of the port of San Jose where they had embarked.

On April 27, the presiding judge in the murder trial, A. Hurtado de Mendoza, wrote to the Mexican secretary of state, Ignacio Mariscal, with an official request to petition the Guatemalan government for the extradition of General Lima and for the rendition of Onofre Bone as a material witness.[91] Despite the public demand for the execution of the killers, the trial would be put on hold while awaiting extradition. Mariscal telegraphed these orders to the Mexican minister in Guatemala City, the writer and diplomat Federico Gamboa. He explained to Gamboa that under the extradition treaty of 1894 between Mexico and Guatemala, the latter country was not legally bound to extradite its nationals to a foreign country, but that given the nature of this crime, they would be bound by the rule of international decency to do so.[92] While most countries that signed such extradition treaties were not legally required to give up their own citizens, they were not prevented from doing so, either.

Several days passed with no response from Gamboa in Guatemala City. Secretary of State Marsical confided to the US ambassador that he feared the Guatemalans were intercepting his messages and asked if Washington would send a coded telegram to their legation in order to test whether this was the case.[93] It turned out that Gamboa was dragging his feet while waiting for an audience with Guatemalan Secretary of State Barrios to deliver the extradition request in person. On April 26, Mariscal wrote again to Gamboa that the official papers detailing habeas corpus were physically being sent, but that in the meantime Lima and Bone should be detained to prohibit their flight from justice.[94] Mariscal, likely realizing that the extradition request would be resisted, impugned the Guatemalan government using what were then highly insulting terms: it should grant extradition "as any Government of a civilized nation that wishes not to leave unpunished such a scandalous crime."[95]

While Gamboa prepared to deliver this potentially volatile request, other events complicated and deepened the crisis. Before he could per-

The trial of Morales and Mora. José Guadalupe Posada, 1907. Courtesy of the University of New Mexico.

form these duties on a Monday morning, an assassination attempt on President Estrada Cabrera unleashed the dictator's secret police in what was labeled a reign of terror against his political opponents in the Guatemalan capital.[96] At seven thirty in the morning, a remotely detonated land mine struck Cabrera's carriage while he was out for his regular morning ride, killing the horses and gravely injuring one of the president's closest aides. Cabrera ran for his life back to the security of his heavily guarded home. A few days later, another bomb was discovered on his regularly traveled route.

Cabrera's military police immediately suspected the hand of Guatemalan political dissidents guided by Mexico. The police, many of whom acted as plainclothes spies in the neighborhood around the Mexican legation in Guatemala City, arrested hundreds of men, women, and children—including several Mexican citizens who had the misfortune of living near the scene of the first bombing, or working for prominent Guatemalans who were suspected by the Estrada Cabrera regime.[97] Gamboa and Mariscal viewed these assassination attempts as a ruse designed to gain more time for the Guatemalans to come up with a response to extradition that would avoid war. Cabrera sent a high-ranking officer to the Mexican legation, who accused Gamboa personally of harboring those responsible for the attack. Gamboa upped the ante by throwing open the doors and challenging the military police to search the premises—a violation, he stressed, of the sacred laws of extraterritoriality. He demanded that the secretary of state, Barrios, be present at this barbaric act to tie him to this violation of Mexican territory—clear grounds for justified war.[98] Gamboa acted decisively, and in so doing shifted the burden of escalation over the heated extradition request. For the moment, the Guatemalans backed down.

Washington kept a close eye on all of this process, counseling President Díaz to cleave to diplomacy to avoid war. At stake for Washington was not just the protection of American investments, particularly railroads and agribusiness, but the likelihood that an attack by Mexico on Guatemala would endanger the fragile Central American peace accords that Roosevelt had helped negotiate the year before. While not stating so in public, Díaz and Mariscal confided to the US ambassador in Mexico City that they were certain that the order for the Barillas assassination came directly from President Estrada Cabrera. The demands of Washington and the counsel of Ambassador Thompson likely contributed to Díaz's decision not to invade. Though the president had dispatched troops to the Guatemalan border, an open conflict was avoided.

While Díaz decided to maintain peace in part to preserve the international perception of him as a modern and moderate leader, the Guatemalan government attempted to moderate its negative portrayal in the international press. The refusal to extradite General Lima had resulted in a public shaming of the nation as an atavistic relic for shielding the instigator of a cowardly assassination. Few readers likely doubted that Cabrera was involved in all of these events. Though he refused the extradition request, he would not deny that Lima had a part in the killing.

In a diplomatic maneuver, the Cabrera government issued extradition demands of its own.[99] It claimed to have evidence that the attempt on Estrada Cabrera's life had been planned and funded by two Guatemalans living in Mexico, associates of the slain General Barillas. In a curt response, the Mexican foreign ministry cabled back that those two individuals were shielded from extradition due to their status as political refugees whose crimes were not extraditable; they had only published unflattering articles on Estrada Cabrera in the Guatemalan press. The Mexican government shamed Guatemala in its strongest diplomatic terms: the world was watching and witnessed Estrada Cabrera's turn away from the rules of civilized nations.

The Aftermath

After Mexico's failure to coerce and shame Guatemala into extraditing General Lima, thereby allowing this perceived assault on Mexican sovereignty to go unpunished, the country's relationship with Guatemala continued to sour until the outbreak of the Mexican Revolution in 1910 and the death of Estrada Cabrera in 1924. The meanings of this near war over modern extradition law and national honor were left for Mexicans to ponder. In June of 1907, Mexico City attorney José Romero published a polemical tract denouncing the decision of the Guatemalan president not to detain or extradite Lima.[100] Romero cited this refusal of a diplomatic request as evidence of Guatemala's backwardness. Mexico, in stark contrast, had through its adherence to international law and diplomatic restraint proven its modernity.

While the purpose of Romero's tract was to embarrass Guatemala into behaving properly, the bulk of its nearly fifty pages constructed Mexican national identity by repudiating what it was not. Its extradition regime situated Mexican diplomacy alongside that of England, France, Switzerland, and the United States. More importantly, the ability to negotiate bilateral agreements with such countries conveyed international approval and faith in the stability that Díaz had built out of the chaos of factionalism. It proved that the nineteenth century was the distant past inhabited by atavistic countries such as Guatemala.

The juridical and diplomatic process of extradition embraced by Romero was an emblem, he reasoned, of Mexican cultural attainment and one of the most important achievements of the Porfirian diplomatic corps. He extended this accolade to the nation as a whole; Mexicans were modern, while Guatemalans remained mired in intrigues and immorality. It was at this point that Romero's Manichean analogy became more nuanced and contradictory: Mexican leaders were members of the civilized world because they simultaneously surrendered to universal law but also knew when to bend that law, particularly when the dictates of national honor demanded a gentlemen's agreements to set aside the law. In Romero's formulation, Guatemalans clung to their legal right not to extradite their own citizens, hiding behind diplomacy to cover their iniquity. Their refusal to extradite an accused accomplice to the murder of former president Barillas was not a simple act of sovereign prerogative; it made a mockery of universal law by using it in bad faith.

The extradition treaty between Guatemala and Mexico had been ratified in 1894 and was used in the intervening decade several times to return fugitives who crossed the porous border. Guatemala's legal objection to Mexico's request for extradition was justified by the language of the treaty, which stipulated that a nation was not legally bound to deliver its own citizens for crimes committed in the jurisdiction of a treaty partner. Romero's argument, and the reasoning of Secretary of State Mariscal, was that while the treaty did not compel the surrender of nationals, it allowed for the voluntary repudiation of that sovereign right in egregious cases such as the conspiracy to assassinate Barillas. The Mexican government had permitted extradition of some of its nationals for crimes committed in the United States, even though the same sovereign prerogative applied in that bilateral treaty.

Extradition between the United States and Mexico had a long history. Mexico's first ratified extradition treaty was negotiated with the United States in 1861. Romero cited this diplomatic achievement as a diamond in the rough: even among the revolts and civil wars of the first half of Mexico's national existence, political leaders managed to care for the state and point toward progress. The 1861 treaty also included an important US concession to Mexican national law: Mexico would not, under any circumstances, return fugitive slaves to the United States—even if they had committed murder in order to escape captivity and crossed the border. Since slavery was illegal in Mexico, insistence on this clause alone had prevented previous extradition treaties between the two countries, going back to the 1820s. Even under the 1861 treaty, the United States had long resisted extradition of its citizens to Mexico, until finally in 1901 it deported a woman accused of murdering her husband.[101] This was used as proof that even the United States bent its sovereignty in special cases.[102] Modern extradition laws were a reaction to technological innovations that expedited travel (fugitive flight and pursuit) and communication. This shifted the traditions of enlightened nations, Romero argued, from one of providing asylum as a function to one of cooperating in an international empire of justice.[103] He illustrated early decisions by the Mexican government to deny extradition to United States that had given way, after midcentury, to regular, juridical, and almost common-place cooperation in the arrest and rendition of accused criminals.

Romero limited himself to a juridical assessment of treaty obligations and extradition precedent, but his exclusion of the broader international and historical context of Mexican-Guatemalan relations makes the document incomprehensible when read in isolation. As the most populous and militarily powerful nation in Central America, Mexico focused its geostrategic policies on containing the irredentist aspirations of Guatemala's aggressive leader Estrada Cabrera in the late nineteenth and early twentieth centuries.[104] While Mexico was by far the larger nation, its leaders realized that a war with Guatemala would be the worst possible outcome of a diplomatic dispute such as the Cabrera-Barillas affair.

This contentious relationship with Guatemala had existed since the beginning of modern Mexican history. When Mexico gained independence and underwent transformation into the short-lived Mexican Empire, all of independent Central America south to Panama was absorbed into the empire. For this brief moment in the 1820s, Mexico was the largest nation in the hemisphere, with territory stretching from California to modern-day Costa Rica. In July of 1823, following multiple rebellions in the five provinces of Central America and the dethroning of Iturbide, the new Mexican Republic offered the region self-determination. Shortly thereafter, the five provinces declared independence from Mexico and established a republican form of government.

From 1823 until 1840, a series of civil wars led by regional caudillos prohibited the establishment of a fixed capital or agreement on the terms of union. Each of the modern nations of Central America had declared its full independence by 1840. During this period the primary concern of Mexico was the status of the border state of Chiapas—a multiethnic and rural region whose leaders vacillated between union with Mexico and absorption into Guatemala. Economically devastated by the wars for independence, nearly constant struggle between liberal and conservative factions, and the amputation of half its territory during the Texas Revolution and the Mexican-American War while facing secessionist and independence movements in the Yucatan peninsula, the border issues with Guatemala figured as a distant concern for successive Mexican governments as they fought to maintain power and sought international legitimacy and recognition.

Out of this chaos, the Díaz regime had brought stability at the expense of political democracy. It had developed Mexico's infrastructure to the point that French, British, and US observers began to take Mexico seriously as a site for investment and as the standard bearer in a region whose people US politicians viewed as racially inferior and largely ungovernable. Extradition treaties, even when contentious, were a cornerstone of international and domestic legitimacy.

Conclusion

As the date of their execution approached, attorneys for Morales and Mora filed multiple appeals for a change of venue. They argued that the assassination was a political crime and therefore the death penalty, as per the 1857 Constitution, was illegal.[105] They claimed that the inability of the Mexican government to produce key witnesses Onofre Bone and José María Lima invalidated the proceedings. They reminded the court that the Mexican government had denied the extradition of the Guatemalans suspected in the attempted assassination of Estrada Cabrera based on the political nature of the crime—a mitigating factor denied Morales and Mora. In all, their lawyers filed over twenty motions for a stay of execution. All were denied.[106] A US observer in the courtroom marveled at what he regarded as the bizarre proceedings of the court, including the *careo* in which the assassins were put face-to-face to argue against each other over inconsistencies in their testimony.[107] None of this helped their case. Porfirio Díaz denied their last request for clemency.[108] The Mexican press, despite the preference of the president for a peaceful execution to end these events, reported the rumor that Guatemala would declare war on Mexico if the death sentences were carried out.[109]

The prisoners had more mundane concerns. Upon learning their appeal was denied, each dictated letters to loved ones in Guatemala. Morales wrote to his girlfriend, asking her to carry out the improbable request that his mother and sisters be kept from knowing how he had died. Mora wrote his wife, asking her to take good care of his young son (*hijito*).[110] *The Mexican Herald* reported that Morales was ready for death; all he wanted was a new suit in which to be shot.[111] Catholic families prepared to say mass for their souls at the moment of their execution.[112]

On September 9, 1907, they were taken from their cells in the infamous Belen Prison. *El Imparcial,* knowing the public appetite for the smallest details would be insatiable, had its photographer build a platform atop a telephone pole in order to capture the moment of death in the execution yard. The editors thought so highly of his work that they published a picture of the photographer on his platform. The day following the executions, they announced that the paper had sold more than 270,000 copies—representing one newspaper for every two people in Mexico City. Enterprising businesses, such as the munitions factory next door to the prison, sold tickets for five pesos to stand on their roofs and take in the events. Journalists lauded such entrepreneurship.[113]

Mora and Morales were awakened before sunrise. Per their request, they drank coffee and cognac and marched to their execution handcuffed with unlit Cuban cigars in their mouths. The female inmates gathered in the chapel to pray for them, and the priest performed last rites before they were led to the wall and shot by ten soldiers. Their bodies lay twitching until the commander delivered the *tiro de gracia,* a mercy shot, behind their left ears. Their bodies were buried in unmarked graves in the sixth-class section of the Dolores Cemetery.

The timing of the execution was not a coincidence. A week later, in his Mexican Independence Day speech before congress, Díaz touted the execution as the closure of an unfortunate series of events. In response, the

The execution by firing squad of Mora and Morales. José Guadalupe Posada, 1907. Courtesy of the University of New Mexico.

leading congressman lauded Díaz's civilized avoidance of war in carefully measured terms. But most writers in the public sphere hated that justice had not been served, that the "intellectual authors of the crime," Lima, Bone, and Estrada-Cabrera, remained free. Díaz had been constrained through his own treaties. Civilization had made him weak. He could not impose his will even on Guatemala—shortly, he would no longer be able to impose his will on Mexico.

Though Morales and Mora had been subject to every imaginable slur, from satanic to simian, the manner of their deaths evoked sympathy and even admiration. Both men had written poems in their heads. They pronounced them to the guards and their lawyers before being led to the execution ground. No longer the scourges of the earth, Guadalupe Posada portrayed them as the hapless victims of nefarious politicians. They were, after all, of the same class of people that consumed his popular prints and ballads. He humanized them by focusing on the pathos of their final moments—savoring cognac and a good cigar and facing death, as it was worded in his caption, "bravely with their eyes open." *The Mexican Herald*, which had first called the Guatemalans atavistic barbarians, summoned surprising comments upon witnessing their execution: "Both men gave proof of remarkable fortitude, courage and native dignity, which, while not atoning for a crime such as was committed by Morales, certainly entitles the men to some consideration." US writers quoted them in their final moments as wanting to prove to Mexicans that "Guatemalans know how to die like men"—which they did with "extraordinary grit."[114]

The anarchist Flores-Magón brothers, writing from the relative freedom of their exile in Los Angeles, portrayed these occurrences in terms that likely resonated with those who had begun to question Díaz's hold on power. They had proven, in stark terms, that Díaz was deficient in nationalism, that the soldier who once defeated the French and dragged Mexico into modernity had lost his way—his xenophilia had displaced his nationalism.[115] His pursuit of civilization and international legitimacy by self-restraint through treaty obligations had left him unable to defend Mexican honor.

The fulcrum of these events was the doctrine of extradition. This chapter has demonstrated how adherence to extradition treaties symbolized the masculine self-restraint that Latin Americans were so often criticized for lacking. The ability to extend the empire of justice beyond national boundaries proved that the nation had achieved the predictability and stability that were benchmarks for making the leap out of the recurrent cycles of violence of the nineteenth century—but at the same time gave rise to new conflicts that undermined this same stability.

Notes

1. *La Voz de México*, April 9, 1907; *El Imparcial*, April 8, 1907.

2. Secretaría de Relaciónes Exteriores, Acervo Historico Diplomatico, Mexico City (hereafter SREAHD), L-E-2047.

3. Ibid.; *El Imparcial*, April 8, 1907; *El Tiempo*, April 9, 1907.

4. Jürgen Buchenau, *In the Shadow of the Giant: The Making of Mexico's Central American Policy, 1876–1930* (Tuscaloosa: University of Alabama Press, 1996), 73–74.

5. Frederick W. Marks, *Velvet on Iron: The Diplomacy of Theodore Roosevelt* (Lincoln: University of Nebraska Press, 1982).

6. On Cabrera's courting US support from 1898–1920, see Walter LaFeber, *Inevitable Revolutions: The United States in Central America*, 2nd ed. (New York: Norton, 1993), 40–41.

7. The best synthetic study on the importance of empire to the perception of national achievement in a competitive international system is Eric J. Hobsbawm, *The Age of Empire, 1875–1914* (New York: Pantheon Books, 1987).

8. Buchenau, *In the Shadow of the Giant.*

9. Two of the best accounts of racial determinism and how the perception of racial backwardness molded domestic and international policy in Latin America are Richard Graham, ed., *The Idea of Race in Latin America* (Austin: University of Texas Press, 2010); and Nancy Leys Stepan, *The Hour of Eugenics: Race, Gender, and Nation in Latin America* (Ithaca, NY: Cornell University Press, 1991).

10. *Nashville Tennessean*, May 26, 1907; *Spokane Press*, December 15, 1908.

11. José Guadalupe Posada, *José Guadalupe Posada, ilustrador de la vida Mexicana* (Mexico City: Fondo Editorial de la Plástica Mexicana, 1963).

12. *El País*, April 11, 1907.

13. For an overview of this consensus, see John Hart, *Revolutionary Mexico: The Coming and Process of the Mexican Revolution* (Berkeley: University of California Press, 1987), 52–73.

14. Mauricio Tenorio-Trillo, *Mexico at the World's Fair: Crafting a Modern Nation* (Berkeley: University of California Press, 1996), 250. See also Josefina Zoraida Vázquez and Blanca Torres Ramírez, *México y el mundo: historia de sus relaciones exteriores* (Mexico City: Senado de la República, 2000), and José C. Valadés, *El Porfirismo: historia de un régimen, el nacimiento 1876–1884* (Mexico City: Universidad Nacional Autónoma de México, 1977).

15. Pablo Piccato, *The Tyranny of Opinion: Honor in the Construction of the Mexican Public Sphere* (Durham: Duke University Press, 2010), 14–15.

16. The best scholarly overview of the Porfirian era remains Daniel Cosío

Villegas, *Historia moderna de México*, 9 vols. (Mexico City: Editorial Hermes, 1955–72). See also Paul Garner, *Porfirio Díaz* (New York: Longman, 2001).

17. On the intersections of class, masculinity, and the press in this period, see Robert Buffington, *A Sentimental Education for the Working Man: The Mexico City Penny Press, 1900–1910* (Durham: Duke University Press, 2015).

18. Garner, *Porfirio Díaz*, 132.

19. Tenorio-Trillo, *Mexico at the World's Fair*.

20. José C. Valadés, *El porfirismo*.

21. Mariscal (Mexico City) to Gamboa (Guatemala City), April 9, 1907, L-E-2047; Bristegui (London) to Mariscal (Mexico City), June 4, 1907, L-E-2050; and Mariscal (Mexico City) to Jiménez (Mobile, AL), June 12, 1907, L-E-2050, all in SREAHD.

22. Thompson (Mexico City) to Secretary of State Root, April 8, 1907, Department of State (hereafter DS), Record Group 59, National Archives and Records Administration, College Park, Maryland, File 5717-5727/30.

23. Clipping from the *Sunday Star*, June 2, 1907, contained in Creel to Mariscal, June 2, 1907, SREAHD, L-E-2050.

24. SREAHD, L-E-2048, Legajo 3, Tomo 3.

25. Mariscal to Mexican Legation in Berlin, SREAHD, L-E-2047, June 19, 1907.

26. See Melesio Parra, *El señor General Porfirio Díaz juzgado en el extranjero* (Mexico City: Oficina Tipográfica de la Secretaría de Fomento, 1900); and Alfonso Luis Velasco, *Porfirio Díaz: estudio biográfico* (Mexico City: Imprenta de la Escuela Industrial de Huerfanos, 1892).

27. See, for example, the dozens of press clippings in SREAHD, L-E-2047 and L-E-2048.

28. Hart, *Revolutionary Mexico*, 233.

29. Ibid., 369.

30. José Romero, *Apuntes sobre extradicón con motive de la solicitud que hizo México a Guatemala, relacionada con la detención provisional del general guatemalteco J.M. Lima* (Mexico City: El Progreso Latino, 1907); Gobierno de México, *Ley de extradición de la republica Mexicana* (Mexico City: Imprenta del Gobierno, 1897).

31. *El Popular*, August 31, 1907; *La Voz de México*, April 11, 1907; *El Tiempo Ilustrado*, April 14, 1907; *El Tiempo*, April 10, 1907; *El Tiempo*, May 2, 1907.

32. Piccato, *Tyranny of Opinion*.

33. Katherine Unterman, *Uncle Sam's Policeman: The Pursuit of Fugitives across Borders* (Cambridge: Harvard University Press, 2015). See especially chapter 3.

34. *El Tiempo*, April 9, 1907.

35. SREAHD, L-E-2047.

36. Ibid.

37. SREAHD, L-E-2050, Tomo VI.

38. *El Tiempo*. April 9, 1907.

39. SREAHD, L-E-2047.

40. Telegram from Mariscal to Creel, in ibid.

41. Ibid.

42. *La Voz de México*, April 9, 1907.

43. SREAHD, L-E-2047.

44. *El País*, April 8, 1907.

45. *El Mundo Ilustrado*, April 14, 1907; *El Tiempo*, April 9, 1907.

46. SREAHD, L-E-2047; *El Mundo Ilustrado*, April 14, 1907.

47. *La Voz de México*, April 14, 1907; SREAHD, L-E-2050, Tomo VI.

48. Testimony of Miguel García, SREAHD, L-E-2050.

49. *Mexican Herald*, April 8, 1907.

50. SREAHD, L-E-2050, Tomo VI.

51. Ibid.

52. Ibid.

53. Ibid.

54. Miguel Ángel Asturias, *El señor presidente* (Madrid: CEP de la Biblioteca Nacional, 2000).

55. *Mexican Herald*, April 13, 1907.

56. *La Voz de México*, April 11, 1907.

57. *El Tiempo*, May 2, 1907.

58. *El Imparcial*, April 8, 1907.

59. *La Voz de México*, April 11, 1907.

60. A. Vidaurre, *Paralelo entre dos administraciones: apuntes para la historia* (Guatemala City: Tip. Sánchez y de Guise, 1907), 7.

61. Ibid.

62. *La República* (Guatemala City), April 29, 1907, clipping in SREAHD, L-E-1378.

63. *El Imparcial*, April 9, 1907; *El País*, April 11, 1907; *Mexican Herald*, May 4, 1907.

64. For an explanation of the scientific discourses that intersected class, race, and crime, see Robert Buffington, *Criminal and Citizen in Modern Mexico* (Lincoln: University of Nebraska Press, 2000); and Pablo Piccato, *City of Suspects: Crime in Mexico City, 1900–1931* (Durham: Duke University Press, 2001).

65. *El Imparcial*, April 9, 1907.

66. *El País*, April 9, 1907.

67. *La Voz de México*, April 11, 1907.

68. *El Tiempo Ilustrado*, April 14, 1907.

69. *El País*, April 14, 1907.

70. For a convincing account of these general stereotypes emanating from the US toward Latin America in this period, see John J. Johnson, *Latin America in Caricature* (Austin: University of Texas Press, 1980).

71. Girón to Mariscal, April 10, 1907, SREAHD, L-E-2050.

72. Thompson to Secretary of State Root, April 20, 1907, DS, File 5717-5727/30.

73. Thompson to Root, April 26, 1907, DS, File 5717-5727/30.

74. Mariscal to Girón, April 11, 1907, SREAHD, L-E-2050.

75. *La Patria*, April 30, 1907.

76. Parra, *El senor General Porfirio Díaz juzgado en el extranjero*.

77. *La Patria*, April 30, 1907.

78. *La Patria*, April 16, 1907.

79. *El Popular*, April 25, 1907.

80. Pablo Piccato, "The Public Sphere and Liberalism in Mexico: From the Mid-19th Century to the 1930s," in *Oxford Research Encyclopedia of Latin American History*, 2016, http://latinamericanhistory.oxfordre.com/view/10.1093/acrefore/9780199366439.001.0001/acrefore-9780199366439-e-266 (accessed November 3, 2016).

81. *La Patria*, April 30, 1907.

82. Ibid.

83. Telegram from Gamboa to Mariscal, May 13, 1907, SREAHD, L-E-2047.

84. *Mexican Herald*, May 14, 1907.

85. Clippings contained in SREAHD, L-E-2048.

86. *Mexican Herald*, May 15, 1907.

87. The best overview of these policies during the Porfiriato is Jürgen Buchenau, *In the Shadow of the Giant.*

88. Quoted in Buchenau, *In the Shadow of the Giant*, 60.

89. Parra to Mariscal, May 27, 1907, SREAHD, L-E-1378.

90. Thompson to Root, April 25, 1907, DS, File 5717-5727/30; *Mexican Herald*, April 24, 1907.

91. Hurtado Mendoza to Mariscal, SREAHD, L-E-2047.

92. Mariscal to Gamboa, April 22, 1907, SREAHD, L-E-2050.

93. Thompson to Root, April 29, 1907, DS, File 5717-5727/30.

94. Marsical to Gamboa, April 26, 1907, SREAHD, L-E-2050.

95. Mariscal to Barrios, April 30, 1907, reprinted in *Boletín official de la Secretaría de relaciones exteriores*, vol. 24 (Mexico City: Tip. de la viuda de F. Díaz de Leon, 1907), 327.

96. Gamboa to Mariscal, April 30, 1907, L-E-1378.

97. Ibid.

98. Gamboa to Barrios, April 30, 1907; Gamboa to Mariscal, April 30, 1907; and Mariscal to Barrios, May 1, 1907, SREAHD, L-E-1378.

99. Appeal of Bernardo Reyes and Florencio Morales, 1907, Caja 0589, folio 103800, Archivo General de la Nación, Tribunal Superior de Justicía del Distrito Federal, Mexico City (hereafter TSJDF).

100. José Romero, *Apuntes sobre extradición con motive de la solicitud que hizo México a Guatemala, relacionada con la detención provisional del General guatemalteco J.M. Lima* (Mexico City: El Progreso Latino, 1907).

101. Daniel S. Margolies, *Spaces of Law in American Foreign Relations: Extradition and Extraterritoriality in the Borderlands and Beyond, 1877–1898* (Athens, GA: University of Georgia Press, 2011), 270–71.

102. Romero, *Apuntes sobre extradición*, 32.

103. Ibid., 40.

104. Buchenau, *In the Shadow of the Giant.*

105. Caja 0589, folio 103800, TSJDF.

106. Ibid.

107. "A Study of Mexican Criminal Procedure as Illustrated in the Barillas Case," *The Green Bag*, no. 9 (September, 1907), 532–39. The *careo* is confirmed in the court documents; see SREAHD, L-E-2050, Tomo VI.

108. *El imparcial*, September 7, 1907.

109. "Si fusilan a mora y morales," *El Dictamen* (Veracruz), August 29, 1907; *La voz de México*, August 31, 1907.

110. *El Imparcial*, September 7, 1907.

111. *Mexican Herald*, September 7, 1907.

112. *Mexican Herald*, September 8, 1907.

113. *El Imparcial*, September 10, 1907.

114. *Mexican Herald*, September 10, 1907.

115. *Regeneración*, September 14, 1907.

4

Undesirable Foreigners

THE DILEMMAS OF IMMIGRATION POLICY
IN REVOLUTIONARY MEXICO

Pablo Yankelevich

Among the many grievances that fed the Revolution of 1910, there was a clear opposition to the place of privilege occupied by individuals and communities of foreign origin in Mexico's economic, political, and social life. Because of their previously established migratory networks but also official favors, small groups of immigrants (primarily of European and North American origin) enjoyed notable upward mobility during the Porfiriato (1876–1911). Some were investors in businesses in the city and countryside, while others directly competed with national businessmen in a variety of commercial and industrial concerns or worked at companies where their privilege and inequality vis-à-vis Mexican workers was evident.[1] The most radical liberals, those who laid the foundation for the revolution, raised their voices against the interference and power of such foreigners. It wasn't for nothing that, starting in 1897, the emblematic opposition newspaper *El Hijo de Ahuizote* carried the subtitle "Mexico for Mexicans." It did not take long for the anti-Hispanic stance of this publication, in which Spaniards were blamed for a good part of the nation's problems, to be generalized into a formula that equated foreigners with rich and powerful businessmen, bankers, and merchants.[2]

While the number of foreigners in Mexico was never high, the growth of these communities at the turn of the century and, above all, their visibility in high society, fed social and ethnic resentments that found their expression with the outbreak of the revolution. In this context, revolutionary violence allowed for xenophobic conduct, primarily against Spanish and Chinese immigrants, with Americans and the English targeted to a lesser degree.[3]

Given this background, the participants in the Constituent Assembly of 1917 understood the popularity of demands to restrict the presence of foreigners in various aspects of the nation's economic and political life. The result was a constitutional text based on what would later be termed revolutionary nationalism. The Constitution served as a revolutionary program that was particularly focused on restoring national sovereignty over not only the nation's resources but also its mechanisms of political representation. It therefore contained a large number of safeguards for Mexicans and strict limitations for noncitizens. Thus Article 8 excluded foreigners from the right to petition in political matters; Article 9 did the same for the right to assembly and free association; Article 11 asserted the government's right to limit freedom of movement through immigration law; the first section of Article 27 limited foreigners' property rights; Article 32 established a legal framework that gave priority to Mexican nationals in government employment; and finally Article 33 prohibited foreigners from intervening in domestic politics, giving the executive branch the right to expel them from the country without the right to appeal if they did so.

In terms of political rights, the Constitution established a clear distinction between the rights of native-born Mexicans and those of naturalized citizens: the latter could not occupy any elected legislative position nor hold positions of responsibility in the executive or judicial branches. The reason for this differentiation was clearly explained by José Natividad Macías, a delegate at the 1917 Constitutional Assembly and the rector of the University of Mexico: "When dealing with questions of national interest, the Mexican heart is stirred…and feels repugnance and abhorrence when the sons of foreigners reach public positions." To explain this repugnance, we must first examine the networks of political power during the Porfiriato and, above all, the influence exercised by those individuals who made up the circle closest to Porfirio Díaz. Macías himself constantly mentioned the name of José Yves Limantour, Porfirio Díaz's influential Secretary of Finance whose French ancestry made him appear to be a clear example of a "foreigner who feels no affection for the republic."[4]

In reality, the grievances caused by foreigners and their children produced so much bitterness because they reanimated a debate begun in the

nineteenth century, and that is still far from over today. The revolution
revived polemics about the role of the Spanish conquest and the colonial
period in the configuration of the Mexican nation.[5] Liberals submitted the
Porfiriato and its most conspicuous representatives to a historical, moral,
and political judgment that associated its actions with three centuries of
rule by Spanish *conquistadores* and *encomenderos*. The aforementioned
constitutional prohibitions therefore laid the basis for a highly restrictive
immigration policy based on a defensive attitude that interpreted aliens
as a threat.

Immigration legislation was also a reaction to a new migratory dynamic
linked to the country's proximity to the United States. Mexico's revolutionaries soon discovered the double migratory character of the country
they were trying to govern. Mexico exported thousands of its own citizens
to the United States, while at the same time it also attracted immigrants
from Europe, Asia, and the Middle East who did not wish to remain in the
country but instead hoped to continue their journey by illegally entering
the United States.[6] The revolutionaries faced a complicated situation: on
the one hand, the economy was too weak to guarantee even minimum
subsistence conditions for a good part of the country's native population, while on the other, the restrictive immigration policies of the United
States encouraged the arrival of immigrants who used Mexican territory
as an indispensable stepping-stone toward the American dream. But
the problem was greater still: the proximity to the United States added
peculiar characteristics to a phenomenon that was becoming ever more
common in the early years of the twentieth century—temporary Mexican
emigration to work in American agriculture.[7] The fulfillment of expectations of a speedy return to Mexico often depended on the will and fortunes of each emigrant, although this was not always the case.

Geographical proximity not only encouraged migratory flows toward
the United States, but also allowed for the return of thousands of emigrants in moments of economic crisis.[8] Emigration was seen as a problem
in both moments of expansion as well as contraction of the US economy. In the first case, it led to predictions of the depopulation of a country
facing a constant drain of its residents toward the United States; in the
second case, times of economic crisis brought with them the return of
Mexicans who the domestic economy could not employ. This created a
vicious cycle marked by an inability to stop emigration and the fear of potential mass repatriations. This double condition as a sending and receiving country distinguishes Mexico's immigration experiences from those

of any other country in the continent, and it is this double condition that explains the government's immigration policy.

A 1927 Immigration Department study provides revealing information: between 1910 and 1926, the annual average number of foreigners who legally entered the country as immigrants was 26,600; however, the average annual number of immigrants who actually put down roots in the country was 7,200. Why did less than a third of Mexico's total annual number of immigrants remain in the country? Andrés Landa y Piña, then the head of the Immigration Department's Statistics Office, explained that the great majority of immigrants "did not have the goal of establishing themselves among us, but of staying here for a short period of time… in order to carry out the procedures, whether legal or unspeakable, that would allow them to legally or secretly enter the United States of America." The magnitude of this phenomenon was a consequence of the increasingly restrictive immigration policies of the United States, which, during the first half of the 1920s, instituted quotas per nation of origin, favoring immigrants from northern and western Europe to the detriment of those from that continent's eastern and southern countries. Virtually all immigration from Asia was also prohibited. Landa y Piña recognized that these restrictions led to an increase in immigration to Mexico, and confirmed the fact that these foreigners continued to see Mexico "as an anteroom, as a bridge" to the United States.[9]

The American labor market was attractive not only to foreigners but above all to Mexicans themselves, with an increasingly large segment of Mexican laborers departing for the United States for the same reasons that dazzled Europeans and Asians: the existence of a strong demand for laborers, accompanied by high wages. Mexico consequently became a nation whose demographic profile was based on mass emigration with a high rate of return and a low rate of permanent immigration. Landa y Piña accurately described the situation as follows: "Our case is different from other countries in the Americas, as we have an apparent immigration flow through the Gulf, but the opposite occurs at authorized crossing points along the northern border: thousands of Mexican laborers leave the country…and it seems paradoxical to give foreigners exceptional benefits when we have not been able to provide these same benefits to our own countrymen so that they do not feel obligated to emigrate."[10]

This was part of the dilemma faced by Mexico's postrevolutionary governments. The revolution provoked tensions regarding immigration in an attempt to balance irreconcilable concerns. One of these tensions revolved around the problem examined by Landa y Piña: that of allowing foreigners the right to make a life for themselves in Mexico while nationals were unable to do the same. But the second and perhaps definitive tension lay in the political and cultural project to homogenize Mexican society by making the *mestizo* the symbol of national identity.

Mestizaje

The defensive cordon around the nation was based on two policies. The first was the administrative restriction on the labor of foreigners. Conditions and procedures were established for immigrants, so as to ensure that their presence did not take jobs away from Mexicans. Secondly, immigration policy assumed a notably racial character. In the apotheosis of *mestizo*-philia, any foreign presence that threatened the desire for ethnic unity was restricted and even prohibited. This is one of the greatest ambiguities of revolutionary Mexico: with a discourse sensitive to matters of social injustice, and under the framework of a permanent vindication of the essential values supposedly held by the Mexican *mestizo*, the government cultivated an exclusive ethnic consciousness that led to intolerance toward some immigrant communities, as well as toward Mexico's indigenous population.[11]

Manuel Gamio, the father of Mexican indigenism, was also a government official committed to the population policies that began to be implemented in the mid-1920s. Although his contributions toward understanding the process of Mexican emigration to the United States are more widely known,[12] his voice was also present in the debates about immigration policy. Gamio argued that, unlike the United States, racism did not exist in Mexico: "It is not racial repugnance that is observed between the white and indigenous populations, but instead social and economic inequality." Exclusion was due to social conditions that needed to be reverted: "In Mexico," he stated, "the native is rejected for his poverty and ignorance, not for his blood." This inequality "between the oppressed indigenous majority and the ruling white minority" could be remediated through two strategies: the first, of "economic character," would include a generous redistribution of land and an efficient system of industrial education that would allow the indigenous population to make ample use of the natural resources at their disposal, guaranteeing a comfortable level of subsistence. Gamio called the second strategy "the eugenic path," which involved the "rapid and total *mestizaje* of the population" and the creation of a "racially homogenous" society. In connection with this point, he asked, "Would it be convenient to form a *mestizo* population by crossing the indigenous majority with the white minority?" with the categorical answer, "We sincerely believe that the answer is no."

> If this racial mixing or miscegenation occurred immediately, the white population would be racially absorbed by the indigenous population, given the numerical proportion between them, and while this is not deplorable in itself, because the anatomical and physiological characteristics of the indigenous population are not inferior to those of whites, this racial absorption would inevitably imply a consequent cultural absorption. In other words, the modern civilization of the white minority would devolve upon being united with the indigenous population, which represents several centuries of retrogression. This would naturally be highly detrimental and therefore unacceptable.[13]

"The eugenic path" was nothing more than the promotion of white immigration, through which the white population would numerically equal or exceed the indigenous population, thereby substantially "whitening" the *mestizo* race. Immigrants, therefore, should be the object of a "profuse selection": the immigration program would require the determination of the geographical regions of Mexico in which they could settle, as well as the "anatomical, psychic and physiological conditions of the Europeans admitted, so that their fusion with the indigenous be fertile and harmonious."[14]

Gamio made these proposals at the beginning of the 1920s, precisely when the rising tide of immigrants (as a consequence of US immigration restrictions) first began to ring alarm bells. Selection was the slogan of the new Mexican immigration policy. Under this concept, there was space for attitudes, ranging from the most xenophobic and ethnophobic to those that insisted immigration controls responded to transitory problems that would soon be resolved. In the first camp, a prominent place was occupied by the anti-Chinese campaigns centered in—but not exclusive to—the northwest of the country. The second camp included figures such as Andrés Landa y Piña, who would soon become the head of Immigration Department: "Our country," he wrote in 1927, "requires a strong immigration flow that should be calculated not in hundreds of thousands but in millions of individuals."[15] In this ambiguous space, there was always a basic agreement on the indispensable need to increase the white contribution to *mestizaje,* creating a mixture that would be "the mold where our nationality will conform and our fatherland solidify," as Gamio had prophesized a decade earlier.[16]

The 1920s witnessed a cult of *mestizaje* that became the pivot of a discourse that sought to redeem the most vulnerable sectors of Mexican society. According to this discourse, *mestizaje* was to be the salvation of a population oppressed by poverty and illiteracy, whom indigenist policies sought to liberate, while the descendants of the old *criollo* caste, symbolically represented by desirable white immigrants, would provide the benefits of European culture. This was an exclusive form of *mestizaje,* as it only included two source populations, but it was nevertheless unequal in its assumption that one of these populations was in a position of civilizational inferiority.

This unresolvable tension between the components of *mestizaje* took hold in the heart of Mexican immigration policy. Therefore, while the government aimed to meet the indigenous population's basic needs, it also sought to promote *mestizaje* through the arrival of white European immigrants who would carry out agricultural activities in regions of low population density. These white Europeans would serve two purposes: to work and invest their capital in the recuperation of "desert land, virgin jungles and currently sterile mountains," and to establish "blood ties with peasants, contributing to furthering the *mestizaje.*" The arrival in Mexico's rural areas of white Europeans "that do not form isolated colonies amongst us" and are capable "of exploiting our natural resources but not our men" would thus allow them to "assimilate themselves to our race and our spirit."[17]

The Outlines of Undesirability

At the start of the Mexican Revolution in 1910, there were little more than 100,000 foreigners living in a country that was home to fifteen million Mexicans. These figures were a marked contrast with other countries in the Americas. The United States, for example, accepted 1,300,000 immigrants in 1907, while immigrants represented 30 percent of Argentina's total population in 1910.[18] The low number of immigrants in Mexico can help explain why the country's first immigration law was only passed in 1908. The coveted European immigration was on the rise in the final third of the nineteenth century and did not require special legislation that would promote immigrants' incorporation into the domestic economy. Their arrival was the result of the economic growth generated by the period's ultraliberal policies on foreign investment and the construction of new transportation infrastructure.[19] Besides, these Europeans, who numbered slightly more than fifty thousand people in 1895,[20] received the protection of their respective immigrant communities and of a manifest official xenophilia that eased their rapid social ascent and consequent integration into the economic and political elite.[21]

The Immigration Law of 1908 was instead a consequence of growing concern over the rise of Chinese immigration, which was originally promoted by the Mexican government and escalated following the US Chinese Exclusion Act of 1882. This prohibition affected Mexico by creating undocumented flows of Asians who either sought to enter the United States or who, having been deported from that country, settled in northwestern Mexico.[22]

Between 1895 and 1910, Mexico's immigrant population doubled.[23] This growth contained a shifting composition of nationalities. While the proportion of European immigrants decreased from 45% of total immigrants in 1895 to 39% in 1910, the proportion of Chinese immigrants increased from 2% to 11% in those same years.[24] A series of health scares accompanied these changes after contagious diseases were detected in ports of disembarkation for Asian immigrants. This situation led to the promulgation of an immigration law that stipulated "the fullest equality for all countries and all races,"[25] but explicitly prohibited the entry of foreigners who were carriers of illnesses associated with Chinese immigration (bubonic plague, cholera, yellow fever, trachoma, beriberi, and so on). It also regulated procedures for documenting and receiving foreign workers aboard ships that were specially designated for such purposes.

The actions of government agencies in charge of immigration policy were marked by a high degree of arbitrariness. Authorities had to deal with the problems of the country's ethnic composition while also considering the grievances of a society that claimed to be negatively affected by the presence of immigrants. Officials had not freed themselves from the prejudices of the times, which they hid behind pseudoscientific arguments that tended to favor white immigration.

In the Immigration Law of 1926, the first law on the matter passed after the revolution, we can see the earliest manifestations of concern for the selection of migratory flows based on the argument that this would prevent the dangers of social, cultural, and political decomposition, as well as the racial degeneration of the Mexican population: "It's undeniable that foreign immigration can constitute an incredibly powerful factor for the nation's progress; but for this to be the case, it's essential that the government have the ability to select between immigrants and exclude those individuals whose morality, nature, customs and personal circumstances would be undesirable or constitute a threat of physical degeneration for our race, moral depression for our people or dissolution of our political institutions."[26]

This legislation established obligatory registration and documentary controls for immigrants for the first time. It also sought to reduce the volume of migration by requiring all immigrants who wished to permanently settle in Mexico to present, upon entry, either a letter from an employer offering them work for no less than one year or proof that they had the financial resources to cover their living expenses (as well as those of their family, when applicable) for a period of ninety days. Immigration authorities could also temporarily prohibit the arrival of immigrant laborers when, in their judgment, there was a domestic work shortage.[27] After enumerating all the cases in which the government could refuse entry to Mexico,[28] a subsection of Article 29 established that the executive branch of the federal government reserved the right to refuse entry to foreigners, even in cases not mentioned textually in the law. On the other hand, it is also worth mentioning that this law established procedures for granting visas to tourists for the first time. The latter was a clear attempt to stimulate the economy, even though, as discussed later, foreigners often entered the country as tourists and then illegally stayed past their expected departure date.

This law replaced the one passed in 1908 and laid the foundations for what would become the agency in charge of immigration policy: the Interior Secretariat's Immigration Department.[29] Breaking with the Porfirian-era legislation that merely sought to watch over ports of entry and inspect passengers and crew, the Immigration Service widened its controls in 1926 to include the paperwork that foreigners had to complete to legally enter and remain in the country. It was only in that year, in other words, that institutional authority was established over the identity and activities of immigrants.

Mexico saw the arrival of a growing number of immigrants in the 1920s, and a good part of this increase was seen as inconvenient. The economic crisis in the United States at the beginning of the decade sparked a wave of "repatriated" Mexican workers, which soon became one of the central concerns of immigration authorities. According to official figures, more than 150,000 Mexicans returned to Mexico between 1921 and 1924,[30] and they were soon perceived as just as much of a threat as the arrival of the tens of thousands of foreigners who, although still a small proportion of the population at large, nevertheless represented a substantial increase compared to the immigration flows seen in the previous decade. In the written justification for the 1926 law, these concerns were made explicit in a section explaining that the executive branch lacked a legal mechanism "to impede or suspend, even temporarily, the entrance of manual laborers into the nation's territory. Our workers are therefore vulnerable to the effects of an excess labor supply and competition from elements which offer their labor in exchange for miserable wages. This situation prevents improvements to the conditions of our working classes and ensures the constant emigration of workers who seek better conditions abroad."[31]

The process of repatriation, though on the wane in 1926, sounded an alarm that would continue to worry those responsible for implementing immigration policy. As a result, though the new law considered immigration to be "an incredibly powerful factor for the nation's progress," it was primarily aimed at restricting the arrival of new immigrants.

In reality, restriction had begun a few years earlier, when the Interior Secretariat initiated a practice based on "confidential circulars" that defined the outlines of undesirability. These orders, which were delivered to immigration agents and the Mexican consular service, are a faithful portrait of the era's phobias and their justifications, and examining them allows us to measure the discretional application of government regulations far from public scrutiny.

Circular No. 33, issued on May 13, 1924, barred "the immigration of individuals of the negro race."[32] When Mexican consulates began to deny visas to African Americans and Afro-Cubans, the consular service itself began to revolt. In October 1926, Manuel Álvarez, the Mexican Consul in Havana, was reprimanded for having authorized visas for a group of Afro-Cubans who were then arrested at the Port of Tampico and deported to Cuba. The Interior Secretariat immediately exhorted the Foreign Affairs Secretary to instruct him to refuse all visas "to individuals of the negro race, as this immigration is not beneficial to our country."[33] Manuel Álvarez took note of his orders but immediately informed the foreign affairs secretary that "this nation has a population with a very high percentage of individuals of the negro race, who are considered to be citizens with full civil rights and even form part of the current presidential cabinet as ministers of state." For these reasons, the consul requested explanations that he could give to visa applicants "in order to avoid resentment, especially when dealing with individuals who form part of the government."[34] The Interior Secretariat's response indicated that the prohibition referred exclusively to "individuals of the colored race that belong to the working class, in light of the fact that our government seeks to protect our manual laborers, who suffer fierce competition for jobs due to the arrival of such individuals."[35]

The vagueness of these criteria soon caused conflict between different government agencies. In 1928 the public education secretariat hired the Englishman Miguel Menbhardt, a professor specializing in tropical agriculture, "to teach in federal schools." A resident of Belize, he attempted to enter Mexico through its border with Quintana Roo, but was arrested at the Payo Obispo border crossing "for being of the negro race." Thanks to the intervention of the director of federal education, he received an "exceptional authorization" to enter the country "for a period of six months upon paying a 1,000-peso bond."[36]

Teams of seasonal black laborers actually crossed the southern border quite frequently, hired by English, American, and Mexican businessmen to work in forestry. This was made possible thanks to an agreement with the agriculture secretariat stipulating that, in the absence of Mexican workers who were willing to work in rain-forest and jungle regions, businessmen were authorized to hire Belizean laborers. Starting in 1924, when the prohibition on the entry of black immigrants went into effect, this conflict was generally resolved in favor of business interests, but only after an intricate lobbying process in which the representatives of companies that wished to hire black laborers had to meet directly with the president himself in order to obtain temporary work visas for hundreds of workers. Against the background of this struggle between government agencies, the Immigration Department explained the true basis for the prohibition in a confidential document: "The general criteria of the government, as it has been manifested in recent years, is one of marked opposition to immigration of the Ethiopian and Mongolian races, which, for well-known ethnological reasons, constitute a threat to our embryonic nationality."

This was the central motive: these were races that, "because of their inferiority, accept work under conditions of slavery...while in every corner of the Republic we find idle laborers who, in search of wages, decide to emigrate to the United States."[37]

The need for selective immigration was a response to a diagnosis of the attributes of a Mexican population that was seen as not yet constituting an authentic nationality. At the 1917 Constituent Assembly, deputy Paulino Machorro Narváez asked rhetorically, "Do the Mexican people currently constitute a true nationality?" His response showed the vigor of a belief that continued to be influential for decades to come: "There are many elements that currently work against the constitution of our nationality: the different races that date back to the Conquest have yet to complete their fusion. We are a collection of races and each of them has its own mentality, and it is this diversity that presents us before the civilized world as a weak people that lacks national unity."[38]

The belief in this constitutive weakness was at the root of immigration policy. The government aimed to defend the Mexican people from the dangers of certain racial mixtures "that have been scientifically proven to produce degeneracy in future generations,"[39] and to protect them from "other races" that, due to their reluctance to miscegenate, were incapable of being broken down in the crucible of *mestizaje*. This marked the appearance of the category of the "inassimilable" races, which, in the mid-1920s, was applied to a varied array of nationalities and ethnicities.

Prohibited Races and Nationalities

Legislation on immigration was both improvised and belated. The revolutionary decade and the problems of institutionalizing the new regime delayed a proper treatment of the problems arising from population movements. The immigration law of 1926 was passed three years after being first presented. At the beginning of 1926, Primo Villa Michel, a legal advisor to the Interior Secretariat, made a scathing criticism of the version of the bill that was finally approved. He argued that Mexico was suffering from an "enormous invasion of harmful foreigners" and the law that was about to be approved did not include any specific mechanisms to address this situation. This invasion was twofold: First, there were the "individuals of the colored race, whose abundance is the origin of the phenomenon of the ethnological depression of our race." Second, there were those immigrants who, regardless of their race or nationality, "arrive in Mexico without the intention of increasing our productive forces and instead only weigh them down." Villa Michel illustrated this problem using three different groups. The first was composed of Spaniards who "came as apprentices to merchants, offering up their labor for a miserable remuneration, to the extent that they have excluded our young countrymen from almost all mercantile activity in spite of their superior training." The second group was made up of Arabs, Armenians, Turks, Syrians, Lebanese, Poles, and Czechoslovaks who "come with neither trade nor profession and engage in a wretched form of commerce, wandering the streets of our cities and towns…carrying all their capital in their hands in the form of stockings, ties and other cheap products." This form of immigration, devoted to "consumption without production," only aggravated the economic situation in urban spaces by limiting the development and operation of serious commercial enterprises and excluding "the humble classes, who could make a living as small-scale merchants, from commercial pursuits." Finally, the third category of harmful immigrants consisted of those who used Mexican territory as a stepping-stone to illegally enter the United States. This was a substantial group "made up of Italians, Poles and many other nationalities." By failing to establish clear mechanisms to impede this "bad immigration," the proposed law of 1926 left only one alternative in Villa Michel's opinion: "arbitrary agreements," such as those established through the confidential circulars.[40]

Such opinions were not taken into account. A few years later, lawmakers began preparing new immigration legislation. The new law, passed in 1930, refined the mechanisms for selecting immigrants and stipulated that authorization to enter the country was subject to criteria based on the defense of *mestizaje*. Though the government continued to consider immigration as beneficial, it was nevertheless restricted to "members of races whose nature would make them easy to assimilate to our society, thus benefitting the race and the country's economic situation."[41]

This law also marked the first appearance of measures to temporarily limit the entry of workers of Syrian, Lebanese, Armenian, Palestinian, Arabian, and Turkish origin.[42] The list of restricted nationalities soon expanded to include Russian, Polish, and Chinese workers.[43] The economic crisis of 1930s and the consequent increase in the repatriation of Mexican workers only reinforced restrictive immigration policies. In April 1929, the Interior Secretariat prohibited "the entry of immigrant laborers" in its

Circular 37.[44] Months later, a new circular announced that this prohibition would be lifted, albeit only for European workers.[45] When the economy crashed later that year, the Interior Secretariat published the terms of a new temporary prohibition on the entry of foreign laborers in the *Diario Oficial de la Federación*—the government would not authorize the entry of any foreigners who arrived with the intention of performing manual labor in exchange for a wage, nor any foreigners who lacked a capital stock of at least 10,000 pesos ($3,000 USD) that they intended to invest in some agricultural, industrial, or commercial enterprise within a period of six months following their arrival in Mexico.[46]

During the 1930s, through a series of secret orders, "ethnic reasons" justified prohibitions on the arrival of immigrants belonging to "undesirable races," while political and economic motivations justified new limits on the total volume of immigrants. Among these orders, two stand out: the first, issued in October 1933 (Circular 250), prohibited the arrival of immigrants of the "black, yellow, Malay and Hindu races" due to "ethnic" objections; it also banned gypsies due to "their bad habits." It also classified Poles, Lithuanians, Czechoslovaks, Syrians, Lebanese, Palestinians, Arabs, and Turks as "somewhat undesirable" due to "the types of activities in which they engage." Visas for Soviet citizens and foreign priests were cancelled for political reasons, and work visas were limited for foreign doctors and teachers.[47]

The second, more wide-ranging set of orders was issued in April 1934 (Circular 157). On the basis of their "ethnic, economic, political and demographic characteristics," it prohibited the "African, Australian, yellow, Hindu and Malay races." Nationalities and ethnic groups associated with street commerce were reclassified from "restricted" to "prohibited." (These included Poles, Lithuanians, Latvians, Czechoslovaks, Syrians, Lebanese, Palestinians, Armenians, Arabs, Turks, Bulgarians, Romanians, Persians, Yugoslavians, and Greeks.) Individuals whose "blood mixture, cultural level, habits, customs, etc. would make them exotic for our psychology" (Albanians, Afghans, Abyssinians, Algerians, Egyptians, and Moroccans) were also prohibited from entering Mexico. Apart from ratifying the prohibitions based on political reasons, a special section was set aside for Jewish immigrants, who were considered to be "undesirable, above all others, due to their psychological and moral characteristics and the types of activities in which they engage."[48] With these orders, Mexican exclusion reached one of its historic heights, with undesirability based on a diverse array of factors:

skin color, nationality, occupation, profession, customs, habits, religion, and political preferences.

New Diagnostics

The 1930s saw the fiercest opposition to exogenous elements of the domestic population. There is no doubt that the impact of the economic crash was of such magnitude that the arrival of thousands repatriated Mexicans was enough to call off any project that insisted on the advantages of immigration. Of the foreigners who already lived in Mexico, their small numbers mattered little; their mere presence, combined with the country's economic difficulties and the political polarization of those years, provided a breeding ground for exclusionary policies justified by a revolutionary nationalism that then expressed its most xenophobic manifestations.

A strident campaign against undesirable immigrants swept Mexico; the old anti-Chinese activists broadened their phobias with the founding of the National Anti-Chinese and Anti-Jew League, an organization led by veterans of the revolution that expressed the grievances of the middle classes, particularly those engaged in commercial activities. "It's a secret to none," a 1934 manifesto stated, "that the Jews (Russians, Poles, Czechoslovaks, and Lithuanians) lack the most elementary moral and hygienic principles and have abused the hospitality that has been offered them, competing against our compatriots in all commercial activities in the most brutal and unequal manner. They aim to take control of our commerce, and they will succeed unless we build a powerful dike against their ungrateful, illegitimate ambitions."[49]

These campaigns had the support of the authorities. In February 1935, the leaders of the National Revolutionary Party demanded that the Interior Secretary "deal with the problem of undesirable immigrants, the Chinese and the Jews, who are a burden for Mexican people."[50] *El Nacional*, the official newspaper of the postrevolutionary regime, had given an official voice to these campaigns ever since it launched in 1929 and, in one 1931 editorial, wrote that "they have won the approval of all the nation's social classes."[51]

The dilemma of confronting a mass repatriation of Mexicans made immigration policy a tense issue. The legal flow of immigrants fell as a result of the aforementioned restrictions, but the composition of the remaining immigrants raised alarms. Nothing was further from the imagined ideal immigrant than the Syrians, Arabs, Turks, Lebanese, and Palestinians, whose immigration rate rose by 170% between 1910 and 1930, together with Jews from central and eastern Europe.[52]

This environment provided the context for the first diagnostics of the nation's demographics. Gilberto Loyo, a disciple of the prestigious Italian demographer Corrado Gini, was in charge of instituting a new way of approaching population issues. Loyo's populationist posture was based on the assumption that, rather than its heterogeneity, it was the lack of density of the Mexican population that was the main obstacle to the country's modernization. Mexico had a mere eight inhabitants per square kilometer and, with this dispersion, "It's impossible to properly exploit the land, develop modern industries, create modern political and social institutions and ensure a quality of life and level of culture appropriate for a truly modern society. With eight inhabitants per square kilometer, even if they be of the most progressive race, it's impossible to organize a modern society."[53]

The alternative was to favor the natural growth of the population by reducing Mexico's high mortality rate. To accomplish this, programs had to be designed that would ensure medical and legal coverage for women and children, and make nutritional advances and improvements to the hygienic conditions of homes, schools, and workplaces. It would also be essential to execute plans to redistribute the population in order to de-concentrate areas of high density and settle people in zones of low density, particularly along the country's borders.

Loyo's proposals signified a radical change by recognizing the failure of previous attempts to use immigration as a means to modernize the country. Loyo arrived at a somber conclusion: a country like Mexico, with its *mestizo* population and its "backwards cultural type," should not try to increase its population through immigration because, "as experience has shown, *mestizo* countries only attract adventurers, social outcasts, unscrupulous elements that would be bad citizens in any country and terrible ones in a country like ours." He continued to see advantages in promoting the arrival of "good immigrants," but his diagnosis was conclusive: Mexico should invest in its own human capital through policies aimed at the country's social and economic integration. "When the material and moral conditions of the great masses improve, immigration could be more abundant and of better quality, although this will not occur for several decades."[54]

These concerns coalesced in the 1936 General Law on Population, the essential criteria of which remained in place for the following four decades. This legislation was designed to respond to what were understood to be substantial demographic problems—namely, "increasing the population; its racial distribution throughout the country; the ethnic fusion of one group with another; the protection of native-born citizens engaged in economic, professional, artistic or intellectual activities through immigration measures; the education of indigenous groups so that they make greater physical, economic and social contributions from a demographic point of view; [and] the general protection, conservation and improvement of the species through the limitations and procedures established by this law."[55] This was the first piece of legislation that aimed to deal with Mexico's population issues in a comprehensive manner. It favored the natural growth of the population through programs for repatriating emigrants and a highly controlled immigration policy based on the potential for assimilation.

The centrality of the state during the presidency of Lázaro Cárdenas can be seen in the design and implementation of a population policy based around the most restrictive immigration statute in Mexican history. The 1936 law prohibited foreigners from exercising professions (Article 31); with the goal of ensuring that control of the country's economic life would remain in the hands of native-born citizens, it restricted the commercial and industrial activities in which foreigners could engage in various parts of the country (Article 32); to guarantee the distribution of foreigners throughout the country, the government reserved the right to dictate their place of residence (Article 7); and to protect jobs for Mexicans, it restricted foreigners from engaging in intellectual and artistic activities in a systematic and remunerated manner (Article 33). The law also prohibited, for an indefinite time, the entry of immigrant laborers and foreigners who engaged in commercial activities, with the exception of those engaged in foreign trade (Articles 84 and 87), and placed limitations on the number of foreign technicians (Article 86).[56]

This assemblage of labor restrictions was complemented by a system of immigration quotas determined annually by the Interior Secretariat. The law stated that these quotas "will be established by considering the national interest, the degree of racial and cultural assimilability and the convenience of their admission so that immigrants don't become a destabilizing factor."[57] Lastly, the 1936 law, after enumerating all the obligations that foreigners must meet in order to be admitted to the country, concluded with the following provision: "Even when they meet all of these requirements, the Interior Secretariat may prevent the admission of certain undesirable foreigners at its discretion" (Article 74). In contrast with these articles, for the first time the law also provided protections for "foreigners who arrive in the country while fleeing political persecution" (Article 58).[58] This established the precedent that, only a few years later, would allow thousands of Spanish Republicans to take refuge in Mexico, a humanitarian action that occurred in the midst of the most restrictive immigration policies in Mexican history.

The restrictions established by the 1936 law led the authorities to judge it illogical to continue a policy of prohibitions and limitations based on the confidential orders of the Interior Secretariat. It was thought that the time had come to establish a rational legal framework, putting all discretion aside. In May 1937, through Circular 930, the federal government repealed all restrictions "based on race, nationality and religion, as established in Confidential Circulars 250 and 157."[59] The consular service, in other words, was free to issue tourist visas without restrictions, given that federal law now established selection criteria for those who wished to permanently reside in the country.

However, ten months later, in March 1938, this measure was repealed. A study conducted by the General Statistics Department, founded by Gilberto Loyo, showed that there was no evidence that the twenty thousand foreigners who entered on tourist visas between 1933 and 1937 had ever left the country. As a consequence, permission to enter the country would be subject to prior authorization by the Interior Secretariat, with the sole exception of tourists from the United States.[60]

Mexico's approval of its first set of immigration quotas made this strengthening of prohibitionist policies possible. In contrast to the United States or Brazil, where quotas were established according to a percentage of the total number of immigrants registered in the census per nation of origin, the low number of immigrants allowed entry into Mexico under its quota system reflected ethnic preferences and a lack of reliable statistics. While there were no limitations placed on immigrants from Spain or the countries of the Americas, only a hundred nationals from the rest of the world were authorized to enter the country annually during the most restrictive period, from 1940 to 1946.[61]

Dangerous Invasions

Halfway through the 1940s, when the magnitude of the Nazi genocide became clear, invocations of racial belonging began to fall out of favor in population policy. These changes did not pass by Mexico. In 1947 on the initiative of President Miguel Alemán, a new General Population Law was approved with the goal of "adjusting the law to present realities, in which the phenomena of the postwar period have affected the demographic problems faced by Mexico." In justifying the law, the president stated, "First of all, I must mention that this project is in no way racially discriminatory, as Mexico defends the equality of all races before the law." He immediately added that the law in question "is fundamentally oriented towards a more effective selection of immigrants." The criteria of "assimilation," which had been used since the end of the 1920s, reappeared in legislation that would remain on the books until 1974. "It's evident," Miguel Alemán said, "that attempts have failed to assimilate a large percentage of those immigrants that have already been admitted. The cases of foreigners who have become authentic nationals through cordial contact with our country, through an identification with the Mexican way of life, and through an adoption of our traditions and customs, are far from numerous and even exceptional."[62]

The state's will to homogenize the population remained strong in the postwar period. Officials raised alarms about the need to "defend ourselves from uncontrolled immigration, which could place us in the clear danger of being substituted or supplanted, and would in any case be anti-economic and antisocial." The law that was finally approved therefore stipulated, in Article 8, that the Interior Secretariat had the responsibility to "subject the entry of foreigners to those measures it deems convenient, according to their greater or lesser ability to assimilate to our environment."[63]

This new legislation eliminated quotas on nationalities but left the door open to reinstate them, whether by nationality, by type of visa, or by activity to be undertaken in Mexico (Article 59). The discretion used in the implementation of immigration policy can be clearly seen in the provisions establishing that the Mexican government had the power to deny entry or visas to foreigners "as it deems appropriate," even when said foreigners had met all the requirements stipulated by law (Article 60). Lastly, the law defined the profile of potential immigrants by establishing that visas would be granted to tourists, technicians, management personnel in domestic firms and institutions, investors, students, and relatives of foreigners already living in Mexico. In the case of professionals, it stated that they would only be admitted in exceptional circumstances. The new legislation did not allow visas to low skilled workers or those who lacked the resources to sustain themselves and their families.

The criteria used to determine "desirability" was based on the immigrant's ability to "assimilate," a euphemism that alluded to ethnic standards that were never made explicit. Secondly, socioprofessional profiles were subject to quotas that favored high levels of training; the possession of the capital needed to make financial, commercial, or productive investments; and lastly, the existence of family ties—the possibility, in other words, of obtaining a temporary or permanent residence visa by proving one's relations with foreigners already living in Mexico.

Desired immigration was restricted to these criteria, under which professionals were particularly distrusted—to the point where their entry was conditional, as mentioned previously, on exceptional authorizations. It is interesting to reflect on this "exceptionality," on the paradoxes of an immigration policy that privileges high levels of training while setting restricted quotas for professionals.

With the outcome of the Second World War still uncertain, the governmental elite arrived at the conclusion that "the turmoil in Europe, the prevailing conditions in that continent's nations and the promise of comfort and ease of advancement in Mexico will direct large flows of foreigners who have lost their fatherland, family and home to our country."[64] Faced with what was considered a looming threat, the government approved legislation that regulated the exercise of the liberal professions. The parliamentary debates on this issue therefore became the arena in which conceptualizations of immigration were confronted.

Starting in 1943, legislators focused on drafting a series of secondary laws for Articles 4 and 5 of the Constitution, which dealt with professions. In the first round of debates, legislators spoke of the need to draft an emergency law that would anticipate the problems of the postwar era and lay "the foundations for the defense of Mexican professionals and Mexican technical and scientific labor." Such problems, it was supposed, would be none other than the arrival of "mass immigration from Europe, which will have us sleeping in the street and ceding our homes to foreigners."[65] The discussions and drafts, as well as the final law approved in May 1945, established in Articles 15 and 18 that the free exercise of professions would be prohibited for all foreigners and naturalized citizens with foreign degrees.[66] The final legislation not only enshrined inequality between native-born Mexicans and naturalized citizens, but also violated Article 4 of the Constitution, which guaranteed the freedom to work for all the country's residents, whether they be Mexicans or foreigners. What had in fact occurred was that Congress passed a law on professions that sought to restrict immigration without taking into account the issue they were dealing with—that is, the legality of professional degrees independent of the nationality of the degree holder. A native-born Mexican educated abroad, unlike foreigners and naturalized citizens, would therefore be able to obtain permission to exercise his or her profession (Article 17).

Though it would be natural to assume that these inconsistencies would have led to a heated debate, this was not the case. They went unmentioned during the technical rulings prepared by the Education and Constitutional Affairs Committees. And when the project reached the floor of the Chamber of Deputies, the only voice raised in opposition was Herminio Ahumada, who, to mitigate the "chauvinist" spirit of the law and to honor "Mexico's traditional generosity," argued that Mexico could not treat all foreigners the same: "It's necessary for us to take into account a special group of foreigners, that is, our Hispanic-American brothers, as well as the Spaniards, who are no less our brothers. Mexican law must establish privileges for these group of foreigners, and I say foreigners because so they are legally considered, but to me and to all Mexicans neither our fellow Hispanic-Americans nor Spaniards can or should be considered foreigners."[67]

Echoes of Arielism could be heard throughout the first half of the twentieth century, ever since the Constituent Assembly of 1917. When restrictions on immigration were first imposed, there were many who begged for exceptions for Hispanic Americans. Though none of these proposals were successful at the Constituent Assembly, the Immigration and Naturalization Law of 1934 stipulated that Latin Americans who requested naturalization would receive special treatment. A similar situation can be observed in the exceptions to the quota system that were granted to immigrants from Latin America and Spain between 1937 and 1946. This appeal to a cultural community and "race," converted into cultural policy by José Vasconcelos during the 1920s, was taken up by his son-in-law Herminio Ahumada in defense of professionals from Spain and Latin America. Nevertheless, Andrés Serra Rojas, Ahumada's legislative colleague, ended the discussion by declaring, "When the interests of my fatherland are at stake, I am generous with none!"[68]

The issues that went unmentioned by the legislature became the subject of a Supreme Court decision in 1948. Faced with an accumulation of appeals by those affected by this law, the Supreme Court ruled that it was unconstitutional to prohibit foreigners from freely exercising their professions or to make distinctions between native-born Mexicans and naturalized citizens.[69] In December of that year, this ruling obligated President Alemán to propose that Congress modify the Law on Professions in order to harmonize it with constitutional precepts. In general, deputies approved of this project, but the modifications proposed by the president were never incorporated into law. Although Articles 15 and 18 of the Law on Professions were declared unconstitutional by a 1954 ruling, they remained in force until 1993.[70]

Examining those voices that opposed the Supreme Court ruling in December 1948 can shed light on why a law that had been declared unconstitutional continued to be applied. The deputies Victoriano Anguiano and Miguel Ramírez Murguía called on Congress to ignore the ruling, as the individual rights guaranteed by the Constitution could be ignored in order to preserve the greater good, such as the defense of "Mexican professionals and the highest values of the fatherland." Anguiano argued: "I believe that it would be unjust for our country, for our people, and for the middle class to approve [the proposed modifications to Articles 15 and 18] simply to satisfy a constitutional article that is itself debatable. I repeat: it would be an injustice to grant this liberty to foreigners."[71]

The issue at hand was one of competition for jobs, in Anguiano's view. The law should legitimize a position of privilege for native-born Mexicans, in accordance with the same discourses and actions that governed immigration policy:

> We can see how, in other activities such as commerce, small-scale industry and other fields, foreigners have invaded the country and displaced Mexicans. They are more audacious still: they have come to a country that they see as a conquest. We, with our romantic love of freedom, with our desire to present ourselves as a generous country, open the doors...[but] they tear down the immigration restrictions and all legal obstacles, taking control of our means of production and our economic activities, displacing Mexicans and relegating us to the condition of pariahs or slaves.[72]

The 1948 debate around the protection of Mexican professionals was not solely based on stale arguments about the limitless avarice of the foreign-

124 *Yankelevich*

ers, but also, once again, on the inherent danger of a "race in formation that is victimized by foreign influences." Four decades after the revolutionary upheaval, Gamio's *Forjando Patria* remained influential. Mexico suffered from an essential ethnic weakness and therefore required a legal architecture capable of guaranteeing its continued existence:

> Painfully, our country has many examples of the lack of culture caused by the irregular distribution of the population and its scarce density attributed to a lack of means of transportation, by the actions of the Church and, fundamentally, by poverty, which have created a spirit of prostration or admiration towards foreigners. We think that a doctor...or a lawyer, because they have a German, English or French last name, is superior to our own professionals, who, despite their modesty or the tragedy of their daily lives, have the same or better intellectual or professional standards as those individuals with ostentatious last names that impress our people. Herein lies the danger.[73]

Judging foreigners as a danger—and further, still, to do so based on the "inferiority" of Mexican culture—was more than just a pretext to defend professional interests by defying constitutional precepts. The arguments employed showed ambivalent sentiments of both distrust and attraction toward foreigners—the same ambivalence in which notions of the differences between Mexicans and non-Mexicans in the postrevolutionary period were rooted.

Conclusion

The immigration policies of the Mexican Revolution contain a number of paradoxes. In a country with such a low level of immigration, what was the purpose of such rigid regulations? And in a nation so injured by the prejudice and racism of others, how can we explain the strong racialization of immigration policies? Answering these questions obliges us to consider at least four issues.

First, among the causes of the revolutionary upheaval of 1910 was a clear displeasure with the presence of foreigners and their influence. When the revolution triumphed, the country's new rulers were required to listen to the demands of the people, demands that were stronger when there was a foreigner involved. The demands of peasants and workers, for example, held more weight if the landowners or company directors in question were foreigners. It was thus necessary to limit the freedom foreigners' freedom of action. This would create a cordon protecting Mexicans by guaranteeing those social and political rights previously violated by powerful merchants, landowners, industrialists, and bankers, among them immigrants who had benefitted from the privileges granted by the Porfirian regime.

Second, this nationalism played out against the background of cyclical economic crises in the United States that, starting in 1920 and with varying degrees of intensity, triggered the repatriation of thousands of Mexicans, causing employment problems that the postrevolutionary government had to deal with. In this context of labor and commercial competition, the struggle of Mexicans to obtain real advantages in a restricted job market reinforced restrictive immigration policies. Initially concerned with protecting working-class jobs, fears of the rising number of immigrants in the 1920s expanded to professional, middle-class sectors after the Second World War.

Third, the growth in immigration starting in the 1920s appears to be directly related to the restrictive immigration policies of the US government. As a result of these restrictions, Mexico became a destination for more immigrants, as well as a transit nation for foreigners who wished to enter the United States. It took some time for Mexican authorities to understand this double condition, and they reacted as if it was a true invasion of foreigners, even though the volume of immigrants never exceeded 0.5% of the total population.

Fourth, Mexico's immigration policies were not just aimed at protecting labor markets, but also toward protecting the biological and cultural constitution of the Mexican people from undesirable racial mixtures or the presence of social groups that would resist assimilation. These eugenic concerns led to the adoption of racial selection criteria that favored white and European immigration.

In conclusion, the paradoxes of Mexican immigration policy are the result of a convergence of twin circumstances. On the one hand, proximity to the United States meant that government decisions and labor market cycles in the US regulated Mexico's outward and return flows of emigrants as well as the arrival of foreigners who came to Mexico when denied entry to the United States. On the other hand, Mexico's postrevolutionary government reacted with a strategy that strove to close the doors to foreign workers. Therefore politics were designed to narrow the criteria of desirability, and racial arguments made their appearance to justify these prohibitions. The figure of the mestizo as an icon of nationality was used as a shield to avoid the entry of undesirables, feeding an exclusive *mestizaje* that was very far removed from José Vasconcelos's dreams of a "cosmic race."

———————

This article forms part of a research project financed by Mexico's National Council of Science and Technology. I would like to thank Santiago de la Mora and Luis Sandoval for all their help on this research project, as well as Gabriela Díaz and Joshua Neuhouser for translating the text into English.

Notes

1. Raymonde Antiq-Auvaro, *L'émigration des barcelonnettes au Mexique* (Paris: Serre, 1992); Mario Cerutti, *Empresarios españoles y sociedad capitalismo en México (1840–1920)* (Colombres: Archivo de Indianos, 1995); Clara Lida, *Tres aspectos de la presencia española en México durante el Porfiriato* (Mexico: El Colegio de México, 1981); Rosa María Meyer and Delia Salazar, eds., *Los inmigrantes en el mundo de los negocios siglos XIX y XX* (Mexico: INAH, 2003); Camila Pastor de Maria y Campos, "The Transnational Imagination: XXth Century Networks and Institutions of the Mashreqi Migration to Mexico," *Palma Journal* 11, no. 1 (2009): 31–72; Carlos Martínez Assad, ed., *La ciudad cosmopolita de los inmigrantes* (Mexico: Gobierno del Distrito Federal, 2010); Luis Alfonso Ramírez, *Secretos de familia: Libaneses y elites empresariales en la Yucatán* (Mexico: Consejo Nacional para la Cultura y las Artes, 1992); Sergio Valerio Ulloa, *Los Barcelonnettes en Guadalajara, siglos XIX y XX* (Mexico: Universidad de Guadalajara, Instituto Mora, 2015).

2. Tomás Pérez Vejo, "La conspiración gachupina en El Hijo del Ahuizote," *Historia Mexicana* 216 (April–June 2005): 1105–53.

3. Moisés González Navarro, "Xenofobia y Xenofilia en la Revolución Mexicana," *Historia Mexicana* 72 (1969): 569–614; Carlos Illades, *Presencia española en la Revolución Mexicana (1910–1915)* (Mexico: UNAM-Mora, 1991); Alan Knight, *Nationalism, Xenophobia and Revolution: The Place of Foreigners and Foreign Interest in Mexico, 1910–1915* (PhD diss., Oxford University, 1974); Juan Puig, *Entre el río Perla y el Nazas. La China decimonónica y sus braceros emigrantes, la colonia china de Torreón y la matanza de 1911* (Mexico: CNCA, 1992); Delia Salazar, ed., *Xenofobia y Xenofilia en la Historia de México* (Mexico: INM-INAH, 2007); and Pablo Yankelevich, "Explotadores, truhanes, agitadores y negros. Deportaciones y restricciones a estadounidenses en el México revolucionario," *Historia Mexicana* 228 (2008): 1155–99.

4. *Diario de Debates del Congreso Constituyente* (hereafter *DDCC*), 2 vols. (Mexico: Instituto Nacional de Estudios Históricos de la Revolución Mexicana, 1960), 491.

5. Tomás Pérez Vejo, "La extranjería en la construcción nacional mexicana," in *Nación y Extranjería. La exclusión racial en las políticas migratorias de Argentina, Brasil, Cuba y México*, ed. Pablo Yankelevich (Mexico: UNAM-ENAH, 2009), 147–85.

6. Theresa Alfaro-Velcamp, *So Far from Allah, So Close to Mexico: Middle Eastern Immigrants in Modern Mexico* (Austin: University of Texas Press, 2007); Jürgen Buchenau, "Small Numbers, Great Impact: Mexico and Its Immigrants, 1821–1973," *Journal of American Ethnic History* (spring 2001): 23–49; Guillermo Bonfil Batalla, ed., *Simbiosis de cultura. Los inmigrantes y su cultura en México* (Mexico: Fondo de Cultura Económica, 1993); Grace Delgado, *Making the Chinese Mexican: Global Migration, Localism, and Exclusion in the U.S.-Mexico Borderlands* (Stanford: Stanford University Press, 2012); Evelyn Hu-DeHart, "Racism and Anti-Chinese Persecution in Sonora, Mexico, 1876–1932," *Amerasia Journal* 9 (1982): 1–28; Corinne Krauze, *Los judíos en México* (Mexico: Universidad Iberoamericana, 1987); Alicia Gojman, ed., *Generaciones judías en México*, 7 vols. (Mexico: Comunidad Ashkenazi de México, 1994); Moisés González Navarro, *Extranjeros en México y mexicanos en el extranjero*, 3 vols. (Mexico: El Colegio de México, 1994); María Elena Ota Mishima, ed., *Destino México: un estudio de las migraciones asiáticas a México, siglos XIX y XX* (Mexico: El Colegio de México, 1997); and Elliott Young, *Alien Nation: Chinese Migration in the Americas from the Coolie Era through World War II* (Chapel Hill: University of North Carolina Press, 2014).

7. Mark Reisler, *By the Sweat of Their Brow: Mexican Immigrant Labor in the United States, 1900–1940* (Westport, Connecticut: Greenwood Press, 1977); Lawrence A. Cardoso, *Mexican Emigration to the United States, 1897–1931* (Tucson: University of Arizona Press, 1980); Linda Hall, "El Refugio: migración mexicana a los Estados Unidos, 1910–1920," *Historias* (January–April 1982): 19–34; David Montejano, *Anglos and Mexicans in the Making of Texas, 1836–1986* (Austin: University of Texas Press, 1988); Camilla Guerrín-González, *Mexican Workers and American Dream: Immigration, Repatriation and California Farm Labor, 1900–1939* (New Brunswick: Rutgers University Press, 1994); Douglas S. Massey et al., *Return to Aztlan: The Social Process of International Migration from Western Mexico* (Berkeley: University of California Press, 1987); González Navarro, *Extranjero*; and María Isabel Monroy Castillo, "Los rastros de una migración antigua," in *La emigración de San Luis Potosí a Estados Unidos. Pasado y presente*, ed. Fernando Saúl Alanís Enciso (Mexico: El Colegio de San Luis, 2001).

8. Fernando Saúl Alanís Enciso, *Que se queden allá. El gobierno de México y La repatriación de mexicanos en Estados Unidos, 1934–1940* (Mexico: San Luis Potosí: El Colegio de San Luis, 2007); Fernando Saúl Alanís Enciso, *Voces de la repatriación. La sociedad mexicana y la repatriación de mexicanos de Estados Unidos, 1930–1933* (Mexico: El Colegio de San Luis, El Colegio de Michoacán, El Colegio de la Frontera Norte, 2015); Neil Betten and Raymond A. Mohl, "From Discrimination to Repatriation: Mexican Life in Gary, Indiana, during the Great Depression," *Pacific Historical Review* 42 (1973): 370–88; Abraham Hoffman, *Unwanted Mexican Americans in the Great Depression: Repatriation Pressures,*

1929–1939 (Tucson: University of Arizona Press, 1974); Mercedes Carreras de Velasco, *Los mexicanos que nos devolvió la crisis* (Mexico: Secretaría de Relaciones Exteriores, 1974); Jorge Durand, "Ensayo teórico sobre la emigración de retorno. El principio del rendimiento decreciente," *Cuadernos Geográficos* 35 (2004): 103–16; Daniel Simon, "Mexican Repatriation in East Chicago, Indiana," *Journal of Ethnic Studies* 2 (1974): 11–23; Reynolds McKay, *Texas Mexican Repatriation during the Great Depression* (PhD diss., University of Oklahoma at Norman, 1982); Vargas Zaragoza, *Proletarians of the North: A History of Mexican Industrial Workers in Detroit and the Midwest, 1917–1933* (Berkeley: University of California Press, 1993); and Francisco Balderrama and Raymond Rodriguez, *Decade of Betrayal: Mexicans Repatried in the 1930s* (Albuquerque: University of New Mexico Press, 1995).

9. Andrés Landa y Piña, "El problema de la migración en México," vol. 1, December 26, 1927, Archivo Andrés Landa y Piña (hereafter AALyP), private collection, Mexico.

10. Ibid.

11. Bonfil, *Simbiosis*.

12. Manuel Gamio, *Mexican Immigration to the United States: A Study of Human Migration and Adjustment* (Chicago: University of Chicago Press, 1931); and Manuel Gamio, *Forjando Patria* (Mexico: Porrúa 1960).

13. Manuel Gamio, "La futura población de la América Latina," April 1921, AALyP.

14. Ibid.

15. Landa y Piña, "El problema de la migración."

16. Gamio, *Forjando patria*, 5.

17. Ricardo Rivera, *La heterogeneidad étnica y espiritual de México* (Mexico: A. Mijares y Hermano Impresores, 1931), 144–49.

18. Roger Daniels, *Guarding the Golden Door* (New York: Hill & Wang, 2004), 5; Cheryl Shanks, *Immigration and the Politics of American Sovereignty, 1890–1990* (Chicago: University of Michigan Press, 2004), 2; and Fernando Devoto, *Historia de la inmigración en la Argentina* (Buenos Aires: Sudamericana, 2003), 434.

19. Stephen Harber and Jeffrey Bortz, "The Mexican Economy, 1870–1930," in *Essays on the Economic History of Institutions, 1870–1930*, ed. Stephen Harber and Jeffrey Bortz (Stanford: Stanford University Press, 2002); and Sandra Kuntz, *Las exportaciones mexicanas durante la primera globalización, 1870–1929* (Mexico: El Colegio de México, 2010).

20. Delia Salazar, *La población extranjera en México (1895–1990): Un recuento con base en los Censos Generales de Población* (Mexico: Instituto Nacional de Antropología e Historia, 1996), 100.

21. González Navarro, "Xenofobia," 569–614.

22. Chan Sucheng, ed., *Entry Denied: Exclusion and the Chinese Community in America, 1882–1943* (Philadelphia: Temple University Press, 1991); Raymond B. Craib, "Chinese Immigrants in Porfirian México: A Preliminary Study of Settlement, Economic Activity and Anti-Chinese Sentiment," Research Paper Series No. 28, Latin American Institute, University of New Mexico, 1996; Robert Chao

Romero, *The Chinese in Mexico (1882–1940)* (Tucson: University of Arizona Press, 2010); Madeline Yuan-yin Hsu, *Dreaming of Gold, Dreaming of Home: Transnationalism and Migration between the United States and South China, 1882–1943* (Stanford: Stanford University Press, 2000).

23. The immigrant population increased from 54,737 individuals in 1895 to 116,526 in 1910. Salazar Anaya, *La población*, 99.

24. Sergio Camposortega Cruz, "Análisis demográfico de las corrientes migratorias a México desde finales del siglo XIX," in *Destino México: un estudio de las migraciones asiáticas a México, siglos XIX y XX*, ed. María Elena Ota Mishima (Mexico: El Colegio de México, 199), 39–40.

25. "Exposición de motivos, Ley de Inmigración de 1909," *Compilación Histórica de la Legislación Migratoria en México, 1821–2002* (Mexico: Instituto Nacional de Migración, 2002), 109.

26. Ibid., 129.

27. "Ley de Migración de los Estados Unidos Mexicanos," *Diario Oficial de la Federación* (hereafter *DOF*), March 13, 1926, 6.

28. Among these general provisions, the law established sanitary regulations aimed at preventing contagious diseases. Moral restrictions were also established that were aimed at children, women under the age of twenty-five, prostitutes, beggars, and others. In terms of political considerations, members of anarchist organizations were banned from entry, as well as those who held doctrines that would predispose them to the violent destruction of governments or the assassination of public officials. Lastly, the law established that all adult male immigrants should know how to read and write.

29. The Interior Secretariat is the federal agency in charge of internal politics. It handles relations between the executive branch and other government branches, as well as coordination between state and municipal governments. This agency is also in charge of national security matters and immigration issues.

30. Andrés Landa y Piña, *El servicio de migración en México* (Mexico: Talleres Gráficos de la Nación, 1930), 23.

31. "Exposición de motivos," 123.

32. Interior Secretariat, Circular No. 33, May 13, 1924, Exp. 4/362.1/76, October 30, 1926, Archivo Histórico del Instituto Nacional de Migración, Instituto Nacional de Migración, Mexico (hereafter AHINM).

33. Interior Secretariat to Foreign Affairs Secretariat, October 30, 1926, Exp. NC 1192-10, Archivo Histórico Diplomático de la Secretaría de Relaciones Exteriores, Secretaría de Relaciones Exteriores, Mexico (hereafter AHDSRE).

34. Letter from Manuel Álvarez to the Foreign Affairs Secretary, November 25, 1926, Exp. NC 1192-10, AHDSRE.

35. Request for information on restrictions on black immigration, November 1, 1926, Exp. 4/350/127, AHINM.

36. Telegram to the Interior Secretariat, June 13, 1929, Exp. 4/362.1/1929/306, AHINM.

37. Instructions to the Interior Secretariat, November 27, 1925, Exp. 4/350/32, AHINM. On Afro-Belizean immigration to Mexico, see Elisabeth Cunin, *Admin-*

istrar a los extranjeros: raza, mestizaje y nación. Migraciones afrobelicieñas en el territroio de Quintana Roo, 1902–1940 (Mexico: CIESAS, 2014).

38. *DDCC*, 134.

39. Secretaría de Relaciones Exteriores, *Memoria de Labores* (Mexico: SRE, 1927), 512.

40. Study on the immigration law, June 11, 1929, Exp. 4/350-1929/426, AHINM.

41. "Ley de Migración de los Estados Unidos Mexicanos," 6.

42. *DOF*, July 15, 1927, 1.

43. Orders of the Immigration Department, December 6, 1929, Exp. 2.360 (29), Capeta 70, Caja 9, AGN-DGG, Secretaría de Gobenación, Mexico.

44. Interior Secretariat, Circular No. 27, April 29, 1929, Exp. 4/350-1229/420, AHINM.

45. Foreign Affairs Secretariat, Circular No. 516, November 21, 1929, Exp. IV-294-41, AHDSRE.

46. *DOF*, July 17, 1931, 1.

47. Interior Secrerariat, Circular No. 250, October 14, 1933, Exp. 4/350.2.33/54, AHINM.

48. Interior Secretariat, Circular No. 157, April 27, 1934, Exp. 4/350.2.33/54, AHINM. On the prohibition of Jewish immigration, see Daniela Gleizer, *El exilio incómodo. México y los refugiados judíos, 1933–1945* (Mexico: El Colegio de México, 2011).

49. Letter to President Lázaro Cárdenas from the National Anti-Chinese and Anti-Jew League, September 9, 1935, Exp. 4/350.264 AHINM. For more on these organizations, see Ricardo Pérez Montfort, *Por la patria y por la raza. La derecha secular en el sexenio de Lázaro Cárdenas* (Mexico: UNAM, 1993); and Alicia Gojman, *Camisas, escudos y desfiles militares. Los Dorados y el antisemitismo en México (1934–1940)* (Mexico: FCE, UNAM, ENEP/Acatlán, 2000).

50. Letter from Matías Ramos to Juan de Dios Bohórquez, February 26, 1935, Exp. 4/350.215, AHINM.

51. *El Nacional*, March 9, 1931.

52. The 1930 census shows that around eight thousand people of Middle Eastern descent lived in Mexico, compared with slightly less than six thousand from central and eastern Europe. Dirección Nacional de Estadística, *Quinto Censo Nacional de Población de 1930*, 2 vols. (Mexico: Secretaría de la Economía Nacional, 1932), 1:98.

53. Gilberto Loyo, *Las deficiencias cuantitativas de la población de México y una política demográfica nacional* (Rome: Tipografía del Senado, 1932), 5–6.

54. Gilberto Loyo, *La política demográfica de México* (Mexico: Partido Nacional Revolucionario, 1935), 373–76.

55. "Ley General de Población," *DOF*, August 29, 1936, 1.

56. Ibid., 4, 6.

57. Ibid., 2.

58. Ibid., 3, 6.

59. Interior Secretariat, Circular No. 930, May 20, 1937, Exp. 4/350.2.34/54, AHINM.

60. Letter from Andrés Landa y Piña to the Interior Secretariat, March 5, 1938, Exp. 4/350.2.33/54, AHINM.

61. Immigration quotas, October 24, 1941, Exp. 4/350.42/948, AHINM. These quotas can be consulted in *DOF*, October 15, 1940, November 15, 1941, December 16, 1942, October 30, 1944, October 31, 1945, and December 13, 1946.

62. *Diario de Debates de la Cámara de Diputados* 5 (December 28, 1945), 23.

63. "Ley General de Población," *DOF*, December 27, 1947, 4.

64. *Diario de Debates de la Cámara de Diputados* 5 (December 28, 1945), 24.

65. *Diario de Debates de la Cámara de Diputados* 30 (December 20, 1943), 26.

66. Article 15 of this law established that "No foreigner may exercise, in Mexican territory, the technical and scientific professions dealt with in this law. Naturalized citizens who completed all of their professional training at the educational centers authorized by this law will be treated the same as native-born Mexicans in terms of their ability to exercise their profession." In turn, Article 18 stipulated that foreigners and naturalized citizens with foreign degrees could only "I. Serve as professors of specialized courses that would otherwise be unavailable in Mexico or in fields in which they have indisputable expertise, as established by the Federal Department of Professions; II. Serve as advisors or instructors in the establishment, organization or installation of civil or military educational institutions, laboratories or scientific institutions; III. Serve as technical directors in the exploitation of the country's natural resources, in accordance with the limitations established by the Federal Labor Law and other relevant legislation" (*DOF*, May 26, 1945, 3).

67. *Diario de Debates de la Cámara de Diputados* 31 (December 21, 1943), 9.

68. Ibid., 9.

69. Ibid., 35 (December 20, 1948), 8.

70. Góngora Pimentel, Genaro David, and Miguel Acosta Romero, *Constitución política de los Estados Unidos Mexicanos: doctrina, legislación, jurisprudencia* (Mexico: Porrúa 1987), 184. In the lead-up to the implementation of the North American Free Trade Agreement, President Carlos Salinas de Gortari signed a decree that reformed, added, and overturned various articles of the Law on Professions. Among them, Article 15 of the 1945 law was modified and Article 18 was overturned. *DOF*, December 22, 1993, 41.

71. *Diario de Debates de la Cámara de Diputados* 35 (December 20, 1948), 32, 35.

72. Ibid., 33.

73. Ibid., 20.

5

The Voyage of the *Buford*

POLITICAL DEPORTATIONS AND THE MAKING AND UNMAKING OF AMERICA'S FIRST RED SCARE

Kenyon Zimmer

The first red scare was an unparalleled period of political repression in the United States. In the years during and immediately following World War I, amid wartime anxieties and fears generated by the Russian Revolution, federal authorities arrested more than ten thousand men and women on the basis of suspected left-wing political beliefs and affiliations. Ultimately the American government deported 979 individuals as "alien anarchists" between July 1918 and June 1925, and an unknown number of additional "alleged anarchists were arrested and deported…on grounds other than the charge of anarchy."[1] It was the only mass deportation of political dissidents in US history.

The largest "deportation party" of the era set sail on the USAT *Buford*, which left New York on December 21, 1919, with 249 Russian citizens onboard—nearly as many foreign-born radicals as were expelled during the entire period between 1946 and 1966, at the height of the Cold War.[2] Aside from celebrity radicals Emma Goldman and Alexander Berkman, scholars have written extraordinarily little about the deportees themselves. Their forgotten stories illustrate not only the arbitrary exercise of state power, but also the limited and conditional nature of that power. The new Soviet government was reluctant to repatriate possible threats to its tenuous hold on power, and also hoped to pressure the United States into officially recognizing its regime. Detained immigrant radicals meanwhile employed every tactic they possessed to subvert the deportation process, from subterfuge and legal campaigns to hunger strikes and threats of insurrection. Both sources of resistance undermined American efforts to expel subversive foreigners and helped bring the deportations of the first red scare to an ignoble end.

Immigrant exclusion and deportation have always been haphazard and inadequate in practice—at any given moment, there are more deportable individuals within America's borders than the state has the capacity to remove. Nevertheless, defining individuals and categories of immigrants as *potentially* deportable left radicals and other excludable groups "suspended in the state of deportability" and therefore vulnerable to state repression and removal. The spectacle of discretionary deportations—"the deportation terror," in Rachel Ida Buff's formulation—also functioned as a cautionary form of "political theater."[3] Foreign-born radicals were intimately aware of its chilling effects. Danish-born E. E. McDonald, detained on Ellis Island in 1919 for membership in the radical Industrial Workers of the World (IWW), observed, "[I]f the capitalists can effectively deport a few hundred of labor's most active defenders they will have killed two birds with one stone—they will have rid the country of men dangerous to capitalist exploitation and at the same time set a precedent which can always be used as a more or less effective weapon over the head of any alien worker who desires to contribute to the working-class movement, either in a financial, moral or physical sense."[4]

The Anarchist Exclusion Act of 1903, as revised by Congress in 1917 and 1918, rendered many foreign-born radicals deportable. Its provisions allowed for the exclusion and deportation of the "anarchistic classes," defined as all aliens who were anarchists, or who advocated, were affiliated with an organization that advocated, or distributed literature advocating "opposition to all organized government," the overthrow by force or violence of the government of the United States, the killing of public officials, the "unlawful damage, injury, or destruction of property," or "sabotage."[5] From 1903 to 1917, authorities effected just twenty such deportations. However, the legal and institutional basis established by this legislation allowed for the mass expulsions of the red scare. In the fiscal years 1920 and 1921, the 760 radicals expelled under the expanded statutes accounted for more than 10 percent of all deportees removed from the United States.[6]

These numbers would have been even larger, had detainees and international events not impeded the machinery of deportation. As several other contributions to this volume demonstrate, deportation is far more than the enforcement of domestic immigration law. It is a process that by definition involves at least two nation-states, as well as a transnational subject: the deportee. The international relations of the United States could determine the form, scale, or even possibility of removals. Commissioner General of Immigration Anthony Caminetti complained in May 1920, "Under existing conditions in Europe...the movement of people of the anarchistic classes, or even of the Communist and kindred divisions thereof, is possible only when the consular authorities of the country through which it is necessary to pass on the way to final destination give the necessary passport or permit. In fact it is difficult and sometimes impossible to get permits for the transfer of the classes mentioned."[7] Furthermore, within the extraordinary constraints imposed by involuntary incarceration and transportation, immigrant radicals also carved out spaces of resistance and exercised agency. The repatriation of these revolutionaries only aggravated international tensions and rebounded back on the United States, as repatriated anarchists' activities in Russia contributed to the Soviet government's refusal to accept further deportees.

Russian Radicals in America

Most of the approximately thousand radicals deported during the red scare were of Russian origin. Yet in 1920, America's 1.4 million Russian immigrants comprised just 1.3 percent of the total population. The wildly disproportionate repression was a direct reaction to the Bolshevik seizure of power and declaration of the world's first Socialist state in late 1917. Every Russian "red" was, in the eyes of the Department of Justice, party to an international Communist conspiracy aimed at overthrowing the government of the United States. In reality, Russian American radicalism encompassed an eclectic array of often-incompatible tendencies. At the time of the red scare there existed more than two hundred "Russian socialistic, anarchistic, and radical clubs" in the United States, and despite official fears, most of these groups espoused syndicalist or anarchist views that were critical of Marxism.[8] The *Buford*'s passengers included 199 members of the anarcho-syndicalist Union of Russian Workers of the United States and Canada (UORW), another forty-three individuals expelled "on anarchistic and kindred charges"—including "about eleven" Socialists and Communists and around a dozen members of the IWW—in addition to seven nonpolitical deportees.[9]

The organization most feared by employers and the government even before the war began was the Industrial Workers of the World. Founded in 1905, the IWW was a militant labor union with a syndicalist ideology: it rejected electoral politics in favor of working-class direct action, and aimed at not just securing better working conditions for its members but also fomenting a revolutionary general strike that would topple the existing economic and political order. The union reached out to workers neglected by the American Federation of Labor (AFL): the unskilled, women, people of color, and immigrants. Recently arrived Russians, few of whom had mastered English, were informally barred from most AFL unions and had "little opportunity to join a labor group other than the I.W.W.," which included Russian-language branches in several cities. In August 1917, the union counted more than 150,000 members and enjoyed the support of many times that from workers and radicals.[10]

Most Russians who carried IWW cards also belonged to the Union of Russian Workers, an organization founded in 1910 by anarchist refugees from the failed revolution of 1905. Originally oriented toward instigating armed uprisings against the czar, in 1912 the UORW adopted an anarcho-syndicalist program and began to focus on the struggles of Russian immigrants. The organization mushroomed in size following the revolutions of 1917, from four thousand members in early 1918 to seven thousand by February of 1919, and more than nine thousand by November of that year.[11] Outside of the more educated leadership, members were typically young men from peasant backgrounds, either single or with wives in the old country, who came to the United States after 1914 to earn money for land back in Russia (and perhaps avoid military service in the process). Although ethnic Russians predominated, the organization included "Hebrews, Polish, Lithuanian and other working men," as well as a handful of women.[12] Many were radicalized in the United States; UORW national secretary Hyman Perkus, for example, contested his deportation warrant on the grounds that "I am an anarchist but not an alien anarchist. I am 4 ½ years in this country and have been an anarchist for 3 years.... Why did I become an anarchist? I have suffered from injustices and oppression [in the United States] and have seen that the people in general also suffer from injustices and oppression."[13]

When arrested, many UORW members—and most historians since—portrayed their organization as a benign club more interested in education and ethnic sociability than radical politics. But these claims cannot be taken at face value; attorneys for foreign radicals advised clients to deny holding anarchistic beliefs to avoid deportation, and as early as May 1917, word circulated internally within the UORW that, in the event of arrest, members should declare themselves believers in "politics" and "industrial freedom" rather than anarchism and revolution.[14] In at least two cases, members claiming to be illiterate and unaware of the organization's principles were later revealed to be recording secretaries for their local branches, and another Russian who claimed he had only stopped by the Newark UORW offices for some tea proved to be that branch's chairman. UORW editor Adolf Schnabel remarked to the organization's 1919 convention, "as long as I can remember, I never met a member of the Union of Russian Workers that did not know he was an anarchist."[15]

Not all Russian-born anarchists joined the UORW. Although a disproportionate number of that organization's members were, like Hyman Perkus, Jews, most Russian Jewish anarchists belonged to small, independent groups that undertook work in either Yiddish or English. America's large but more moderate Yiddish-speaking anarchist movement aroused little interest from authorities, and therefore weathered the red scare largely unharmed.[16] English-language activism, however, attracted more attention. Alexander Berkman and Emma Goldman, in particular, spent many years popularizing anarchism among native-born American workers and intellectuals, and young Justice Department official J. Edgar Hoover took special interest in the deportation cases against them.[17]

Ironically, Socialists and Communists were least affected by the red scare's deportations. Russian membership in the Socialist Party of America lagged behind that of the IWW or UORW; the party established a Russian Federation only in 1915, and it counted fewer than eight hundred members in early 1918. Membership expanded to seven thousand in 1919, but that same year the moderate leadership of the Socialist Party expelled the Russian Federation and other "left-wing" language groups over disagreements regarding tactics and affiliation with the Communist International. The expelled groups then helped form the new Communist Party of America, into which their members were transferred en masse.[18] The Department of Justice, however, did not target the Communist Party until January 1920, and few of those members apprehended in federal raids were expelled before mass deportations became impossible. Those radicals most likely to embrace—and be embraced by—the Soviet regime were, therefore, the least likely to be repatriated.

Making the Red Scare

Coordinated repression of radicals commenced as soon as the United States entered the First World War in April 1917. The federal government imprisoned hundreds of leftists and labor organizers for violating the Selective Service, Espionage, and Sedition Acts. As historian William Preston Jr. has shown, the antiradical campaign then changed in scope, strategy, and focus as Justice Department officials came to view deportation "as the most flexible and discretionary weapon available for their attack upon radical labor agitators," since immigration hearings are considered "administrative" proceedings and circumvent the constitutional protections granted in criminal trials.[19]

On June 16, 1917, the day after the Espionage Act went into effect, federal agents arrested Emma Goldman and Alexander Berkman for obstructing military conscription as organizers of the No-Conscription League. Each was sentenced to two years in federal prison, with the recommendation that they be deported as alien anarchists upon completion of their terms. Police arrested other members of the League, including young Russian Jewish anarchist Morris Becker, for refusing to register for the draft. Becker later joined Goldman and Berkman on the *Buford*.

In July, President Woodrow Wilson authorized federal agencies to coordinate "a systematic push to crush the IWW." The union had led a number of strikes in war-related industries, including mining and lumber, and the Justice Department launched simultaneous raids against IWW offices nationwide on September 5. The following year a federal court sentenced ninety-three of the union's leaders and organizers to between one and twenty years for allegedly conspiring against the war effort, and state and local authorities continued to imprison hundreds of IWW members during and after the war.[20]

The Union of Russian Workers first caught the Justice Department's attention for its role in labor unrest within the rubber industry in Akron, Ohio. Although wartime demand had improved wages for most rubber workers, recent Russian immigrants were excluded from the AFL's Amalgamated Rubber Workers Union and confined "to dirty, heavy jobs such as opening and washing bales of crude rubber." The local UORW branch grew to two hundred to four hundred members (out of a local Russian population of just one thousand), and began working with the remnants of the local IWW organization, which had led a failed rubber strike in 1913.[21]

Justice Department agents arrested six UORW members on November 20, 1917, at a secret meeting convened "for the purpose of devising ways and means to bring about a strike of the Russian workers employed in the various [rubber] plants in this city." The Bureau of Immigration issued deportation warrants for five of the men as alien anarchists (the sixth was a government informant), but had to release the suspects on bail pending arrangements for their expulsion to Russia—a tricky proposition, as the United States refused to officially recognize the new Bolshevik government. In the meantime, one of those arrested, Daniel Kuts, turned informant for the Justice Department, and the case against Mike Elick was dropped because he had a wife and child in Akron. Of the remaining Russians, B. F. Goodrich Company employees Ivan Kabas-Tarasiuk and Naum Stepanuk were deported on the *Buford*, followed by Firestone employee Paul Krachie, deported in 1921.[22]

Russian radicals were not the only group targeted by authorities. In January 1918, federal officials in Seattle concocted plans to round up all IWW members in the region, and immigration agents immediately detained some 150 immigrants belonging to the union for deportation as "anarchists." Over the following months authorities also arrested dozens of Italian anarchists affiliated with Luigi Galleani's revolutionary newspaper *Cronaca Sovversiva*, including Galleani himself. These schemes foundered, however, at the desk Secretary of Labor William B. Wilson, within whose Labor Department the Bureau of Immigration resided. According to Wilson's interpretation of existing statutes, mere membership in a radical organization was insufficient cause for deportation; instead, proof of individual advocacy of proscribed views was necessary. The Justice Department—with Secretary Wilson's backing—therefore drafted new legislation that, when passed into law as the Immigration Act of 1918, expanded the legal definition of deportable radicals to explicitly include all members and affiliates of organizations that promoted such ideas. In July 1918, two months before the new act went into effect, the Justice Department and Bureau of Immigration began preparing for the mass expulsion of alien anarchists, including members of the Union of Russian Workers.[23]

The Armistice of November 11, 1918, did not alter these plans. Instead, postwar labor unrest and violence accelerated them. The Seattle General Strike of February 1919, in which members of both the IWW and UORW played minor roles, stoked new fears of a "Soviet America." That same month, the Justice Department announced that the "United States is to be swept clean of its alien anarchists and trouble makers," and it formulated plans to deport some seven to eight thousand radicals.[24] Then, in April, May, and July, a series of homemade bombs were mailed to or placed at the homes of a number of antiradical, antiunion, anti-immigrant public figures, including Attorney General A. Mitchell Palmer. In leaflets left at several of the sites, the bombers—identified by historian Paul Avrich as associates of Luigi Galleani, who was deported that June—cited ongoing government repression as the rationale for these explosive reprisals: "We have been dreaming of freedom, we have talked of liberty, we have aspired to a better world, and you jailed us, you clubbed us, you deported us, you murdered us whenever you could."[25] The bombings only expedited plans for further raids.

Although the Bureau of Investigation built a strong circumstantial case against Galleani's followers, it was soon sidetracked by increasingly wild theories of Soviet involvement. This led it back to the Union of Russian Workers, which, Andrew Cornell notes, "seemed to mark the exact political location where the anarchist bombers, Wobbly general-strike organizers, and Russian Bolsheviks intersected." In addition, the little-known organization presented a convenient target for an attention-hungry Department of Justice. The UORW suddenly became the federal government's number-one domestic enemy.[26]

Under Attorney General Palmer's direction, federal and local authorities launched mass arrests of UORW members on November 7, 1919. Federal agents and New York City Police ransacked the Russian People's House at 133 East 15th Street, which contained the UORW's national offices, a library, a meeting hall, and several classrooms. It was, according to the *New York Call*, "one of the most brutal raids ever witnessed in the city.... Clubs and, according to some, blackjacks were used without mercy," and passersby "heard heavy thuds of clubs descending on human flesh" from within the building. Roman Andriuk, a twenty-six-year-old sailor and UORW member, was attending a popular automobile repair class when "six men broke in the door and [each] began to use clubs on the heads of those who were nearest him. I was also hit on the head and I don't know what happened after that." Benjamin Afanasievitch, a student in an after-hours arithmetic course, described the scene as he was herded out of the classroom: "The door...was occupied by two men who were beating with blackjacks every one that passed. Then when we got down stairs they were also beating us, and those of us who fell down were trampled on by the detectives." Anarchist dressmaker Ethel Bernstein described it as a "wholesale clubbing. The name 'red' was in place, for blood was everywhere, blood of our comrades! Such a scene I have never witnessed before." Those who could not produce evidence of American citizenship—360 in all—were arrested and detained for possible deportation. Andriuk, Afanasievitch, and Bernstein all wound up on the *Buford*.[27] Detroit, home to five UORW branches, saw less violence but nearly a thousand arrests. With jails overflowing, "the upper floors of the Post Office building were converted into a prison in which hundreds of men were held." Authorities eventually moved the detainees to the Fort Wayne prison barracks, where they engaged in a two-day hunger strike to protest inhumane conditions.[28]

Class Conflict and Private Intelligence

Sensational as the "Palmer raids" may have been, they were incredibly inefficient. Of the 1,182 suspects seized nationwide on November 7, only 439 were held for a deportation hearing, and less than half of those resulted in removal. Most of the eventual deportees—including Bernstein—had been detained and interrogated at least once previously, and already had outstanding deportation warrants against them.[29] Nearly a third of those arrested in the raids proved to be American citizens, and in the other cases the Bureau of Investigation found that "it quite often is next to impossible to prove actual membership with the organization alleged to be anarchistic."[30] Immigration law required what federal agents were frequently unable to provide: accurate intelligence. Authorities were instead forced to rely on confidential informants and, increasingly, concerned business owners. The latter proved an especially valuable resource, as American capitalists and federal agents found mutual benefit in utilizing each other to compensate for their own limitations: employers called on the state to quash labor unrest, and the Department of Justice outsourced much of its intelligence-gathering to private businesses.

According to Attorney General Palmer, after the armistice, "it became evident that there was at work in the United States certain forces determined to handicap the Government in its work of reconstruction and to embarrass the Congress of the United States and the public officials charged with the administering of the law in every way possible." As an example, Palmer pointed to a series of strikes in Connecticut led by members of the Union of Russian Workers. "It was necessary to adopt drastic methods by the State and city authorities, [with] the department [of Justice] working in close cooperation. A number of the most active leaders at Asonia were arrested on deportation warrants; some were included in the passenger list of the *Buford*.... The strike failed after the Federal and State prosecutions." The Justice Department thus took upon itself the task of disciplining the postwar labor force, and "participated in deportation arrests explicitly initiated by employers in order to rid themselves of agitators and troublemakers."[31]

In Michigan, the Ford Motor Company's Sociological Department worked hand-in-hand with the antiradical American Protective League to establish a surveillance apparatus "which included about 100 operatives in forty-five different departments and shops of the Ford factory," and reported suspected radicals to federal authorities. One of these, a stock-keeper and UORW member named Alexay Nishancoff, was terminated "for making Bolshevik and I.W.W. speeches to his fellow workmen," and held under guard by Ford's Service Department for nine hours until the Bureau of Investigation took him into custody. His admitted admiration for the Bolsheviks earned him a bunk onboard the *Buford*.[32]

New Hampshire businessmen had no reservations about "opening their employee files upon request and volunteering any bit of rumor or gossip that they had heard about radicals employed by their company," in addition to passing along the names of workers they had terminated for suspected radical sympathies. Some employers lent their own undercover detectives to the Justice Department, including E. H. Hunter, an operative for the New Hampshire Association of Manufacturers who "worked at the Nashua Manufacturing Co. and informed the Bureau [of Investigation] of union and radical activities among Polish and Lithuanian workers there." In Youngstown, Ohio, the Mahoning Valley Employers' Association likewise had "under-cover men throughout their plants and also have under cover men watching the activities of the I. W. W., Socialists, Bolsheviks and other Anarchistic Associations," and the association forwarded copies of these operatives' daily reports to the Bureau of Investigation.[33]

The Special Agent in Charge at the Bureau's Akron office explained to Assistant Director Frank Burke how he had "established a system of checking up [on] members of the Union of Russian Workers at all the rubber factories in Akron. The officers of the factories are cooperating in this work and they are from time to time giving me information as to the

location of these subjects and also information pertaining to their activities.... Yesterday the B. F. Goodrich Co. sent to this office a list of names
which were believed to be members of the above union." When agents
rounded up these suspects, "the B. F. Goodrich Company was appealed
to for assistance, and Mr. M. A. Flynn, Director of Labor, of this Company,
instructed his assistant, Mr. W. A. Garrigan, to use all the facilities of
the Company to cooperate with this office to the fullest possible extent."
Garrigan provided not only a company interpreter, but also his personal
stenographer, "without compensation."[34]

Authorities arrested other UORW members in 1919 for participating
in AFL-led strikes in steel and coal. But as the interchurch movement's
investigation of the steel strike noted, of all of the participants arrested for
radicalism, "None...was arrested on charges of radical agitation during
the strike but for being members of organizations, such as the I. W. W. and
various Russian societies or for professing Communist beliefs. That is,
the arrests might have been made, so far as the charges were concerned,
at any time irrespective of the strike." Leveraging radicals' deportability
to undermine labor struggles was a strategy utilized by both employers
and federal agents. As one early study concluded, the red scare therefore
consisted, in part, of "anti-labor operations," in which the Department of
Justice "functioned as a national strikebreaking agency."[35]

However, the interests of business and the state did not entirely coin-
cide. Employers invoked the threat of deportation as a method of *disciplining* unruly workers, whereas federal authorities harbored grandiose
plans to *remove* all foreign-born radicals. In one particularly poignant
case, Louis D. Brodsky of the Nelson Pants Manufacturing Company in
St. Louis reported his employee Max Brazelia, a Jewish immigrant from
Warsaw, to the Department of Justice for "spreading Bolsheviki propaganda in the workroom." But Brodsky also stated that Brazelia "was a
good workingman and that he wouldn't like to lose him," and he therefore asked that "a government man be placed in his factory to watch [the]
subject." Instead, Brazelia was handed over to immigration officials,
who obtained a warrant for his deportation the following day. Brodsky
immediately protested and subsequently testified in defense of his employee, calling Brazelia "foolish" but trustworthy. Several coworkers likewise testified that Brazelia, although a Socialist, had never advocated the
overthrow of the US government. Regardless, Brazelia ended up on the
Buford.[36]

As Brazelia's case illustrates, immigration enforcement was unpredictable, haphazard, and capricious. Many outspoken anarchists walked free, and many deportation cases that agents believed were "somewhat weak" were nevertheless pushed through to completion. The specter of uncertainty lay at the heart of deportability. Immigration officials could, at their discretion, find grounds for deporting—or not deporting—virtually any suspected alien radical. Often it was simply a matter of how one chose to interpret legal terminology, and whether or not institutional capacity and will existed to pursue a given case.[37]

In a number of cases inspectors exploited the most subjective and ambiguous clause of the 1918 immigration law, which authorized the deportation of aliens who advocated "sabotage." Because the term was not defined in the statute, it could mean anything from arson and bombings, to more benign forms of property destruction, to simply "the conscious withdrawal of the workers' industrial efficiency," as IWW organizer Elizabeth Gurley Flynn defined it. Admitting belief in any one of these was grounds for removal. For example, although it was unclear if Andy Sereck of Youngstown, Ohio, belonged to the Union of Russian Workers as alleged (even Commissioner General Caminetti confessed, "This is not a particularly strong case"), his stated acceptance of "sabotage," regardless of how he may have understood the tactic, secured him a place on the *Buford*.[38]

A few too many drinks landed IWW member Harold Berger a bunk on the same ship. Fresno police arrested Berger in September 1917 for a bout of public intoxication, during which he "damned the government," and detained him as an alien radical after discovering his IWW membership card. At his immigration hearing Berger freely admitted that he "was a syndicalist since I was a lad of 13 or 14," and believed "in sabotage as taught by Walker Smith and Elizabeth Gurley Flynn." In a subsequent interview, he further admitted to being an anarchist who advocated "overthrowing the capitalist system through a general strike or walk out, folding our arms," but not through violence. The Bureau of Immigration issued a deportation warrant, charging him as an advocate of sabotage, an alien anarchist, and for good measure (and without a shred of evidence), as someone "likely to become a public charge" at the time of his 1913 entry.[39]

Likely to become a public charge (LPC) was an even more subjective term than sabotage. The utility of the LPC statute lay in its unfalsifiability: the determination that an individual was LPC at the time of entry was, by definition, a conjecture—a guess—on the part of an immigration agent, and one that no amount of evidence could definitively refute. Moreover, if an immigrant became a public charge within five years of entry, regardless of his or her financial circumstances at the time of arrival, the law defined them *ex post facto* as LPC. As in Berger's case, inspectors often added LPC charges to the warrants of alleged radicals lest the evidence of anarchism proved inconclusive. For example, when Seattle's Immigration Inspector requested deportation warrants for every known alien IWW member in his district, he included LPC charges on all of them as a matter of course. And when immigration officials were "unable to find that the anarchistic charges in the warrant are substantiated by the evidence" in the case of *Buford* passenger Paul Pawlas, a Russian-born Czech and itinerant laborer arrested in Cleveland for distributing Socialist Party literature, they simply charged him as likely to become a public charge instead.[40]

Authorities exercised more creativity in the cases of Mikhail Gernet and Nicolai Omelianchuk, arrested in Detroit for causing "a disturbance" at a talk given on April 28, 1919, by Russian Socialist Catherine Breshkovsky, a critic of the Bolsheviks whom Gernet labeled a "reactionary." Despite Gernet's rough treatment ("The Police beat me up until I was unconscious," he testified, "I cannot raise my arms, and I can't eat"), he admitted only to membership in Russian Branch No. 3 of the Socialist Party, not itself a deportable offense. The inspector in charge, however, concluded, "While the evidence is hardly sufficient to substantiate any of the anarchistic charges, it does show that the alien is an agitator and trouble maker and therefore one likely to come in conflict with our laws," and to end up in prison—and thus to become a public charge. This tortured line of reasoning landed Gernet on the *Buford*. In the case of Omelianchuk, who had crossed into the United States from Canada just days before the incident, "Some evidence of radical tendencies developed at hearing, but anarchy charge [was] not preferred." He was instead charged as LPC because at the time of his entry he was carrying only $30, and was deported to Russia in 1921.[41]

The government took this logic to its ludicrous extreme in the case of twenty-three-year-old Ukrainian Alexander Shkilnuk, who was arrested by military police in 1918 and court-martialed after refusing to be drafted in the United States armed forces—despite the fact that, as an immigrant who had not submitted a declaration of intent to naturalize, he was not eligible for conscription and not subject to military law. The War Department, apparently realizing its mistake, released Shkilnuk early from Fort

Leavenworth, but immigration agents immediately rearrested him as likely to become a public charge. Even though Shkilnuk claimed to have been carrying $400 when he entered the country, the charge stemmed from the fact that he had become a federal prisoner—and *ipso facto* was likely to become such at the time of his entry, regardless of the illegality of his incarceration. Although "Evidence of radical tendencies developed at hearing," it was not the legal basis of his deportation on the *Buford*.[42]

Gendering Immigration Enforcement

Federal agents focused their efforts overwhelmingly on male radicals, and more than 95 percent of those detained and deported during the red scare were men. This in part reflected the male dominance of the American left, as well as the heavily skewed gender ratio among Russian and Italian immigrants. But it was also a product of authorities' tendency to ignore female activists and to view unattached males as a particularly danger- ous group. Antiradicals of the time believed "that single men…were more likely to lean toward socialism. Marriage and families stabilized married men; thus married men were more likely to become 'real Americans.'"[43] Even in the case of radical couples, typically only men were targeted for arrest and deportation.

The most famous exception was Emma Goldman, yet even her expul- sion was predicated upon the citizenship status of her estranged husband, Jacob Kershner. Under America's gendered naturalization laws, a mar- ried woman's citizenship status derived from that of her spouse. Because Kershner had lied about his age in order to be naturalized years earlier, Goldman's own American citizenship, bestowed through Kershner, was declared void. It was the first politically motivated denaturalization in America's history, but also a rarity, as denaturalization was a cumbersome bureaucratic process.[44]

Authorities' preoccupation with the patriarchal family unit could also work in radicals' favor. Most immigration agents "conscientiously sought to avoid breaking up families," especially if the removal of breadwinners might render wives and children destitute—and thus create possible public charges. This necessitated either the discretionary reprieve of mar- ried aliens like Akron's Mike Elick, or arranging for deportees to volun- tary depart with their family members. For this reason, Secretary Wilson instructed that no deportees with wives or children in the United States were to be included on the *Buford*, pending arrangements for their families' repatriation. This shielded many Russian radicals detained throughout the country from being transferred to Ellis Island for removal.[45]

However, the inspector at Ellis Island either ignored or never received Wilson's directive, and thirteen of the detainees under his supervision left wives behind when deported on the *Buford*. A group of these detainees' wives and sweethearts made headlines the day of the ship's departure when, upon learning at the office of the Ellis Island ferry that their loved ones had been deported earlier that morning, they staged an angry demonstration. Police arrested Clara Brook, whose husband Abe was a UORW member aboard the *Buford*, for breaking a window with her fist. Brook spent five days in jail where "the other women prisoners—prostitutes, pickpockets, etc.—jeered at her, calling her the wife of 'a Bolsheviki.'" She and the other "Buford widows," as the press dubbed them, appealed to Commissioner General Caminetti, "*Send us to Soviet Russia with our husbands!*" Several insisted that they be deported on the same charges as their spouses, and some swore out affidavits attesting to their own membership in the Union of Russian Workers and belief "in the overthrow of the government of the United States by means of forcible revolution." Although Ellis Island Assistant Commissioner Bryon Uhl complained that these women were seeking "a free trip to Russia," they had forced the law's hand: five were subsequently deported (four with children in tow), while a sixth "left the country voluntarily at her own expense."[46] Their husbands, meanwhile, caused even more trouble for authorities.

Subversives on Land and Sea

By May 1919, Ellis Island was bursting at the seams with hundreds of radicals awaiting deportation, and more arrived every day from detention centers throughout the country. Like Leavenworth Penitentiary, the island's detention block inadvertently became a state-created "convergence space" that "threw together prisoners of different races, ethnicities, nationalities, political orientations, and ideologies."[47] From within the belly of the deportation beast, immigrant revolutionaries forged new solidarities and found new ways to resist the state.

Radicals from different camps organized friendly political debates, including a May Day discussion "which lasted for hours and covered the history of the old International, Socialism, Anarchism, Bolshevism, [and] I.W.W. centralization and decentralization." They also handwrote several issues of a prison newspaper, *Gazeta*, featuring articles in German, Russian, Lithuanian, Yiddish, and additional languages, and boasted that behind bars, free from the postal censors who banned so many radical publications during the war, they finally enjoyed "real freedom of speech." The detainees instituted "full Communism" among themselves, with the self-proclaimed "Ellis Island Soviet" collecting voluntary weekly contributions to purchase food and other goods from the island's overpriced canteen and distributing them according to need.[48]

Nervous officials quarantined the radicals to prevent the spread of their subversive ideas to other immigrants. Romanian Jewish anarchist Shmuel Marcus (later known as Marcus Graham) responded by producing another clandestine newspaper, handwritten in pencil, with the brazen title *Ellis Island Anarchist Weekly*. "If we [cannot] talk and argue with the other immigrants openly—this paper will reach them secretly," Marcus wrote, "and we hope they will pass it around, discuss it and send us all questions secretly and we will answer them through this paper." Launching a one-man campaign of civil disobedience against immigration authorities, Marcus also refused to divulge his real name or place of birth to them, resulting in his release on bond because exasperated authorities could not determine to which country they could deport him.[49]

Other detainees attempted to transform the physical space of the island. Some resisted anonymity by scratching their names into the walls of their cells, or carving defiant messages like "Viva l'Anarchia!" Others took collective action. In late November 1919, around seventy members of the "Ellis Island Soviet" launched a five-day hunger strike. Represented by the "Committee of Room 203," whose members included former UORW national secretary Peter Bianki and female UORW members Ethel Bernstein and Dora Lipkin, the strikers demanded the removal of an iron screen that separated detainees from loved ones in the visitors' room.[50] Less than a month later most of the strikers were loaded onto the *Buford*, where they continued to engage in similar practices.

The process of boarding the ship began in the predawn hours of December 21. In a letter intercepted by the Bureau of Investigation, Ivan Novikov, a former contributor to the UORW's paper *Golos Truda*, detailed how he had been roused from his bed and escorted to a large hall filled with detainees.

The USAT *Buford*, 1915. Courtesy of the Library of Congress Prints and Photographs Division.

It was noisy and the room was full of smoke. Everybody knew already that we are going to be sent out. People were sitting around the tables and nervously, many with tears in their eyes, were writing telegrams and letters.... Many of the comrades, especially those who were sent from Hartford, Youngstown, Manhassan [*sic*] and other cities were in the literal sense of the word without clothes or shoes.... I, myself, when I sat down to write a letter to my wife and son, have stopped involuntarily and wiped the rolling tears.... Pale, afflicted people were roaming about.... There was no laughter.... Sometimes it seemed as though these people are burying somebody, a relative, a dear one.... Every one of us was living through his own tragedy. One left a mother, the other a wife and son, one a sweetheart, the other a dear friend.

At four o'clock in the morning, the order came to move. Outside, Emma Goldman recalled, "Deep snow lay on the ground; the air was cut by a biting wind. A row of armed civilians and soldiers stood along the road to the bank.... One by one the deportees marched, flanked on each side by the uniformed men, curses and threats accompanying the thud of their feet on the frozen ground." They were "packed...like herring in a barrel" onto a ferry that transported them to where the *Buford* lay at anchor. By six o'clock the ship had commenced its transatlantic journey.[51]

The 249 deportees were a diverse group; Berkman counted "about ten different dialects spoken by the men: Russians, Ukrainians, Polish, one Tartar from the Caucuses, Letts, Lithuanians, etc." The passengers also included thirteen Jews, a "Bohemian" (Paul Pawlas), and a Persian from Russian-ruled Armenia.[52] Supervising Inspector F. W. Berkshire, on a brief reprieve from his post on the US-Mexico border, oversaw the voyage, accompanied by eight immigration agents, fifty-eight US soldiers, and six army officers.[53] More than once during the *Buford*'s nearly month-long trip, this maritime hierarchy threatened to turn upside-down.

The *Buford* was a slow, leaky transport ship left over from the Spanish-American War and specially charted by the Bureau of Immigration for this voyage. The three female passengers—Goldman, Bernstein, and Lipkin—were confined to a single cabin, while the male deportees crowded into three steerage sections below deck, where several inches of water stagnated on the floor. "The light was so bad that it was impossible to read without causing pain to the eyes," Novikov recalled. "It was smelling with paint, mouldness [sic] and some kind of specific stench." Three days into the trip, Berkman noted in his diary, "Men getting sick." His entry for Christmas Day simply read, "Men very sick." That night, rough seas sent the *Buford* "lulling on all sides, everything squeaked and the bow, going down every minute, was overflowed with water, penetrating into all crevices, deluged the rooms and formed entire lakes in the corners. Everything was wet and there was no place to dry it." In these conditions, seventeen-year-old UORW member Thomas Bukhanov, Peter Bianki's nephew, lost his hearing as a result of "a severe cold."[54]

Deportees nevertheless found ways to put their beliefs into action and exert control within their floating prison. The ship's physician asked Berkman, one of the few men in good health, to act as his "interpreter and nurse," giving the anarchist freedom to move about the ship. Berkman also received permission for himself and Hyman Perkus, Dora Lipkin's companion, to regularly visit the three female passengers. Next, the deportees organized a committee to take a census and, in what Berkman called "our first attempt at practical communism," collect all extra clothing and supplies and distribute them to those in need. They also elected a committee, composed of Berkman, Perkus, Novikov, Bianki, and Adolf Schnabel, to negotiate with Supervising Inspector Berkshire on their behalf.[55]

Buford passengers Peter Bianki, Emma Goldman, Dora Lipkin, and Alexander Berkman, 1919. Courtesy of the Library of Congress Prints and Photographs Division.

The ship's baker was not aboard due to an illness, and Berkshire admitted, "his assistants were not competent bakers." Berkman therefore persuaded the inspector to allow two of the deportees—cooks by profession—to take over the bakery and, in Berkshire's terse assessment, "it may be said that they performed the service in a satisfactory manner." Next Berkshire suspended the passengers' daily three hours of access to the deck while the *Buford* passed through the Kiel Canal on its way to the Baltic Sea. Berkman and Bianki warned that the men would "raise hell" if not allowed fresh air, and threatened that "in case of refusal we will go on deck by force." Berkshire again conceded to their demands.[56]

Deportees meanwhile fraternized with the guards and began to undermine military discipline aboard the ship. Many of the soldiers were upset by their surprise deployment over the Christmas holiday; another was "sore as hell" because he had missed his own wedding. Soon, Berkman recorded, guards were "selling us their extra clothing, shoes, and everything else they can lay their hands on. Our boys are discussing war, government, and Anarchism with the sentinels. Some of the latter are much interested, and they are noting down addresses in New York where they can get our literature." Eighteen-year-old Ethel Bernstein attracted special attention; according to Goldman, "The soldiers were wild about her, discussed anarchism every free moment at their disposal, and became greatly interested in our fate." One soldier, known as "Mac," passed messages between the male and female passengers and smuggled extra food to the deportees. "We've gotten so friendly with our guards now," Berkman boasted, "that we do as we please below deck.... Berkshire has repeatedly hinted his displeasure at the influence I have gained." On the night of January 10, military discipline broke down. Many soldiers were drunk on alcohol purchased from a German ship, and Berkman had his "hands full to keep the men out of trouble." Mac then introduced Berkman to a group of guards who "proposed that I take charge of the ship. They would arrest their officers, turn the boat over to me, and come with us to Russia." Order was only restored after the ship's officers arrested four soldiers and two crewmen, and Mac was given "strict orders to keep away from" Berkman. Three days later, however, Berkman's diary records a payment of $25 "to Mac" for unspecified purposes.[57] Subversion, it seemed, was indeed contagious.

Two weeks into the *Buford*'s voyage, the entire venture nearly collapsed. The cause, however, was external: the government of Latvia, the ship's original destination, withdrew permission for the ship to land there for fear of domestic Communist opposition, as well as an alleged lack of available trains for transporting the deportees overland. A week of frantic negotiations secured rail passage through Finland, where the redirected *Buford* landed on January 16, 1920. The passengers were escorted into stifling, windowless train cars and endured a three-day trip to the Russian border with little food or water. Finnish soldiers then unloaded the deportees and ordered them to proceed on foot to the border, where Berkshire was forbidden from dealing directly with the Red Army guards whose government the United States refused to recognize. Instead, he stood back as Berkman, the deportees' elected representative, stepped forward. The anarchist, rather than the US official, negotiated the terms of the group's repatriation.[58] The scene poignantly illustrated the limits of American state power.

Disillusionment in Russia

The *Buford* passengers entered a country wracked by civil war, peasant uprisings, economic turmoil, plummeting production, and famine, as well as escalating suppression of those critical of the new Communist regime.[59] Although most deportees quickly disappeared into the chaos of war or anonymity, many left documentary trails. Some spoke out against Soviet authoritarianism and once again became targets of government repression, facing imprisonment, exile, or death. Others eagerly joined the Russian Communist Party and worked on behalf of the Soviet state, only to fall victim to Stalin's purges. Either way, few found long-term joy or comfort in their homecomings.

Almost as soon as they arrived, the head of the Petrograd Cheka (All-Russian Extraordinary Commission for Combating Counterrevolution, Profiteering, and Corruption) warned Goldman and Berkman, "anarchist foolishness would not be tolerated." The shocked repatriates also learned from comrades that the Bolsheviks had begun to suppress their erstwhile anarchist allies as early as April 1918.[60] *Buford* passenger and UORW member Theodore Kushnarev "did not even have time to orient and familiarize himself with the Russian reality, when he was arrested in Crimea" in the fall of 1920 and sentenced to five years in a prison camp "for propaganda of libertarian ideas." He was later released after authorities deemed his incarceration an "error," but did not enjoy his freedom for long. Kushnarev found work with the American Relief Administration offering aid against the famine, but then contracted typhus and died in 1925. Akron UORW member Ivan Kabas-Tarasiuk took an active role in the anarchist Nabat Federation in Kharkov after his arrival, likewise leading to his arrest and imprisonment in November 1920.[61]

For most deportees, even securing basic employment was a grim proposition. According to Goldman, most of the men from the *Buford* spent months "walking from department to department, trying to be placed where they might do some good. They were a sorry lot, those men who had come to Russia with such high hopes, eager to render service to the revolutionary people. Most of them were skilled workers, mechanics— men Russia needed badly; but the cumbersome Bolshevik machine and general inefficiency made it a very complex matter to put them to work." War resister Morris Becker finally secured a factory job in Petrograd, but when he complained of "the unbearably putrid air in the shop where he was working, the unnecessary filth and dirt," he was berated for being "a pampered *bourgeois*" who "pine[d] for the comforts of capitalist America." Becker, however, was not alone in his dissatisfaction. Russia suffered an epidemic of strikes between 1918 and 1921, and the Soviet regime, viewing labor unrest as a counterrevolutionary and existential threat, routinely suppressed it with violence. By 1921, with strikers in Saratov, Moscow, and Petrograd demanding equitable food rations, an end to government suppression of the black market, democratic representation, and freedom of speech and assembly, "the Communist Party faced what amounted to a revolutionary situation."[62]

This unrest culminated at the beginning of March, when the more than fifteen thousand sailors of the Kronstadt naval base rebelled in solidarity with striking Petrograd workers and demanded, among other reforms, "freedom of speech and press to workers and peasants, to anarchists and left socialist parties." On March 5, as Red Army soldiers prepared to assault Kronstadt, a committee composed of Goldman, Berkman, Hyman Perkus, and a voluntarily repatriated anarchist from America named Petrovsky petitioned the Petrograd Soviet to negotiate a peaceful settlement with the sailors. Their appeal was ignored, and three days later the government launched a twelve-day offensive, involving some fifty thousand troops, that drowned the Kronstadt rebellion in blood. Berkman, who could hear the artillery fire from his Petrograd apartment, wrote in his diary, "My heart is numb with despair; something has died within me."[63]

In the aftermath of Kronstadt, Soviet authorities initiated a new wave of mass arrests and reprisals directed against perceived threats to the regime—including many *Buford* passengers. For example, in July 1921 a police informant within Baltimore's Workers' Relief Society obtained a letter smuggled out of Russia, using invisible ink to evade Communist censors, notifying members of the organization that Paul Holowkin, a former UORW member and shipyard worker deported on the *Buford*, had been "shot by the Bolshevik authorities as an active counter-revolutionist." By 1923, comrades abroad had recorded 181 cases of anarchists imprisoned, killed, or deported by the Soviet regime, and of these nearly 10 percent had been living in the United States at the time of the 1917 revolution.[64] Those not executed faced decades of incarceration. Ivan Kabas-Tarasiuk endured years of imprisonment, beatings, forced labor, and internal exile. Berkman, who helped document the fate of Kabas-Tarasiuk and others, referred to him as one of many Russian anarchists "who have now for years been buried alive in prison or exile. No charges have ever been made against them, no trial ever given them."[65]

By the end of 1921, Berkman and Goldman were desperate to leave Russia. In December they obtained passports to leave for Germany, with the implicit understanding that they would never return—and they never did. In exile, they dedicated themselves to dispelling the "Bolshevik myth" and aiding their comrades in Russia, while continuing to spread their anarchist ideals. Berkman spearheaded international efforts to aid anarchists in Soviet prisons and labor camps, eventually leading to the creation of the Alexander Berkman Aid Fund, named in his honor. One of the hundreds of cases this organization tracked was that of Ivan Novikov, who had been almost too ill to travel on the *Buford*, and in 1932 was serving a three-year sentence at a labor camp in Kudymkor.[66]

Deportees who embraced Soviet Communism fared better, but only in the short term. Former Union of Russian Workers secretary Peter Bianki considered himself a syndicalist rather than an anarchist, and in Russia he joined the Communist Party and served in a variety of government posts. In 1928 he relocated to Siberia to direct a requisition squad, and was killed two years later in an armed peasant uprising against the hated government seizures. The Communist Party celebrated him as a martyr, and a street in the village of Charyshskoye still bears the name "Bianki."[67] Most others who joined the Communists did not survive the purges of "old Bolsheviks" that began in 1934. Hyman Perkus, who before his deportation declared his opposition to Bolshevism, in 1920 founded the small Union of Russian Anarchist Workers Repatriated from America, which argued for the necessity of revolutionary dictatorship to combat counterrevolutionaries, and therefore urged that anarchists "must not have a hostile, but only a critical, attitude" toward the Bolsheviks. Perkus worked with Goldman and Berkman to negotiate on behalf of the Kronstadt sailors, but later reportedly joined the Communist Party, only to be executed in the 1930s.[68] Ethel Bernstein and her husband Samuel Lipman, a Socialist deported from the United States in 1921, likewise made peace with Communism. In 1920 Ethel went to work for the People's Commissariat for Foreign Affairs, and in 1927 Lipman joined the Communist Party. The following year he obtained a prestigious position as head of the department of political geography at Moscow's Communist University of Toilers of the East, a training center for Communist activists from the colonial world. In the 1930s, however, Lipman too was executed. An anarchist friend who visited Bernstein in the Soviet Union in 1970 recalled, "She told me how Stalin had killed her husband in the purge, how her son had been killed in the war, how she had spent ten years at hard labor in a Siberian prison camp. Her whole life had been a tragedy, and she was now a broken woman."[69]

Deportation and Diplomacy

The effects of deportation on domestic and foreign conditions are, in theory, of no consequence to immigration enforcement. However, the repatriation of political dissidents can destabilize their countries of origin, sometimes in ways contrary to the interests of the deporting nation. Furthermore, although the voyage of the "Soviet Ark" was a public relations triumph for American authorities, it ultimately demonstrated the futility of efforts to solve domestic political unrest through mass deportations.

Attorney General Palmer promised New Yorkers a "second, third and fourth Soviet Ark sailing down their beautiful harbor in the near future," and claimed the government had already prepared an additional 2,720 "perfect cases" for deportation. But it was not to be. The *Buford's* trip strained the Bureau of Immigration's financial and organizational resources to their limit. The cost—not including the return trips of the soldiers and government agents aboard—was nearly $76,000 and, according to Labor Department Solicitor John W. Ambercrombie, "all the other work of the Bureau of Immigration had to be suspended" to coordinate the enterprise.[70] Moreover, the United States learned in early 1920 that Russia was willing to receive just five hundred additional deportees, and only on the condition that they be issued visas by Russia's appointed representative in the United States, Ludwig Martens. As this would implicitly recognize the Soviet regime, the Americans did not comply. Instead, they at last secured permission to transport Russian deportees through Latvia beginning in December 1920. The six *Buford* wives were among the 120 Russians transported on the SS *Estonia* via this route beginning on February 1, 1921, as was Soviet representative Martens, now a deportee himself. The total number of Russian radicals repatriated in this manner, however, did not exceed 350.[71]

Shifting public opinion and resistance from the leadership of the Department of Labor brought the mass arrests of the red scare to a close by the end of 1920, though previously approved deportations continued to be carried out.[72] But on March 4, 1921, three days before the Red Army launched its assault on Kronstadt, the Soviet consul at Libau barred six deported anarchists from entry. Mayer L. Nehring, a Jewish IWW member from Cleveland, was told "You are not Russian," and the others were informed, "Russia does not need bomb-throwers." Nehring and another of the deportees returned to the United States on bail, and Nehring's impossible status as an undeportable illegal alien was eventually resolved by a presidential pardon in 1930. The fates of the four anarchists who remained stranded in Europe are unknown. A month after excluding Nehring and his comrades, the Soviet government announced that its borders were closed to further deportees until the United States granted its regime formal diplomatic recognition.[73]

In the summer of 1921, the Commissioner General of Immigration complained, "Considerable difficulty has been experienced in effecting the deportation of aliens of the anarchists and kindred classes. The majority of the aliens ordered to be deported because of their beliefs or activities along these lines were of Russian nationality."[74] The United States, in fact, would be unable to deport all but a few Russian citizens until Franklin D. Roosevelt belatedly recognized the Soviet Union in 1933. The American government's anti-Communist foreign policy, in other words, prevented it from carrying out its domestic antiradical agenda. The role of the radicals themselves in creating this contradiction should not be overlooked. Russia's closure of its borders was a direct outgrowth of its crackdown on left-wing critics, including returned Russian-American radicals who refused to accept Soviet authority, just as they had refused to accept that of American officials.

Conclusion

"Ideas, thoughts cannot be banished." So Ivan Novikov reassured his comrades in 1920. By one conservative estimate, at the time of the red scare at least fifty thousand immigrants met the criteria for deportation under the Anarchist Exclusion Act, and the actual number is certainly many times higher.[75] The wholesale expulsion of America's foreign-born "reds" was therefore never more than a fantasy, and federal repression failed to destroy American radicalism. However, in combination with devastating internal quarrels sparked, in part, by the emergence of the Soviet Union and the Communist Party, it did diminish the anarchist movement and cripple both the Union of Russian Workers and the IWW. "Ironically," Beverly Gage notes, by doing so "it also helped to secure the position of the Communist Party as the defining organization of the revolutionary left."[76] Judged on its own terms, the first red scare was a miserable failure.

Nevertheless, it did demonstrate that any immigrant could at any time face deportation on the basis of political ideas or affiliations. The forcible removal of radicals provided a model for later deportations of immigrant labor organizers and radicals, and established a legal precedent for the suspension of aliens' constitutional rights that later justified the internment of Japanese Americans during World War II, the deportation of Communists during the Cold War, and a wide array of legislation and practices targeting alleged terrorists in the late twentieth and early twenty-first centuries.[77]

The fates of Emma Goldman and Alexander Berkman illustrate the ambiguous lessons of the first red scare. After escaping Soviet Russia, Berkman lived the remainder of his life as an unauthorized migrant in

France and neighboring countries, perpetually stateless and deport-able. In 1931, amid one of many struggles to avoid expulsion, he wrote to American comrades, "My case certainly illustrates most strikingly the brutality and stupidity of government. The situation is actually such that I have no right to exist anywhere on this earth."[78] In June 1936, following two painful and unsuccessful prostate surgeries and living in poverty, the despondent anarchist committed suicide. Goldman, by contrast, lever-aged gendered naturalization laws through a marriage of convenience to a Scottish anarchist that granted her British citizenship. She divided her time between England, Canada, France, and Spain, writing and deliv-ering lectures virtually nonstop. In 1933 Goldman even received special permission from liberal Secretary of Labor Frances Perkins to visit the United States for a ninety-day lecture tour, provided she did not speak on overtly political topics. Appropriately, at the time of her death in Toronto in 1940, Goldman was spearheading a successful effort to save anarchist Attilio Bortolotti, who had fled to Canada to elude American immigration authorities in 1929, from expulsion to Fascist Italy. Her resistance to de-portation and attempts to silence her was total.[79] The perilous journeys of Goldman and her shipmates on the *Buford* revealed that the immigra-tion enforcement regimes emerging in the United States and elsewhere were powerful, but not nearly as powerful as they imagined themselves to be.

The author wishes to thank Torrie Hester and Cristina Salinas for their thoughtful suggestions and comments on this chapter.

Notes

1. United States Congress, Senate, Committee on the Judiciary, *Charges of Illegal Practices of the Department of Justice*, 67th Congress, 2nd Session (Wash-ington, DC: Government Printing Office, 1921), 2, 26; *Annual Report of the Com-missioner General of Immigration to the Secretary of Labor*, 1929, 224; *Annual Report of the Commissioner General of Immigration to the Secretary of Labor*, 1919, 34 n.

2. Ellen Schrecker, "Immigration and Internal Security: Political Deportations during the McCarthy Era," *Science & Society* 60, no. 4 (1996–1997): 393–426.

3. Nicholas P. De Genova, "Migrant 'Illegality' and Deportability in Everyday Life," *Annual Review of Anthropology* 31 (2002): 419–47; Natalia Molina, "Con-

structing Mexicans as Deportable Immigrants: Race, Disease, and the Meaning of 'Public Charge,'" *Identities* 17, no. 6 (2010): 641–66, quote on 657; Rachel Ida Buff, "The Deportation Terror," *American Quarterly* 60, no. 3 (2008): 546. See also Carole Boyce Davies, "Deportable Subjects: U.S. Immigration Laws and the Criminalizing of Communism," *South Atlantic Quarterly* 100, no. 4 (2001): 949–66.

4. *New Solidarity*, May 31, 1919.

5. E. P. Hutchinson, *Legislative History of American Immigration Policy, 1798–1965* (Philadelphia: University of Pennsylvania Press, 1981), 423–25.

6. *Annual Report of the Commissioner General of Immigration to the Secretary of Labor* (hereafter cited as *Annual Report*), 1917, 84; *Annual Report*, 1920, 10; *Annual Report*, 1921, 14.

7. A. Caminetti, Memorandum for the Secretary, May 19, 1920, in File 54344/275, Records of the Immigration and Naturalization Service (hereafter INS), Record Group 85, National Archives and Records Administration (hereafter NARA), Washington, DC. See also Donna R. Gabaccia, *Foreign Relations: American Immigration in Global Perspective* (Princeton: Princeton University Press, 2012); Torrie Hester, *Deportation: The Origins of U.S. Policy* (Philadelphia: University of Pennsylvania Press, 2017).

8. United States Bureau of the Census, *The Statistical History of the United States: From Colonial Times to the Present* (New York: Basic Books, 1976), 117; Jerome Davis, *The Russian Immigrant* (New York: Macmillan Company, 1922), 114.

9. *Annual Report*, 1920, 32; Alexander Berkman, *The Bolshevik Myth (Diary 1920–1922)* (New York: Boni and Liverlight, 1925), 15. Slightly different numbers are given in Louis F. Post, *The Deportations Delirium of Nineteen-Twenty: A Personal Narrative of an Historic Official Experience* (Chicago: Charles H. Kerr, 1923), 27.

10. Salvatore Salerno, *Red November, Black November: Culture and Community in the Industrial Workers of the World* (New York: State University of New York Press, 1989); Davis, *The Russian Immigrant*, 40 (quote); Eric Thomas Chester, *The Wobblies in Their Heyday: The Rise and Destruction of the Industrial Workers of the World during the World War I Era* (Santa Barbara: Praeger, 2014), xii.

11. File 325570, Bureau Section Files (hereafter cited as BS), Records of the Federal Bureau of Investigation (hereafter cited as FBI), Record Group 65, NARA, College Park, Maryland; File 54616/115, INS; New York State Senate, Joint Legislative Committee Investigating Seditious Activities, *Revolutionary Radicalism: Its History, Purpose and Tactics with an Exposition and Discussion of the Steps Being Taken and Required to Curb It* (Albany: J. B. Lyon, 1920), 1:861.

12. Davis, *The Russian Immigrant*, 77, 197; Charles H. McCormick, *Seeing Reds: Federal Surveillance of Radicals in the Pittsburgh Mill District, 1917–1921* (Pittsburgh: University of Pittsburgh Press, 2003), 159; Paul Avrich, *Anarchist Voices: An Oral History of Anarchism in America* (Princeton: Princeton University Press, 1995), 369; translation of *Golos Truda*, May 25, 1917, in File 54379/100, INS.

13. File 54709/116, INS.

14. See Files 54616/115A and 54709/201, INS; William Preston, Jr., *Aliens and Dissenters: Federal Suppression of Radicals, 1903–1933* (New York: Harper & Row, 1963), 215; Regin Schmidt, *Red Scare: FBI and the Origins of Anticommunism in the United States, 1919–1943* (Copenhagen: Museum Tusculanum Press, 2000), 288; translation of *Golos Truda* to J. Medvedeff, May 23, 1917, in File 54235/158, INS. See also Mark Grueter, "Red Scare Scholarship, Class Conflict, and the Case of the Anarchist Union of Russian Workers, 1919," *Journal for the Study of Radicalism* 11, no. 1 (2017): 53–81.

15. Files 54709/117, 54709/210, 54709/112, and 54616/115A, INS; File 325570, BS, FBI.

16. Kenyon Zimmer, *Immigrants against the State: Yiddish and Italian Anarchism in America* (Chicago: University of Illinois Press, 2015), chapter 5.

17. Paul Avrich and Karen Avrich, *Sasha and Emma: The Anarchist Odyssey of Alexander Berkman and Emma Goldman* (Cambridge: Harvard University Press, 2012); Richard Gid Powers, *Secrecy and Power: The Life of J. Edgar Hoover* (New York: The Free Press, 1987), 80–86; Kenneth D. Ackerman, *Young J. Edgar: Hoover, the Red Scare, and the Assault on Civil Liberties* (New York: Carroll & Graf, 2007), chapter 12.

18. Theodore Draper, *The Roots of American Communism* (New York: Viking Press, 1957), 138, 158, 189.

19. Preston, *Aliens and Dissenters*, 100.

20. Chester, *The Wobblies in Their Heyday*, 156 and passim; Philip Taft, "The Federal Trials of the IWW," *Labor History* 3, no. 1 (1962): 57–91; Preston, *Aliens and Dissenters*, chapters 4–5.

21. Daniel Nelson, *American Rubber Workers and Organized Labor, 1900–1941* (Princeton: Princeton University Press, 1988), 23–43, 52, 54; "Nationalities in the United States," *Foreign-Born*, December 1919; File 372181, Old German Files (hereafter cited as OG), FBI; File 54248/20, INS.

22. Files 8000-350826 and 372181, OG, FBI; Files 54248/20, 54235/160, and 54235/158, INS.

23. Preston, *Aliens and Dissenters*, 162–72, 182–89; Chester, *The Wobblies in Their Heyday*, 138–43; Paul Avrich, *Sacco and Vanzetti: The Anarchist Background* (Princeton: Princeton University Press, 1991), chapter 8; Schmidt, *Red Scare*, 249.

24. Schmidt, *Red Scare*, 134; Stanley Coben, *A. Mitchell Palmer: Politician* (New York: Columbia University Press, 1963), 199.

25. Avrich, *Sacco and Vanzetti*, quote on 81.

26. Andrew Cornell, *Unruly Equality: U.S. Anarchism in the Twentieth Century* (Berkeley: University of California Press, 2016), 71; McCormick, *Seeing Reds*, 155. On the investigation, see Avrich, *Sacco and Vanzetti*; Charles H. McCormick, *Hopeless Cases: The Hunt for the Red Scare Terrorist Bombers* (Lanham, MD: University Press of America, 2005); Beverly Gage, *The Day Wall Street Exploded: A Story of America in Its First Age of Terror* (Oxford: Oxford University Press, 2009).

27. *New York Call*, November 8, 1919; Files 54709/272 and 54709/277, INS; *Anarchist Soviet Bulletin*, April 1920; Schmidt, *Red Scare*, 268.

28. Agnes Inglis, "The Raids on the Union of Russian Workers," unpublished manuscript, box 27, Agnes Inglis Papers, Joseph A. Labadie Collection (hereafter cited as Labadie), University of Michigan, Ann Arbor; Constantine M. Panunzio, *The Deportation Cases of 1919–1920*, reprint ed. (New York: Da Capo Press, 1921), 81–82.

29. Schmidt, *Red Scare*, 268; Powers, *Secrecy and Power*, 77; *Annual Report, 1920*, 32.

30. National Lawyers Guild, "Political Deportations in the United States: A Study in the Enforcement Procedures: 1919–1952," *Lawyers Guild Review* 14, no. 3 (1954): 111; Preston, *Aliens and Dissenters*, 217.

31. United States Congress, House of Representatives, Committee on Rules, *Attorney General A. Mitchell Palmer on Charges Made Against Department of Justice by Louis F. Post and Others* (Washington, DC: Government Printing Office, 1920), 156, 157; Preston, *Aliens and Dissenters*, 166. See also Bruce B. Shubert, "The Palmer Raids in Connecticut, 1919–1920," *Connecticut Review* 5, no. 1 (1971): 53–69.

32. Stephen Meyer III, *The Five Dollar Day: Labor Management and Social Control in the Ford Motor Company, 1908–1921* (Albany: State University of New York Press, 1981), 175; File 54649/62, INS.

33. David Williams, "'Sowing the Wind': The Deportation Raids of 1920 in New Hampshire," *Historical New Hampshire* 34, no. 1 (1979): 14–15; File 8000-350826, OG FBI.

34. H. W. Kage to Frank Burke, November 18 and November 24, 1919, in File 372181, OG, FBI.

35. File 54709/478, INS; McCormick, *Seeing Reds*, chapter 7; Grueter, "Red Scare Scholarship," 56–60; Interchurch World Movement of North America, *Report on the Steel Strike of 1919* (New York: Harcourt, Brace and Howe, 1920), 38; Labor Research Association, *The Palmer Raids*, ed. Robert W. Dunn (New York: International Publishers, 1948), 22, 24.

36. File 352388, OG, FBI; File 54616/25, INS.

37. File 54709/604, INS; Bonnie Honig, "Bound by Law? Alien Rights, Administrative Discretion, and the Politics of Technicality: Lessons from Louis Post and the First Red Scare," in *The Limits of Law*, ed. Austin Sarat, Lawrence Douglas, and Martha Merrill Umphrey (Stanford: Stanford University Press, 2005), 209–45.

38. Elizabeth Gurley Flynn, *Sabotage: The Conscious Withdrawal of the Workers' Industrial Efficiency* (Cleveland: I.W.W. Publishing Bureau, 1916); File 54709/185, INS.

39. File 54407/17, INS.

40. Preston, *Aliens and Dissenters*, 177–78; File 54616/16, INS.

41. File 54616/172, INS.

42. File 54616/239, INS.

43. Panunzio, *Deportation Cases*, 17; Kim E. Nielsen, *Un-American Womanhood: Antiradicalism, Antifeminism, and the First Red Scare* (Columbus: Ohio State University Press, 2001), 17.

44. Martha Gardner, *The Qualities of a Citizen: Women, Immigration, and*

Citizenship, 1870–1965 (Princeton: Princeton University Press, 2009), chapter 1; Patrick Weil, *The Sovereign Citizen: Denaturalization and the Origins of the American Republic* (Philadelphia: University of Pennsylvania Press, 2012), 58–62.

45. McCormick, *Seeing Reds*, 162; File 54235/36E, INS.

46. Post, *Deportations Delirium*, 5; Panunzio, *Deportation Cases*, 89; Winthrop D. Lane, "The Buford Widows," *The Survey*, January 10, 1920; Files 54235/36E, 54709/273, 54616/115A, and 53108/66, INS.

47. Christina Heatherton, "University of Radicalism: Ricardo Flores Magón and Leavenworth Penitentiary," *American Quarterly* 66, no. 3 (2014): 559.

48. *Ellis Island Anarchist Weekly*, May 10, 1919, Miscellaneous Manuscripts, Labadie; Zosa Szajkowski, *Jews, Wars, and Communism* (New York: Ktav Publishing House, 1972), 2:13; Ludovico Caminita, *Nell'isola delle lagrime: Ellis Island* (New York: Stabilimento Tipografico Italia, 1924), 45.

49. *Ellis Island Anarchist Weekly*, May 10, 1919; Cornell, *Unruly Equality*, 72, 322 n.75; Kenyon Zimmer, "Positively Stateless: Marcus Graham, the Ferrero-Sallitto Case, and Anarchist Challenges to Race and Deportation," in *The Rising Tide of Color: Race, Radicalism, and Repression on the Pacific Coast and Beyond*, ed. Moon-Ho Jung (Seattle: University of Washington Press, 2013), 128–58.

50. Caminita, *Nell'isola*, 131; *New York Times*, November 26, 1919; *New York Tribune*, November 30, 1919.

51. Ivan Novikov to Dear Friends, January 16, 1920 (hereafter cited as Novikov letter), in File 379190, OG, FBI; Emma Goldman, *Living My Life* (1931; reprint, Salt Lake City: Peregrine and Gibbs M. Smith, 1982), 717.

52. Alexander Berkman, "The Log of the Transport Buford," *The Liberator*, April 1920; Szajkowski, *Jews, Wars, and Communism*, 2:13; Files 54616/16 and 54616/82, INS.

53. Supervising Immigrant Inspector to Commissioner General of Immigration, February 11, 1920, in File 53108/66, INS. Numerous historians cite the inflated figure of 200 or 250 soldiers aboard the *Buford*; the original source of this error appears to be the *New York Times*, December 22, 1919.

54. Novikov letter; Alexander Berkman, "Russian Diary," 1919–1922, unpublished manuscript, n.p., Alexander Berkman Papers, International Institute of Social History, Amsterdam, The Netherlands.

55. Berkman, *Bolshevik Myth*, 17, 19; Novikov letter.

56. Supervising Immigrant Inspector to Commissioner General of Immigration, February 11, 1920, in File 53108/66, INS; Novikov letter; Berkman, "Log of the Transport Buford"; Berkman, *Bolshevik Myth*, 23.

57. Berkman, *Bolshevik Myth*, 19, 22–24; Goldman, *Living My Life*, 720–22; Berkman, "Log of the Transport Buford"; Berkman, "Russian Diary." There is some discrepancy regarding the date of this incident, but Berkman's unpublished diary places it on January 10.

58. US Department of State, *Papers Relating to the Foreign Relations of the United States*, vol. 3 (Washington, DC: Government Printing Office, 1920), 693–96; Supervising Immigrant Inspector to Commissioner General of Immigration, February 11, 1920, File 53108/66, INS.

59. Orlando Figes, *A People's Tragedy: A History of the Russian Revolution* (New York: Penguin, 1996), chapter 15.

60. Goldman, *Living My Life*, 785; Paul Avrich, *The Russian Anarchists* (Princeton: Princeton University Press, 1967), 184–85, 222–25.

61. Groupe des anarchistes russes exilés en Allemagne, *Répression de l'anarchisme en Russie Soviétique*, trans. Voline (Paris: Éditions de la "Librairie sociale," 1923), 63; Elaine J. Leeder, *The Gentle General: Rose Pesotta, Anarchist and Labor Organizer* (Albany, NY: State University of New York Press, 1993), 26–29; Avrich, *Anarchist Voices*, 383; *Bulletin of the Relief Fund of the International Working Men's Association for Anarchists and Anarcho-Syndicalists Imprisoned or Exiled in Russia* (hereafter cited as *Bulletin of the Relief Fund*), November 1927.

62. Emma Goldman, *My Disillusionment in Russia* (London: C. W. Daniel, 1925), 39; Goldman, *Living My Life*, 742; Jonathan Aves, *Workers against Lenin: Labour Protest and the Bolshevik Dictatorship* (London: Tauris Academic Studies, 1996), quote on 155.

63. Paul Avrich, *Kronstadt, 1921* (Princeton: Princeton University Press, 1970); Israel Getzler, *Kronstadt 1917–1921: The Fate of a Soviet Democracy* (Cambridge: Cambridge University Press, 1983); Berkman, *Bolshevik Myth*, 301–3.

64. File 202600-2386-1, BS, FBI; Groupe des anarchistes russes exilés en Allemagne, *Répression de l'anarchisme*.

65. *Bulletin of the Relief Fund*, December 1926, May 1929, November-December 1929; G. P. Maximoff, *The Guillotine at Work: Twenty Years of Terror in Russia (Data and Documents)* (Chicago: Alexander Berkman Aid Fund, 1940), 461–62, 525–26, 548, 566, 592, 597; *Freedom* (London), March 1927.

66. Avrich, *Russian Anarchists*, 235–36; *The Tragic Procession: Alexander Berkman and Russian Prisoner Aid* (Berkeley/London: Alexander Berkman Social Club/Kate Sharpley Library, 2010); Avrich and Avrich, *Sasha and Emma*, chapters 23–29; Maximoff, *The Guillotine at Work*, 597.

67. File 54616/115, INS; Avrich, *Anarchist Voices*, 365; Malcolm Archibald, "Peter Bianki: The Soviet Years," *Kate Sharpley Library*, 2015, http://www.kate sharpleylibrary.net/pnvzh1.

68. File 54709/116, INS; Victor Serge, "New Tendencies in Russian Anarchism," in *Anarchists Never Surrender: Essays, Polemics, and Correspondence on Anarchism, 1908–1938*, ed. and trans. Mitchell Abidor (Oakland: PM Press, 2015), 188–89; Avrich, *Anarchist Voices*, 342, 365.

69. Alexander Berkman to Fitzie [M. Eleanor Fitzgerald], November 22, 1920, in "Berkman, Alexander, 1879-1936," Miscellaneous Manuscripts, Labadie; Paul Avrich, "Anarchist Lives: Mollie Steimer (1897–1980) and Simon (Senya) Fleshen (1894–1981)," in *Fighters for Anarchism: Mollie Steimer and Senya Fleshin*, ed. Abe Bluestein (New York: Libertarian Publications Group, 1983), 14; Avrich, *Anarchist Voices*, 339, 342.

70. *New York Times*, February 29, January 4, January 5, 1920; File 53108/66, INS.

71. US Department of State, *Papers*, 3:700; Hester, *Deportation*, 138-39; *Annual Report*, 1921, 14. On Martens's deportation, see Todd J. Pfannestiel, *Re-*

thinking the Red Scare: The Lusk Committee and New York's Crusade against Radicalism, 1919–1923 (New York: Routledge, 2015), chapter 3.

72. Post, *Deportations Delirium*; W. Anthony Gengarelly, "Secretary of Labor William B. Wilson and the Red Scare, 1919–1920," *Pennsylvania History* 47, no. 4 (1980): 310–30; Honig, "Bound by Law?"

73. *Freedom* (London), May 1921; *Free Society*, October-November 1921; Stephen M. Kohn, *American Political Prisoners: Prosecutions under the Espionage and Sedition Acts* (Westport, CT: Praeger, 1994), 120; Hester, *Deportation*, 139.

74. *Annual Report*, 1921, 14.

75. Novikov letter; Kate Holladay Claghorn, *The Immigrant's Day in Court* (New York: Harper & Brothers, 1923), 459.

76. Zimmer, *Immigrants against the State*, chapters 5–6; Cornell, *Unruly Equality*; Chester, *The Wobblies in Their Heyday*; Gage, *The Day Wall Street Exploded*, 311.

77. Nathaniel Hong, "The Origin of American Legislation to Exclude and Deport Aliens for Their Political Beliefs, and Its Initial Review by the Courts," *Journal of Ethnic Studies* 18, no. 2 (1990): 1–36; Julia Rose Kraut, "Global Anti-Anarchism: The Origins of Ideological Deportation and the Suppression of Expression," *Indiana Journal of Global Legal Studies* 19, no. 1 (2012): 169–93; Molina, "Constructing Mexicans"; Arleen de Vera, "Without Parallel: The Local 7 Deportation Cases, 1949–1955," *Amerasia Journal* 20, no. 2 (1994): 1–25; Deirdre M. Moloney, *National Insecurities: Immigrants and U.S. Deportation Policy since 1882* (Chapel Hill: University of North Carolina Press, 2012); David Cole, *Enemy Aliens: Double Standards and Constitutional Freedoms in the War on Terrorism* (New York: New Press, 2003).

78. *Road to Freedom*, September 1931.

79. Alice Wexler, *Emma Goldman in Exile: From the Russian Revolution to the Spanish Civil War* (Boston: Beacon Press, 1989); Avrich and Avrich, *Sasha and Emma*, chapters 23–29; Travis Tomchuk, *Transnational Radicals: Italian Anarchists in Canada and the U.S., 1915–1940* (Winnipeg: University of Manitoba Press, 2015), chapter 6.

6

Deportable Citizens

THE DECOUPLING OF RACE AND CITIZENSHIP IN THE CONSTRUCTION OF THE "ANCHOR BABY"

Natalia Molina

In 2014 a group of nearly thirty Latino immigrant families filed a lawsuit because the Texas Department of State Health Services would not issue birth certificates for their American-born children. These immigrant parents argued that this caused significant hardship: even though a birth certificate is technically not necessary for a host of activities, the parents had nonetheless been refused when attempting to set up baptisms for their children, or to enroll them in daycare, school, and special education services, for lacking birth certificates. These refusals compromised the parents' ability to work, to obtain health insurance, and even to move about the state freely for fear that, without documentation proving their parental rights, their children could be taken from them should they be stopped. The parents also pointed to future harm that would be caused when these children become adults and wished to obtain worker's permits, driver's licenses, or passports; to board domestic flights; or to obtain Social Security cards. The Texas Department of State Health Services argued that it was only protecting private and confidential information from being released to those who had not presented adequate proof that they were qualified to obtain it. Since 2013, however, Texas had made such proof increasingly difficult to obtain for immigrant parents, most of them hailing from Mexico and Central America. Mexican consular identification cards, which had once been acceptable forms of identification, were now being rejected, as were Mexican voter identification cards if they had expired (and immigrant parents living in the United States cannot renew these cards).[1] After two years of courtroom battles, a settlement was reached in the US District Court for the Western District of Texas, in which the state of Texas agreed to expand the list of acceptable forms of identification.[2]

At the heart of this controversy are explicit and implicit assumptions of who deserves US citizenship. Legally it is clear that these children have the right to be citizens: under the Fourteenth Amendment, anyone born in the United States is a US citizen. But the legal definitions of citizenship do not always overlap neatly with the cultural and social understandings of what it means to be an American. The long, contested history of US citizenship demonstrates that citizenship and whiteness were often equated, both legally and symbolically, which made it difficult for some to accept nonwhites as American citizens.[3] After the Mexican-American War (1846–48), the Treaty of Guadalupe Hidalgo extended US citizenship to Mexicans living in the ceded territory, something not afforded to any other nonwhite group at the time. This was seen as a political concession only—while Mexicans were legally citizens, many did not consider them full citizens because of their indigenous blood. Critics fought the legal classification of Mexicans as white beginning from the time that the United States incorporated Mexican lands and peoples, and they would continue to do so for generations on the basis of the argument that Mexicans should be considered neither white nor black but in a "race of their own."[4] The struggle over Texas children's birth certificates shows the long shadow cast by this history extends even to this day.

The battle over birth certificates is an extension of a pattern, rooted in popular discourse and cultural representations, that advances the image of pregnant Mexican pariah-mothers strategically entering the United States to give birth at US taxpayers' expense. Critics argue that the mothers are playing the system, intentionally giving birth in the United States with the goal of securing citizenship for themselves. Such critics—nativists and centrist politicians alike—dub these US-born children "anchor babies," despite the term's offensive implication that mothers birth children first and foremost for their own gain. Not only is the mother delegitimized in this scenario, but so is the child, who is not constructed as an American citizen but as a simple (and unfair) means for undeserving immigrants to gain US citizenship. Indeed, the very term "anchor baby" obscures the fact that we are talking about a US citizen.

While the term "anchor baby" does not reference a specific ethnic or racial group, Latino children generally, and Mexican American children specifically, were the groups most conjured in discussions and media stories on the topic.[5] In part, this reflects the demographics of immigration: Mexicans represent more than half of the undocumented immigrants in the United States, making them a highly visible population. Yet while other immigrant groups certainly give birth in the United States, the anchor baby stigma is not extended to those groups in any kind of sustained or visible way.[6] The fact that Mexicans bear the brunt of the anchor baby stigma is only the newest iteration of an old story that depicts Mexican immigrants as unworthy of inclusion in the United States.

This chapter pushes back the timeline of this tale to the late 1920s and 1930s, with the "birth" of the anchor baby concept, in order to demonstrate that then, as now, even when Mexicans were US citizens, they were not seen as truly legal. In doing so, I demonstrate how the popular concept of the anchor baby, regularly discussed and advanced by the media today, is mistaken. These children do not provide an "anchor" for their undocumented parents and never have. Undocumented parents have never automatically been extended citizenship on the basis that their children were born in the United States. Nor have parents of American-born children received automatic reprieve from deportation as part of immigration law or policy.[7] Indeed, the first comprehensive US immigration law, the Johnson-Reed Immigration Act of 1924, did not even consider family reunification. It took more than forty years, until the passage of the 1965 Immigration and Nationality Act, for family reunification to become an important consideration (though far from a trump card) in immigration policy.

Nonetheless, the idea of the anchor baby persists. Many trace the anchor baby discourse and the visible targeting of women to the early 1990s and the passage of California's Proposition 187, which sought to deny public services to undocumented immigrants. Ostensibly, Proposition 187 targeted all undocumented immigrants, but within California's political and cultural climate, it was understood that the referendum's primary target was Mexicans and that Mexican women and children would be disproportionately affected. During the campaign, the two public services most discussed were education and nonemergency medical care, specifically infant and maternal care.[8]

Proposition 187 was certainly not the first time the public expressed concern that Latina mothers and children were products of a "culture of poverty." This concept, originally formulated in the 1950s by anthropologist Oscar Lewis, explained Mexicans' and Puerto Ricans' poverty as arising from their own supposed bad choices—choices that became incorporated into their culture and passed down generation after generation. This theory thus bypassed any discussion of racism and structural discrimination.[9] Then Assistant Secretary of Labor Daniel Patrick Moynihan subsequently popularized the concept in a 1965 report discussing the roots of black poverty in the United States (now commonly referred to as "the Moynihan Report"). As he discussed the disintegration of the black family during slavery and traced its effects into the post–civil rights era, Moynihan squarely put the blame on black matriarchs for this "tangle of pathology." The welfare queen stereotype is a contemporary incarnation of this "culture of poverty" argument. The "welfare queen" is usually depicted as a poor woman of color, assumed to be sexually irresponsible and morally questionable, and suspected of deliberately bearing children in order to increase her welfare payments. As such, these women are viewed with suspicion and derision, just as many poor women of color before them have been accused of having children primarily to increase their monthly welfare benefits.[10] Mexican women and their children have become the latest version of the "welfare queen," this time with an anti-immigrant twist—and their representation demonstrates how gender plays a key role in shaping the contours of anti-immigrant discourse. Whether "welfare queen" or the mother of an "anchor baby," black or Mexican, native- or foreign-born, the through-line of these archetypes is the same: women of color irresponsibly breed in hopes of obtaining government handouts, and their children are mere collateral in the process.

In order to demonstrate the roots of the anchor baby myth, I begin my analysis with the passage of the 1924 Immigration Act and the decade that followed, which saw the first sustained popular national discussion regarding birthright citizenship for the US-born children of Mexican immigrants.[11] I argue that these citizen children were seen as less than fully American, in large part because before they were born their mothers were already vilified by a host of people in authority, including politicians, health officials, and social workers. These authorities' opinions then became institutionalized into laws, policies, and practices that circulated widely as cultural representations in the media, reinforcing the cycle of stigmatization. Though citizens, there was no guaranteed process for these children to "become Mexican American" in a cultural or social sense.[12] They inherited the stigma of illegality imposed on their immigrant parents, despite their citizenship status, demonstrating the ways in which race and citizenship are unyoked for Mexican Americans, generation after generation, belying the popular American assimilation myths from the melting pot to color blindness.[13]

I then move to a discussion of the Great Depression, a time of mass re-patriations, deportations, and general scapegoating of Mexicans. During this time, US-born children were not merely referred to as anchor babies; instead, their citizenship rights were ignored as they were deported along with their families. In fact, it was citizen children who risked bringing their undocumented parents to the attention of the state and putting them at risk of deportation. I examine legislation proposed during the Depression that would have kept mixed status families deemed "worthy" from being deported (often white families) while constructing others as "unworthy" (often Mexican families) as deportable.

Furthermore, I turn to a set of Los Angeles County Department of Char-ities cases that would have been affected by said legislation. These depor-tation case studies show that a child's citizenship was easily trumped by an immigrant parent's "illegal" status, to the extent that the child could not access resources intended for citizens without in effect having her own citizenship revoked through deportation. Various mechanisms were used to enforce and justify this practice: particularly charges of immoral-ity, being a public charge, and delinquency. The upshot was to exclude Mexican Americans and their families from American soil and American identity. I argue that such disregard of these young people's rights would have long-term implications for how race and citizenship continue to be culturally decoupled for Mexican Americans.

Gendering the Long Immigration Debate Era

One hundred years ago, Mexican immigration was not the hotly debated topic it is today. Mexicans immigrated in smaller numbers, were confined mainly to the Southwest, and many were sojourner laborers who worked for a season and then returned home to Mexico. They did not threaten the status quo: they did not tend to settle down, join unions, naturalize, or vote. These reasons, coupled with the lobbying power of large-scale employers in agriculture and industry, as well as diplomatic and trade in-terests, ensured that no quotas were imposed on Mexico under the 1924 Immigration Act, which established a national origins quota for southern and eastern Europeans and banned immigration from Asia, but placed no such restrictions on immigrants from countries in the Western Hemisphere.[14]

After the passage of the 1924 Immigration Act, lawmakers began to question why the United States had curtailed immigration from Europe and not from Mexico. In its aftermath, the discourse around Mexican immigration shifted. For one, as immigration from other countries declined in the wake of the new law, Mexicans came to make up a larger percentage of those on the immigration rolls. In the two years leading up to the 1924 Immigration Act, Mexicans constituted 10.9 percent of the total number of admitted immigrants. In the three years after the passage of the act, their numbers jumped to 16.1 percent. By 1927, Mexicans were second only to Germans in terms of the number of new immigrants. A long view of the 1920s reveals that in that decade, Mexicans composed more than 11.2 percent of all immigrants admitted to the United States.[15] With this increase in numbers came greater anxiety about the nature of Mexican immigrants. Long seen as a racially inferior but generally malleable workforce, during this era the public increasingly stereotyped Mexicans as social burdens: criminal, diseased, and unassimilable. As a result, attempts to curtail Mexican immigration after 1924 increased, ushering in what I term the *long immigration debate era*, during which restricting Mexican immigration continued to be debated after the passage of the 1924 Immigration Act through the onset of the Depression.[16] Between 1925 and 1930, the House and Senate proposed nearly two dozen bills restricting immigration from countries in the Western hemisphere.[17] These years mark the period immediately after the passage of the 1924 Immigration Act, when many expressed their outrage that Mexican immigrants were not subject to the same quotas as Europeans. By 1930, however, the Depression had set in and repatriations, voluntary and involuntary, as well as restrictions on visas, had severely curtailed Mexican immigration. Nevertheless, these long, intense, and sustained conversations on race shaped the meanings of "Mexican" during these years, and for years to come.

Mexican women and children were often central to these immigration debates. They became the symbol for what was wrong with a more open immigration policy with Mexico. Until the midtwenties, the growth of the Mexican population in the United States had been attributed mainly to immigration. But with the increased arrival of Mexican women, the Mexican family (as opposed to the single, sojourning Mexican male) became

"Chita" Luque (holding child) and her grandchildren, circa 1933. Courtesy of Shades of L.A. Collection, Los Angeles Public Library.

the favorite target of those who advocated immigration reform. The representation of Mexican women at this time as "excessive breeders" signaled the dangers of an open immigration policy, as opposed to painting immigrants as an economic threat or job stealers.

With the onset of the Depression, immigration restrictionists intensified their campaigns identifying Mexican women's reproductive capacity as a reason to end immigration. The belief that Mexican women were unusually "fecund" and anxieties over the potential for "race suicide," in which the middle- and upper-class white population would be eclipsed by racialized groups, helped focus attention on birth rates during the

1930s.[18] For example, in congressional hearings over immigration restriction, Louisiana congressman Riley Wilson drove home the point that even if Mexicans returned to their home country, "they have children, and a child born in California is an American citizen."[19]

Such concerns were not limited to the political realm but also circulated in academia, public health, and popular media. "They bring their women, their children," warned C. M. Goethe, a California philanthropist, conservationist, and eugenics advocate, adding that Mexicans were "a group that is most fecund."[20] Samuel Holmes, the Berkeley zoologist and eugenicist, echoed Goethe's contentions. In one article, Holmes cited a survey from San Bernardino, California, that found that "three out of every eight babies born [here] were Mexican."[21] "The menial laborers of today produce the citizens of tomorrow," he warned in another article.[22] The shift in focus from immigration flows to birthrates confirms the role that fears about "race suicide" played in fueling immigration reform efforts.[23]

While this was the first time lawmakers singled out Mexican women in particular and proposed legislation to deal with the threat they supposedly posed, we need only to pull the lens back to see how this image of Mexican women as transgressive was in keeping with earlier images of other immigrant women. To take just one example, consider the first federal immigration law, the Page Act of 1875, which (among other restrictions) prohibited the entry of Chinese prostitutes on the assumption that all Chinese women wishing to immigrate to the United States were sex workers.[24] A generation later Progressive reformers, often women themselves, targeted immigrant women as members of backward cultures in need of rehabilitation and pressured them to take courses to assimilate into American culture, such as language and cooking classes. Though many of these programs meant well, the idea that immigrant women needed to be taught how to be proper mothers pointed to how they were seen as deviating from accepted gender roles.[25]

The Making of the White "Anchor Baby"

The Depression marked a major turning point in the treatment accorded to Mexicans living in the United States. The marginal acceptance that stemmed from being a source of cheap labor evaporated as rapidly as the jobs Mexican laborers had been hired to fill. As jobs disappeared, so too did the justification for allowing an open immigration policy with Mexico.

Opponents of unrestricted immigration began insisting that Mexicans return home and followed up those demands with political pressure at the local, state, and national levels, often providing funds for "voluntary" deportation programs, called "repatriation." As work by pioneering scholars in Chicano history has shown, officials perceived Mexicans as overburdening city resources by relying too much on relief programs.[26] These early studies all examine how deportations pivoted on the image of the Mexican as a charity seeker. Less examined in these rich histories of deportation and repatriation programs are the children of those deported, many of whom were Mexican Americans.[27]

Deportation to Mexico was devastating. Many of these families had been settled in the United States for years, and the abrupt deportation

Central Station, Los Angeles, January 12, 1932. "Photo shows a crowd of 1,400 Mexicans at Central Station when they departed today for their old homes in Mexico. The families, with their babies, guitars, blankets, shawls and bundles, left on three special Southern Pacific trains chartered by Los Angeles county, which set aside about $15,000 to aid them in their repatriation. Officials estimated that this sum spent on transportation would have recovered within six weeks in savings on charity." Courtesy of *Herald-Examiner* Collection, Los Angeles Public Library.

process did not allow them to transplant their lives easily to Mexico. First, their available modes of transportation to Mexico, either in their own vehicles or on trains sponsored by counties to encourage people to repatriate, limited the amount of things they could take with them. In addition, those who were transported by train were not necessarily returned to their hometowns. Instead, they were delivered to far-flung cities where most had no family members to help cushion their transition. Repatriates were not necessarily looked upon with favor by their countrymen, either. As in the United States, Mexico's economy was faring poorly, and it was difficult to find employment. Many of these children felt more comfortable speaking English, and some could not speak Spanish at all, for which they were singled out and denounced. Also, repatriates found themselves viewed as traitors who had defected to the United States and were now being forced to return to Mexico, where they would compete with locals in the struggling economy. One repatriate was asked, "What you doing here for, to eat the little bread we have. Why you no stay there?"[28] Thus Mexican American children were treated with particular disdain, as they were American citizens and people questioned their rights to access any Mexican government resources.

Regardless of these difficult conditions, repatriated Mexicans had very little choice but to stick it out. Crossing the US-Mexico border was arduous. While the border was fairly porous early in the early twentieth century, it quickly solidified, with an increase in fees and medical exams starting in 1917, the development of the Border Patrol in 1924, and the increased difficulty of obtaining a visa after the passage of the 1924 Immigration Act. Moreover, repatriates often lacked the money, resources, and sometimes the health to make such a journey. They also were not making the journey as single sojourners optimistically looking for jobs, but as families, which only made the trek more expensive and challenging.[29]

By the mid-1930s, US lawmakers were attempting to deal with the reality of mixed-status households composed of deportable parents and their US-born children. In May 1935, the House of Representatives introduced the Kerr Bill (H.R. 8163), which was meant to prevent immigrants of "good moral character" and with no criminal offenses from being separated from their families. Proponents argued the bill could help 2,862 "hardship cases" that had been identified by immigration officials.[30] Under the bill, the Secretary of Labor would be able to consider a stay of deportation if the individual's deportation would have serious consequences for his family or for "the best interests of the United States."[31] In order to stay a deportation, the petitioner needed to prove either he had been a resident of the United States for at least ten years or he had been a resident for one year and had close relatives who were citizens or permanent residents. Residency had to be verified by a letter from a citizen known to the applicant.[32] Moreover, the bill would offer a path to citizenship for those who received the stay of deportation. The committee that would be formed to review the stays of deportations would also have the authority to grant legal residency status. The bill did not pass, because its detractors expressed concern that it would grant too much discretionary power to the special "interdepartmental committee."[33] Nonetheless, it still contributed to a national conversation on who was and was not fit to be a citizen. Forty-one other bills were introduced in the 74th Congress (1935–36) and 75th Congress (1937–38) that were some variation of the Kerr Bill and the Coolidge Bill (the counterpart bill in the Senate), further illustrating how the nation weighed which immigrants it felt worthy of help. Taken in the aggregate, this proposed legislation sheds light on a moment when the state needed to reckon with the increasing number of mixed-citizenship families and where (and if) they would fit in the nation.

The Kerr Bill was intended to help those with no criminal history who had come to the attention of the state because they had fallen on hard times and become a "public charge." This language of "public charge" dates from the 1882 Immigration Act, which prohibited entry to any "convict, lunatic, idiot, or any person unable to take care of himself or herself without becoming a public charge."[34] The 1891 Immigration Act expanded the phrase to include "persons *likely* to become a public charge" (emphasis added), which included anyone suffering from a "loathsome or dangerous contagious disease." The act also created the possibility of deportation on "likely public charge" (or LPC) grounds, even after an immigrant's initial arrival in the United States: "[A]ny alien who becomes a public charge within one year after his arrival in the United States from causes existing prior to his landing therein shall be deemed to have come in violation of law and shall be returned as aforesaid."[35] Subsequent immigration laws in 1903, 1907, and 1917 extended the period of jeopardy to two years, then three years, and then five years. Like a disease diagnosis, the LPC charge could be used to stigmatize undesirable immigrants.

The potent history of the LPC clause and the influence those in power could exert when they wielded it against immigrants long after they settled in the United States has, until now, been relatively unexamined.[36] It effectively made all Mexicans living on the border potentially deportable. The arbitrary, adaptable, and open-ended nature of the LPC designation created great uncertainty for all new arrivals, but Mexican immigrants were especially vulnerable. Not only were they frequently employed in seasonal low-wage agricultural work, but Mexicans (unlike other immigrants) were close to their home country, not needing the resources to cross large bodies of water or travel thousands of miles to visit. Particularly in the Southwest, many Mexican laborers crossed into and out of the United States frequently, returning home to visit family and friends. Doing so incurred risk, however. The LPC "clock" started anew with each border crossing—and there were no legally defined criteria for establishing who was "likely to become a public charge." Thus, even after decades of living in the United States, Mexicans who lost their jobs and sought charity or got sick and sought medical assistance could be deported if they had been to Mexico within the previous five years, even if it was simply for a day. This combination created a near-continuous potential for deportation that could eclipse all other aspects of Mexican immigrants' identity in the United States, as workers, homeowners, neighbors, churchgoers, and long-time members of local communities. Lawfully admitted immigrants, and especially those who tried to maintain social networks on both sides of the border, could thus find themselves suspended between becoming American and becoming deportable.

The Kerr Bill, in theory, would protect all mixed-status families, but both the origins of and debates around the bill suggest that it was intended to offer a path to citizenship for European immigrants who would otherwise be separated from family members through deportation. In effect, the bill would turn white ethnic children into "anchor babies." In a humanitarian gesture, Commissioner of Immigration and Naturalization Daniel MacCormack stayed deportation in 465 cases involving mixed-status families in June of 1934 until the bills could be introduced and heard in Congress the following session. These cases were all drawn from Ellis Island, where the vast majority of cases were Europeans.[37] Commissioner MacCormack was himself an immigrant from Ireland, and while at first Irish immigrants in America were not quite considered white and fought to distance themselves from blacks, who were also low on the US racial hierarchy, by the mid-1930s Irish and other European immigrant groups were well into the process of what Matthew Frye Jacobson calls "becoming Caucasian."[38] The majority of Mexicans lived on the opposite coast from lawmakers and administrators like Commissioner MacCormack; Representative Kerr (D-NC); Senator Coolidge (D-MA), who sponsored the counterpart bill in the Senate; or Chairman of the House Immigration and Naturalization Committee Samuel Dickstein (D-NY), who also supported the legislation.[39] For these officials, the deserving beneficiaries of the bill were to be European immigrants coming through Ellis Island.

The intent of the Kerr Bill was therefore in keeping with past legislation that had offered a path to citizenship for European immigrants but not to others. For example, the 1924 Immigration Act removed the statute of limitations on deportations for entering without a visa, rendering some immigrants "illegal" with the stroke of a pen. Historian Mae Ngai, however, demonstrates how the act was applied unevenly, allowing "illegal" European immigrants to avoid deportations through loopholes in the law that allowed them to visit Canada, thereby enacting a voluntary departure; obtain the necessary visa; and then legally cross back into the United States, thus wiping the slate clean of their illegal status. Simultaneously, immigration officials enforced the law against Mexicans, and hence linked them to illegality.[40]

Unless they had a criminal record, white European immigrants were seen as worthy of the stays of deportation to keep their families intact. Headlines and newspaper stories declared that the bill would "Exempt the Worthy Here Illegally."[41] One senator argued it was inhuman to send immigrants back to Germany or Russia, given the political situations in those countries.[42] Another described a Canadian mother who had entered the country legally with her baby in her arms but had not registered the child, who was thus now deemed "illegal" and would have to be deported.[43] In addition, newspapers ran stories about families of deportees that were "shattered, lives broken, and the possibilities of producing worthwhile citizens...routed, all without reason." An article entitled "Congress Asked to Revise Abusive Deportation Laws" described the woeful tale of Natalia Odlin, a "white Russian" who was at the mercy of "an untractable [sic], unfeeling law that treats criminals and babies alike." The article featured a large picture of twenty-two-year-old Natalia, "whose name was as pretty as she was"; her American husband, Clifford Odlin; and one child, their fair-haired toddler son. The article plainly stated that the Odlins were "poor," yet even this did not get in the way of its sympathetic portrayal— at the same time that Mexicans were being deported for receiving charity and were not allowed into the United States if they were perceived as poor and thus "likely to become a public charge."[44]

The Odlin family's tale of woe differed from the stories about Mexican families that ran in newspapers during the Depression. A *Los Angeles Times* article discussed how "Uncle Sam" was attempting to force thirty-nine "unwanted visitors" to leave the United States, twenty-six of whom were said to be "illegal." What of the other thirteen detainees? They included, the article noted, Simon Alvarado, his wife (no first name given), and their eight American-born children. (The remaining three immigrants were to be deported to Canada and Europe.) There was no discussion of the Alvarado children's rights as citizens to remain in the United States, or of what it meant to deport citizens. Instead, the story went on to quote an immigration officer, M. H. Scott, who described the deportations as "just part of the work that the Immigration Bureau [was] doing in cooperation with the County Department of Charities to relieve taxpayers of the burden of supporting persons not entitled to relief." Officer Scott's comments reveal how laws that do not blatantly discriminate against specific groups are instead "racialized upon enforcement," meaning that racialized groups are targeted or disproportionately affected by the application of the law.[45] In this case, we see how the federal government cooperated with municipal agencies to deport racialized immigrants—and citizens— seen as "unworthy" at the local level.

Not only did the article obscure that these were US citizens, but it further depicted Mexicans as undesirable by portraying them as welfare burdens. Officer Scott explained that the government was working to "eliminate this class of aliens."[46] Scott's comments were in keeping with a long genealogy of officials across the twentieth century who viewed certain groups as "worthy" of government aid, like the Odlins mentioned previously, and others as unworthy, like the Alvarados, in ways that broke along racial lines. Scholars have documented how time and time again receiving government aid has disproportionately stigmatized people of color more than whites, and how debates about poverty, welfare, and remedies for both have been value laden with moral ascriptions.[47]

Furthermore, a picture of the Alvarado family accompanied the article, with a headline separate from and preceding the article that read, "Family of Ten Sent Back to Mexico." The Alvarados' picture was taken in the street, suggesting that they were poor or working-class, as they stood dressed in their everyday clothes. The caption read, "[Alvarado] and his wife acquired eight children in the eleven years they have been here and the county has spent more than $7,000 on them," depicting the children as liabilities rather than assets to American society. The emphasis on the number of children played on the eugenic fears of the late 1920s, discussed previously, but now also helped to link the issue of immigration to welfare. These kinds of visual representations of Mexicans contributed greatly to the notion that the Mexican family, regardless of citizenship status, was a threat.[48]

The fact that no examples of Mexican or Asian families were used in the Kerr Bill hearings to solicit sympathy from Congress, therefore, comes as no surprise. At the time, the United States was still directing mass deportation campaigns against Mexicans, and Asians were banned from immigrating or naturalizing. Of the fourteen members of the congressional immigration committee, only one hailed from California, home to the largest population of Mexicans and Asians, while the rest were from the Midwest or East Coast. None expressed concerns or hopes that the potential act would allow Mexicans or Asians to remain in the country.

Making Deportable Families

Although the Kerr Bill did not ultimately pass, a closer look at the people it would have affected gives a sense of the era's racial logic of citizenship. California in particular was instrumental in shaping general US attitudes about Mexican immigrants. As a hotbed for scientific, medical, and public health standards, programs, and policies, California shaped the meaning of "Mexican" and Mexicans' place in the US racial hierarchy for generation after generation.

For example, while they awaited Congress's decision on the Kerr Bill, the Transportation Division of the Los Angeles County Department of Charities (the innocuous term for the deportation division) took it upon themselves to pull the case files of mixed-status Mexican families that were receiving charity to see how the passage of the bill might impact the Department. Los Angeles was home to the largest population of Mexicans outside of Mexico City, but the fact that it singled out mixed-status Mexican families, even though there were other immigrants receiving charity, reveals the ways in which the enforcement of these laws played out according to local perceptions of who constituted a racial threat; in other words, the law was "racialized upon enforcement."

The Transportation Division worked with the local Immigration and Naturalization office to collect charity and immigration histories for the families flagged for deportation. Although the original county relief records were not preserved, much of the information from these case files was collected in a 1939 University of Southern California (USC) master of social work thesis by Carrie Belle MacCarthy, "A Survey of the Mexican Hardship Cases Active in the Los Angeles County Department of Charities." MacCarthy examines 72 cases of families with one or more deportable members, comprising a total of 313 people. While she groups some cases together for analysis, she discusses many individual case files in great detail, including the reason for deportation, number of children, years in the United States, and how much charity was requested. These accounts make MacCarthy's "Survey" an invaluable source.[49]

MacCarthy was a student in the School of Social Work at USC, established by Emory Bogardus. Bogardus was one of the leading race and immigration experts of his time and had been a student of the sociologist Robert Park, who established the first theory of "race relations." Bogardus coined a theory and method to gauge "social distance," a way of measuring how willing (or unwilling) people were to engage with people dissimilar to them, particularly across racial and ethnic lines. At USC, he established a cottage industry of MA theses looking at Los Angeles's racial and ethnic communities. Like more readily accessed sources produced by leading sociologists of the time, such as the "Survey of Race Relations" archived at Stanford, the USC master's theses reveal how race came to be defined as a problem to be solved.[50] While not housed neatly together in one archive, taken in the aggregate, these are some of the richest extant sources we have that give insight into how racial formation operated during this period for Mexican immigrants. The Transportation Division singled out the cases discussed in the "survey" as potentially deportable based on the fact that they received charity from the county. Charity was defined as assistance in any form from a source funded by taxation. As such, it could involve monetary compensation, but it might also consist of receiving medical care at a city or county hospital, clinic, or sanatorium, even if the patient was referred there by a doctor. In Los Angeles County, receiving assistance from the Bureau of Indigent Relief would clearly qualify as charity, but so did getting care from Rancho de Los Amigos (medical services), Olive View Sanatorium, or the Los Angeles County Hospital. Even seeking aid to bury a family member constituted a form of charity.

Simply receiving charity was not a deportable offense. Receiving charity within five years of immigrating to the United States, however, was. Most of the Mexicans described in the MacCarthy "Survey" had fallen into this trap and were found deportable because they received public assistance within five years of entry.[51] Of the 124 adults involved the cases, only five were born in the United States.[52] Though many had actually lived in the United States for more than five years, sometimes even for decades, a trip to Mexico would restart their LPC clock, essentially reverting their status to the same as recent immigrants, thus making them deportable. In one particular case, a Mrs. Salazar (wives' first names are not provided in the case files) had come to the United States as a child and lived there all of her life. After her husband died, she traveled to Mexico to comfort her mother-in-law. This family obligation restarted her LPC clock, and thus when she sought charity upon her return, she became deportable.[53] Similarly, Ricardo Ramirez had lived in the United States since 1919. He was married with three children, including one from his wife's prior marriage. Ramirez had been gainfully employed until the Depression. In 1932 the family moved to Mexico to try to make a living there, but after four months lawfully returned to the United States. At some point after his return, Ramirez applied for relief. Though he had lived in the United States for twenty years and had only returned to Mexico once in all of that time, his four-month sojourn made him—in addition to his dependent American-born children—deportable.[54]

Many of the children subject to deportation in the survey were Mexican Americans. Of the 184 children in the study, 145 (78.8%) were born in the United States.[55] For example, in the case described previously, Mrs. Salazar, who was found deportable, had three children, all US-born.[56] The cases of these mixed status families again highlight the fact that while the Kerr Bill did not pass, examining the questions and reactions it raised shines a light on one of the first recorded instances of the state grappling with the issue of mixed status families.

Many of the parents who requested aid did so on behalf of their children. Some of this assistance, such as medical care, was solely or mainly for the children; in other words, tax dollars were going to citizens, yet the parents of these citizens were being labeled as public charges and in the process became deportable. In other cases, the aid was not as neatly earmarked for the children: in most of these cases, the parents, who were usually employed in low-paying or part-time jobs, needed to supplement their income to support their family and only at that point sought aid. Since the aid was being used to support the household, which included the children, this was again another example of public assistance being used "properly" (e.g., going to citizens) and the parents being punished for it. We see then not that children were deported along with their parents, but parents were deported because of their children. Thus these children's citizenship did not offer *protection* for their parents, but instead parents were penalized for seeking benefits for their children. One might even go so far as to suggest that the parents were deported for the crime of seeking to uphold their children's rights as citizens.[57]

During this time period, when citizen children were deported along with their immigrant parents, there were no public outcries about "anchor babies." In fact, if we examine the families in the survey, we see that in the case of family deportations, parents often had come to the attention of the county because they sought aid on behalf of their US-born children. In other words, these were not anchor babies but quite the opposite: citizen children who made their immigrant parents deportable. Furthermore, in making their parents deportable, they also became deportable.

Of the seventy-two families listed in the survey, there were eight instances where the mother and father were immigrants and all of the children were citizens. The parents' immigrant status put them in a precarious position. First, when the Depression hit, many immigrants who had been gainfully employed for many years now had no choice but to seek assistance. Any residents who had crossed the border within the past five years were now caught in the LPC window and made vulnerable to deportation. Second, many of the adults in the families had immigrated prior to 1924, when entering the country without a visa did not make immigrants subject to deportation. The 1924 Immigration Act changed the requirements around residency, legal status, and so on, and individuals who could not prove when they entered the country or that they did so legally became "illegal" overnight.

The survey does not contain detailed records on each of these eight cases, but we can gain some insights for the two cases where we have the most details.

Mr. and Mrs. Jesus Garcia had lived in the United States since 1915 and raised six American-born children, settling and becoming firmly rooted in Los Angeles. Except for Mrs. Garcia's mother, who lived in Mexicali, a Mexican border town just a few hours from Los Angeles, most of the

Garcias' relatives lived in Los Angeles and other parts of California. When the Depression hit, Jesus lost his full-time job but eventually secured work as a "yard man" and "laborer." His new wages were not enough to support the family, and so he applied for relief for the first time in 1935. Within a year, the family repatriated to Mexico seeking a better life, but soon returned to Los Angeles. In 1936 they came to the attention of the county when they sought treatment for their twelve-year-old daughter, Dolores, who was suffering from meningitis. She did not recover and received a burial from the county. The bulk of the relief received by the family came in the form of medical and burial services for Dolores, a US citizen; nonetheless, that relief made her parents deportable.

The Mesas moved to the United States as a married couple in the early 1920s (exact year unknown). The couple had four children while living in the United States and "occasionally received relief" beginning shortly after the birth of their first child, Elisa. In 1931 the county repatriated the family to Mexico. The file does not state the reason for repatriation, but given what we know, it is relatively safe to assume it was because they received relief within five years of entry into the United States. Despite being repatriated, the family returned to the United States, which was an immigration violation. For that reason alone, the Mesas were deportable. They did not, however, come to the attention of the county until they sought medical help for their two minor daughters, Elisa and her younger sister Berta. Both girls suffered from tuberculosis and sought care in the county sanatorium.[58]

The Los Angeles County Hospital records reveal that families were sometimes deported directly from the hospital, where the Transportation Division set up a station. For example, in the case of Altagracia Oliva and her children, the outcome was bleak. After being labeled as "mental," she and her seven children, ranging in age from one to fourteen, were deported from the hospital to Mexico City.[59] The records do not indicate the citizenship of anyone in the family. In other cases, children were deported without their parents. In 1938 the Arias girls (ages four, five, and seven), the Miranda boys (ages six and nine), and the Robledo children (ages three, eight, ten, twelve, and fifteen) were deported, along with other patients from the general hospital, after being identified by the Child Welfare Department as good candidates for deportation. Since all were minors, the Department of Charities assigned a "matron" to travel with the children.[60] Emilia Mesa and her newborn (the baby was described as

Deportee Carlos Tamborrell with his children Mary Louise and Carlos Jr., Los Angeles, 1935. Courtesy of the *Los Angeles Times* Photographic Archive, Library Special Collections, Charles E. Young Research Library, UCLA.

being in an incubator) were deported in 1939. In Mesa's case, it appears clear that using the county general hospital's services to give birth to her American citizen child made her deportable.

The state was not concerned with the practice of deporting US-born children because it did not view deporting its own citizens as a moral issue; it was more concerned with the cost of raising those children, should their parents be deported. This was evident in the case of the Rojo family.

Juan Rojo had returned to Mexico in 1930 after the brickyard where he worked closed. He worked odd jobs but could not support his family, and returned to the United States but could find only irregular and low-paying employment. When he then applied for charity assistance to help support his family, the county brought deportation charges against him.[61] Juan Rojo stated he would not take his three minor US-born children to Mexico with him, meaning the county would be left responsible for supporting them, which county officials did not want. (The case record does not state if Mrs. Rojo would also be deported or why she was not able to care for the children.) As a result, the county considered allowing Rojo to stay, deeming this a less expensive and less complicated option. (The case study does not indicate what the county ultimately decided.) It is not clear why Rojo's threat of leaving his children was taken seriously enough to prompt the county to consider a reprieve. Perhaps his threat was deemed credible because he was a father, whereas the idea of a mother leaving her children would seem inconceivable and unpardonable. Or perhaps it was simply because Rojo leaving his children behind would have cost the county money; this had happened in at least one prior case, and the county incurred the expense of hiring someone to look after the abandoned minors.[62]

The Second Generation

The fact that there was no uproar at the time over Mexican Americans being regularly repatriated and deported along with their parents strongly suggests that these children's American citizenship was not readily acknowledged.

Furthermore, this is the period in which long-standing associations between Mexican racial identity and criminality started being extended to Mexican American youth. Illegality had been central to racial constructions of Mexicans already, but this had mainly been reserved for adults and most prominently in relation to border crossing. But in the "survey" cases, twelve of the seventy-two families had youths who were or had been interned in a state school (juvenile hall) or were now wards of the court.[63] While the case files do not provide much information (they do not include the violation and only sometimes state where the youth was interned), these cases represent one of the earliest incidences linking Mexican youth with delinquency.

While youth described in the "survey" were not deported for juvenile delinquency, their record put their families in a precarious position. First, it helped mark the entire family as immoral at a time when morality (long a prerequisite for immigration to the United States generally) was being upheld as one of the conditions of staying a deportation under the Kerr Bill. Second, spending time in a county or state institution (including youth detention) was considered as receiving a form of relief, which again was a deportable offense if a family had been in the United States for five years or less. As such, not only did violations committed by a youth cast aspersions on the entire family; it was also a way that young citizens (Mexican Americans) helped negatively racialize their own immigrant parents (Mexicans). Had the person who committed the crime been an immigrant, he would have been immediately deported. In these cases, however, illegal activity on the part of citizens became part of an immigrant's deportation case file—yet another link between criminality and immigration, in which immigrant parents were made deportable by their children.

Conclusion

The Los Angeles County Department of Charities deportable cases serve as a window into the 1930s and how during this key moment the public failed to recognize the rights of Mexican Americans. In the 1930s, for the first time, the second generation demographically eclipsed the first generation of Mexican immigrants. Yet the acquisition of de jure citizenship did not readily translate into social citizenship for this new generation. The dramatic growth in the number of US-born Mexican Americans coincided with the most massive deportation of Mexicans the United States had seen up to that time—the second generation arrived on the scene at a time of intense contestation over who was fit to be a citizen. Throughout this chapter, I have demonstrated it was not only the rights of adults, many of them immigrants, that were violated, but also those of US-born children of Mexican descent. While the historiography has highlighted that Mexican American children were deported with their parents, it is rarely merited more than a passing reference. However, the "Survey" cases—compiled from data produced by an agency in the largest receiving city for Mexican immigrants at the time—suggest that this was much a more widespread problem than previously understood. Nearly 80% of the deported children in that sample were US-born, demonstrating the ease with which American citizenship can be ignored when the dominant culture does not want to recognize it.

———————

This essay is dedicated to the memory of my father, Héctor Molina. I would like to thank Kenyon Zimmer, the participants and audience members at the "Deportation in the Americas: Histories of Exclusion" symposium at UT Arlington, and the participants in the Tepoztlán Institute for the Transnational History of the Americas, as well as Ian Fusselman and Isabella Furth for their editorial artistry and librarians Harold Colson and Annelise Sklar for their research expertise.

Notes

1. Molly Hennessy-Fiske, "Texas Denying Children Rights, Suit Says," *Los Angeles Times*, July 18, 2015; Manny Fernandez, "Immigrants Fight Texas' Birth Certificate Rules," *New York Times*, September 17, 2015.

2. Julia Preston, "Texas Is Forced to Ease a Policy on Immigrants," *New York Times*, July 25, 2016.

3. Ian Haney-López, *White by Law: The Legal Construction of Race* (New York: New York University Press, 1996).

4. Natalia Molina, *How Race Is Made in America: Immigration, Citizenship, and the Historical Power of Racial Scripts* (Berkeley and Los Angeles: University of California, 2014), chapter 2; Reginald Horsman, *Race and Manifest Destiny: The Origins of American Racial Anglo-Saxonism* (Cambridge: Harvard University Press, 1981).

5. On deviant cultural representations of Latina motherhood, see Laura Briggs, *Reproducing Empire: Race, Sex, Science, and U.S. Imperialism in Puerto Rico* (Berkeley: University of California Press, 2002); Leo R. Chavez, *The Latino Threat: Constructing Immigrants, Citizens, and the Nation* (Stanford University Press, 2008); Laura E. Gomez, *Misconceiving Mothers: Legislators, Prosecutors, and the Politics of Prenatal Drug Exposure* (Philadelphia: Temple University Press, 1997).

6. For example, in March 2015, Homeland Security cracked an illegal ring that offered to help Chinese women secure tourist visas to the United States as well as medical care and a place to stay (dubbed "maternity hotels") for the purpose of giving birth and securing US citizenship for their children. Taiwanese, Korean, and Turkish women had also utilized these services. These activities, however, did not lead to any kind of long-term stigmatization for these groups, perhaps because these were middle-class and wealthy women, or because Asians are today considered a "model minority" in the United States. Thus the stigma did not

hold in the same way it does for Mexicans, who are generally associated with illegality. "'Maternity Tourism' Raids Target California Operations Catering to Chinese," *Los Angeles Times*, March 3, 2015.

7. Legally there is no such thing as an anchor baby, since the US-born child of an immigrant woman would need to wait until he or she was an adult to sponsor his or her parents for citizenship; see Kevin R. Johnson, "'Aliens' and the U.S. Immigration Laws: The Social and Legal Construction of Nonpersons," *University of Miami Inter-American Law Review* 28, no. 2 (1996): 263–92.

8. While the proposition passed by an overwhelming majority in 1994, the courts immediately barred implementation of the law, pending settlement of the legal challenges lodged against it. On the gendered implications of Proposition 187, see Pierrette Hondagneu-Sotelo, "Women and Children First: New Directions in Anti-immigrant Politics," *Socialist Review* 25, no. 1 (1995): 169–90.

9. Oscar Lewis and Oliver La Farge, *Five Families: Mexican Case Studies in the Culture of Poverty* (New York: Basic Books, 1959); Oscar Lewis, *La Vida: A Puerto Rican Family in the Culture of Poverty* (New York: Random House, 1966).

10. See Rickie Solinger, *Wake Up Little Susie: Single Pregnancy and Race before Roe v. Wade* (New York: Routledge, 1992); Rickie Solinger, *Pregnancy and Power: A Short History of Reproductive Politics in America* (New York: New York University Press, 2005); Dorothy Roberts, *Killing the Black Body: Race, Reproduction, and the Meaning of Liberty* (New York: Vintage, 1997).

11. While there was a backlash against Mexicans' ability to become US citizens in the aftermath of the US war with Mexico, court cases contesting Mexicans' citizenship focused on adults and their rights to naturalize. Natalia Molina, "The Long Arc of Dispossession: Racial Capitalism and Contested Notions of Citizenship in the U.S.-Mexico Borderlands in the Early Twentieth Century," *Western Historical Quarterly* 45, no. 4 (2014): 431–47; Arnoldo De León, *In Re Ricardo Rodríguez: An Attempt at Chicano Disenfranchisement in San Antonio, 1896–1897* (San Antonio, TX: Caravel Press, 1979). On expansion and contestation of birthright citizenship, see the discussion of *United States v. Wong Kim Ark* (1898) in Erika Lee, *At America's Gates: Chinese Immigration During the Exclusion Era, 1882–1943* (Chapel Hill: University of North Carolina Press, 2003). In my book, I examine the long history of birthright citizenship in the nineteenth century leading up to *United States v. Wong Kim Ark* (1896) and efforts to further broaden the parameters of birthright citizenship in the twentieth century. See Molina, *How Race Is Made in America*, chapter 3.

12. George Sánchez, *Becoming Mexican American: Ethnicity, Culture, and Identity in Chicano Los Angeles, 1900–1945* (New York: Oxford University Press, 1993); William V. Flores and Rina Benmayor, *Latino Cultural Citizenship: Claiming Identity, Space, and Rights* (Boston: Beacon Press, 1997).

13. Eduardo Bonilla-Silva, *Racism without Racists: Color-Blind Racism and the Persistence of Racial Inequality in the United States* (Lanham: Rowman & Littlefield, 2006).

14. A few years earlier, the 1921 Immigration Act had initiated a quota system that became known as the national origins principle. Immigration from eastern

and southern Europe was limited to 3 percent of the population of each designated European country's citizens in the United States at the time of the 1910
census. That amount was reduced to 2 percent of the population in the 1890
census under the 1924 Immigration Act.

15. Mexican Fact-Finding Committee, *Mexicans in California: Report of Gover-
nor C. C. Young's Mexican Fact Finding Committee* (Sacramento: California State
Printing Office, 1930), 20–23; Mark Reisler, *By the Sweat of Their Brow: Mexican
Immigrant Labor in the United States, 1900–1940* (Westport, CT: Greenwood
Press, 1976), 183, n. 4.

16. Molina, *How Race Is Made in America*, 22–23.

17. The bills proposed different formulas for restriction; see Reisler, *By the
Sweat of Their Brow*, 198–226.

18. On eugenic anxieties about white births being eclipsed by immigrants, see
Alexandra Minna Stern, *Eugenic Nation: Faults and Frontiers of Better Breeding
in Modern America* (Berkeley: University of California Press, 2005).

19. House Committee on Immigration and Naturalization, United States Con-
gress, *Seasonal Agricultural Laborers from Mexico. Hearings January 28 and 29,
February 2, 9, 11, and 23, 1926, on H.R. 6741, H.R. 7559, H.R. 9036* (Washington,
DC: US Government Printing Office, 1926), 14, 15.

20. C. M. Goethe, "Other Aspects of the Problem," *Current History* (August
1928): 767.

21. Samuel J. Holmes, "Peon Immigrants," *Eugenics: A Journal of Race Better-
ment*, November 1928, 36.

22. "Perils of the Mexican Invasion," *North American Review*, May 1929, 227.

23. Elsewhere, I argue that public health issues, including disease rates and
birth rates, became central to scapegoating Mexicans during the Depression.
Natalia Molina, *Fit to Be Citizens?: Public Health and Race in Los Angeles, 1879–
1939* (Berkeley: University of California Press, 2006), chapter 4.

24. On the Page Law, see Eithne Luibheid, *Entry Denied: Controlling Sexuality
at the Border* (Minneapolis: University of Minnesota Press, 2002); Leti Volpp,
"Divesting Citizenship: On Asian American History and the Loss of Citizenship
through Marriage," *UCLA Law Review* 53 (2005): 405–83.

25. Sarah Deutsch, *No Separate Refuge: Culture, Class, and Gender on an Anglo-
Hispanic Frontier in the American Southwest, 1880–1940* (New York: Oxford Uni-
versity Press, 1987); Vicki L. Ruiz, *From Out of the Shadows: Mexican Women in
Twentieth-Century America* (New York: Oxford University Press, 1998); George
Sánchez, "'Go After the Women': Americanization and the Mexican Immigrant
Woman, 1915–1929," in *A Multi-cultural Reader in U.S. Women's History*, ed. El-
len DuBois and Vicki Ruiz (New York: Routledge, 1990), 284–97.

26. Francisco Balderrama, *In Defense of La Raza: The Los Angeles Mexican Con-
sulate and the Mexican Community, 1929–1936* (Tucson: University of Arizona
Press, 1982); Francisco E. Balderrama and Raymond Rodríguez, *Decade of Betrayal:
Mexican Repatriation in the 1930s* (Albuquerque: University of New Mexico Press,
1995); Abraham Hoffman, *Unwanted Mexican Americans in the Great Depression:
Repatriation Pressures, 1929–1939* (Tucson: University of Arizona Press, 1974).

27. A notable exception is Marla Ramirez, "Contested Illegality: Three Generations of Exclusion through Mexican 'Repatriation' and the Politics of Immigration Law, 1920–2005" (PhD diss., University of California, Santa Barbara, 2015).

28. Camille Guerin-Gonzales, *Mexican Workers and American Dreams: Immigration, Repatriation, and California Farm Labor, 1900–1939* (New Brunswick, NJ: Rutgers University Press, 1991), 107.

29. Ibid.; Balderrama and Rodríguez, *Decade of Betrayal.*

30. The Senate counterpart bill was 2.2969, and both collectively were known as the Kerr-Coolidge Bill. The bill was introduced three times but did not actually come up to a vote until the third time. The provisions were slightly modified in the different versions, but the basic proposal remained the same.

31. I deliberately refer to the potential deportee as "he," since it was usually men who were considered the "head of the household" and thus whose cases could come before the Secretary of Labor.

32. At the same time, the Kerr Bill also gave more power to the federal government to deport immigrants convicted of a crime. According to sociologist Cybelle Fox, the Roosevelt administration supported the bill in an attempt to look tough on crime when it came to immigrants, hoping that this would deflect criticism of its more liberal proposals, such as those including aliens in relief projects. Cybelle Fox, *Three Worlds of Relief: Race, Immigration, and the American Welfare State from the Progressive Era to the New Deal* (Princeton, NJ: Princeton University Press, 2012), 205.

33. Committee on Immigration, United States Senate, *Deportation of Criminals, Preservation of Family Units, Permit Noncriminal Aliens to Legalize Their Status, Second Session, on S. 2969, a Bill to Authorize the Deportation of Criminals, to Guard Against the Separations from Their Families of Aliens of the Noncriminal Classes, to Provide for Legalizing the Residence in the United States of Certain Classes of Aliens, and for Other Purposes* (Washington, DC: Government Printing Office, 1936), 19. Organized labor also protested potentially not deporting immigrants who could be taking American jobs, and there were some concerns that immigrants might try to marry or have a child in order to remain in the United States.

34. See Sec. 2, Immigration Act of 1882, 47th Congress, Sess. I (22 Statutes-at-Large 214).

35. See Sec. 11, Immigration Act of 1891, 51st Congress, Sess. II (26 Statutes-at-Large 1086).

36. Elsewhere I demonstrate how the LPC charge was wielded against Mexican labor activists in the 1940s. Molina, *How Race Is Made in America*, chapter 4.

37. Coleman Jones, "Five Immigration Bills Seek Easier Criminal Deportation, Humane Rules for Desirables," *The China Press*, August 18, 1934.

38. Matthew Frye Jacobson, *Whiteness of a Different Color: European Immigrants and the Alchemy of Race* (Cambridge, MA: Harvard University, 1998). See also David Roediger, *Working toward Whiteness: How America's Immigrants Became White: The Strange Journey from Ellis Island to the Suburbs* (New York: Basic Books, 2005); David Roediger, *The Wages of Whiteness: Race and the Mak-*

ing of the American Working Class (London: Verso, 1991).

39. Samuel Dickstein, "Condemns Moves to Harass Aliens," *New York Times*, June 30, 1935.

40. Mae M. Ngai, *Impossible Subjects: Illegal Aliens and the Making of Modern America* (Princeton: Princeton University Press, 2004), chapter 2. Khalil Gibran Muhammad demonstrates that once settled in cities, white ethnics continued to receive differential treatment from Progressive Era reformers and policy makers who attempted to Americanize them while simultaneously linking blacks to criminality. See Khalil Gibran Muhammad, *The Condemnation of Blackness: Race, Crime, and the Making of Modern Urban America* (Cambridge, MA: Harvard University Press, 2010).

41. For example, see "Senators Approve Bill to Oust Aliens: Committee Reports Plan to Deport Criminals, Exempt the Worthy Here Illegally," *New York Times*, March 29, 1936; and "Alien Deportation Bill is Approved," *Washington Post*, March 29, 1936.

42. "Deporting Aliens Called 'Inhuman,'" *New York Times*, April 23, 1936.

43. *Deportation of Criminals, Preservation of Family Units*, 16–17.

44. Robert T. DeVore, "Congress Asked to Revise Abusive Deportation Laws," *Washington Post*, May 13, 1934.

45. Molina, *Fit to Be Citizens?*, 35, 39, 150, 214.

46. "Thirty-Nine Deported as Unwanted Visitors," *Los Angeles Times*, October 23, 1935.

47. Alice O'Connor, *Poverty Knowledge: Social Science, Social Policy, and the Poor in Twentieth-Century U.S. History* (Princeton, NJ: Princeton University Press, 2001); Ira Katznelson, *When Affirmative Action Was White: An Untold History of Racial Inequality in Twentieth-Century America* (New York: W.W. Norton, 2005); George Lipsitz, "The Possessive Investment in Whiteness: Racialized Social Democracy and the 'White' Problem in American Studies," *American Quarterly* 47, no. 3 (1995): 369–87; Michael B. Katz, *The Undeserving Poor: From the War on Poverty to the War on Welfare* (New York: Pantheon Books, 1989); Robin D. G. Kelley, *Yo' Mama's Disfunktional!: Fighting the Culture Wars in Urban America* (Boston: Beacon Press, 1997).

48. On the importance of visual representations on informing racial categories, see Natalia Molina, "Illustrating Cultural Authority: Medicalized Representations of Mexican Communities in Early-Twentieth-Century Los Angeles," *Aztlán: A Journal of Chicano Studies* 28 (2003): 127–43; John Tagg, *The Burden of Representation: Essays on Photographies and Histories* (Amherst: University of Massachusetts Press, 1988); Laura Wexler, *Tender Violence: Domestic Visions in an Age of U.S. Imperialism* (Chapel Hill: University of North Carolina Press, 2000).

49. I use MacCarthy's "survey" primarily as a source of data; I do not draw on her analysis except where stated.

50. On the "Survey of Race Relations" and the role it played in defining the "Oriental Problem," see Henry Yu, *Thinking Orientals: Migration, Contact, and Exoticism in Modern America* (Oxford, NY: Oxford University Press, 2001).

51. Carrie Bell MacCarthy, "A Survey of the Mexican Hardship Cases Active in the Los Angeles County Department of Charities, Los Angeles, California" (MA thesis, University of Southern California, 1939), 21.

52. Ibid., 22. There were a total of 313 people in the study.

53. Ibid., 39.

54. Ibid., 77–78.

55. Ibid., 22.

56. Ibid., 39.

57. Ibid., 54.

58. Ibid., 52.

59. Letter to Board of Supervisors from Department of Charities, August 9, 1938, Board of Supervisors' Minutes, Los Angeles County Board of Supervisors, hereafter cited as B of S.

60. Letters to Board of Supervisors from Department of Charities, August 9 and May 16, 1938, B of S.

61. MacCarthy, "A Survey of the Mexican Hardship Cases," 37.

62. Balderrama and Rodríguez, *Decade of Betrayal*, 81.

63. MacCarthy, "A Survey of the Mexican Hardship Cases," 26.

7

A Half-Century of Defending Migrants

THE AMERICAN COMMITTEE FOR THE PROTECTION OF THE FOREIGN BORN AND THE REPURPOSING OF IMMIGRANT RIGHTS ADVOCACY, 1959–1980

Rachel Ida Buff

Introduction: Repurposing Walter Prescott Webb

Walter Prescott Webb, after whom this book series is named, inaugurated a spatial approach to the study of American history. Following Frederick Jackson Turner, he argued for the transformative power of frontiers in American as well as global history. In work that in many ways paralleled that of his European contemporaries of the Annales School, Webb proposed a synthetic narrative of economic and political modernity emanating from the central process of "civilized people advancing into wilderness."[1] For Webb as for Turner, frontier encounters infused American politics with freedom, individualism, and equal access to citizenship in a sovereign and independent nation. Progress westward involved the colonization of the lands beyond what Webb deemed the "great frontier," which bounded the "known" or "civilized" world. Webb saw colonization as a positive process, leading to emancipation and progress. Since his central narrative concerned the development of Anglo-American national culture, Webb's work took little notice of indigenous inhabitants or of other denizens who did not benefit from the institutions he celebrated.

Much of Webb's work about the West has itself been eclipsed by the moving frontier of historical scholarship. Contemporary Western historians have been among the many voices challenging his vision of predestined Anglo-American ascension in the region, as well as his categorizing of the denizens of the region as "wild Indians" and racially degenerate Mexicans. Indigenous cultures and ecosystems flourished well west of Webb's boundary of the ninety-eighth parallel long before Euroamerican contact. Scholars have illuminated the hybrid and contested process of multiracial settlement in the West, supplanting the idea of the frontier with the centrality of the border. The ninety-eighth parallel appears now to have bounded a particular historiographic imagination more than it delimited settlement and progress.[2] So what remains of Webb's legacy? What of his vision can be productively repurposed and applied to contemporary scholarship? How does this imagining of "frontiers" jibe with evolving awareness of the central role of empire in shaping US history? Is this legacy of any use to an immigration historian like myself, who focuses on the stories of those whose global migrations pitched them up against established national boundaries—what Webb himself called "the sharp edge of sovereignty"?[3]

This chapter documents the existence of an immigrant rights movement that thrived in the twentieth-century United States across frontiers of space as well as time. This movement sought to blunt the deployment of this "sharp edge of sovereignty" against multiracial communities through immigration enforcement. Activists organized against the cutting blade of what they called "the deportation terror." Working under the umbrella of the American Committee for the Protection of the Foreign Born (ACPFB), this movement brought migrants from a wide range of national origins together on the West and East Coasts, in the Southwest and the Midwest, in cities as well as in rural communities. Originating in 1932 out of a Popular Front–era coalition between liberal and left-wing advocacy organizations, the organization survived repression during the early Cold War to become actively engaged in the emergence of new forms of community organizing and politics in the 1970s. The ACPFB functioned with a tiny national office in New York City and satellite committees that arose around the country in response to deportation crises. With support from the national office, these local committees represented individuals against deportation and denaturalization, while the national office continued to press for broad reforms in immigration policy. While the ACPFB faced persecution during the Cold War, being listed as a subversive organization between 1958 and 1965, it survived to continue advocating for new cohorts of the foreign born, becoming involved in the origins of the contemporary immigrant rights movement in the early 1980s.

The ACPFB represented migrants from around a world transformed, in Webb's account, by the "discovery" and subsequent exploitation of the West. Their twentieth century struggles for access to democratic rights were quite different than the narrative Webb delineated, in which European encounters with the West shaped democratic institutions. At the same time, in a way that Webb could not quite see from his westward-looking orientation, immigrant rights advocates also responded to global and hemispheric transformations by struggling to assert democracy. This essay repurposes Webb's signal concern for the expansion of democratic institutions in the American West by looking at the development of immigrant rights activism across the nation.

Immigrant Rights Advocacy and the "Sharp Edge of Sovereignty"

At first glance, discussion of the ongoing existence of an immigrant rights movement across the twentieth century seems to run counter to Webb's insights about the ways western settlement transformed American culture. As Webb laid out in *The Great Frontier*, the American experience until the twentieth century was characterized by uncontested possession of empty lands and the democratic potential of their occupation. The "great boom" of accumulation enabled by the wealth of the West fueled modernity in the United States as well as Europe. And while the economic benefits of the boom were not equally distributed, the institutional democracy that came about as a result of this encounter was available to all. Webb wrote: "The settlers were citizens moving into territory owned by the nation. The only thing that distinguished these citizens and this territory from the older region was the fact that the processes current were a step or two behind the processes of the older region, say in Virginia or Massachusetts."[4]

Webb himself was aware that this democratic abundance was historically finite. In *The Texas Rangers: A Century of Frontier Defense*, he wrote a heroic narrative that pitched the vigilante Rangers against the "sharp edge" of a now-defined US-Mexico border. Viewed another way, frontier democracy was staged against the development of the Texas Rangers and subsequent Border Patrol, founded in 1924. Immigrant rights activists contended with the increased power of immigration enforcement, both at the border and, increasingly, further inland in what legal historian Daniel Kanstroom has called "postentry social control." As the border migrated inland, migrants were compelled to reinvent and defend democracy.[5]

Of necessity, the ACPFB worked at the frontiers of the nation, whether those frontiers existed physically in the Southwest and Texas, or political-ly in the lines drawn between foreign and native-born denizens. Just as Webb's West contained unprecedented wealth, the strength and wealth of the ACPFB lay in its expanse: the organization was able to persist because it survived in diverse migrant communities separated by space and time. Precisely because of the agility of the organization's networked, diffuse structure, there were practical impediments to extinguishing it. Perhaps the "wide open spaces" represented for Webb in the lands west of the ninety-eighth meridian from the sixteenth through nineteenth centuries were to be found in immigrant spaces in the twentieth.

Writing a half-century after Webb, Ethnic Studies scholar George Lipsitz wrote of the "long fetch" of history—the ways that particular episodes re-verberate through time and space, coming back around to reshape seem-ingly unrelated moments. Lipsitz used this term to describe the power of music, but perhaps frontiers, too, can have long fetches.[6]

By contemplating issues of regional and historical difference, my work on the ACPFB takes a page out of Webb's book. Immigrant rights organiz-ing took various forms in different places and times, in ever-changing cir-cumstances and among disparate migrant communities. Although united under the ACPFB umbrella and by an analysis of global colonialism that in some ways resembled Webb's map of the world, advocates confront-ed quite different situations on the ground. Racial hierarchies and local allegiances had the potential to cause division; such rifts, in turn, could be exploited by various disciplinary agents bent on undermining immi-grant organizing. The ACPFB created collaborative channels that allowed disparate immigrant rights advocates to connect and to repurpose strate-gies originating in one particular space and time for use in another. Such repurposing was central to the long immigrant rights movement of the twentieth and twenty-first centuries.

In repurposing immigrant rights, we might also repurpose the geo-graphical vision of Walter Prescott Webb. While Webb and the ACPFB occupied the same historical time, they inhabited separate worlds that were connected only though the support of some of Webb's colleagues in academia for the work of the ACPFB. Webb's unique concern with space can be instructive about not just a singular experience of democracy, but of the importance of place, and about the ways these geographic differences shape history. Just as Webb saw the frontier reinvigorating national democratic institutions, successive cohorts of migrants, familiar with the "sharp edge of sovereignty," infused the ACPFB with innovations in new campaigns for rights and justice.

Certain episodes in immigration enforcement recur across time, space, and migrant cohorts, requiring from immigrant rights advocates both an awareness of the past and new strategies to combat repression. The urbanization of immigration enforcement began with surveillance of Chinese American communities in the West during the early twentieth century and was reinvented to suit subsequent crises: during the era of the Palmer raids, the Cold War militarism of Operation Wetback, the Nixon-era counterinsurgency-influenced Area Control dragnets, and contemporary Homeland Security practices. Though deemed illegal by the US Supreme Court in 1975 in a case supported by the ACPFB, arrests of individuals based on foreign-born appearance recurred in Arizona under State Bill 1070 in 2011.[7]

Incidences of urban dragnets against the foreign-born crisscross the continent as well as the twentieth and twenty-first centuries. Contending with each, advocates responded to local conditions with specific alliances and resources. At the same time, they deployed the ACPFB's collaborative channels to access an archive of discourses and strategies, repurposing those left over from prior struggles to suit conditions on the ground.

The sections that follow detail the repurposing of a specific document, and subsequently the ways that ACPFB activists drew on the organization's collaborative channels to forge new coalitions against the deportation terror. This geographic and historical repurposing shaped immigrant rights advocacy in the 1970s, a time in which global migration was being transformed by national immigration policy as well as shifting economic structures. Finally, I consider the way in which the repurposing of immigrant rights advocacy across space and time might add to our understanding of immigration history.

Repurposing Immigrant Rights Discourse:
"Our Badge of Infamy"

In 1971 the Los Angeles Center for Autonomous Social Action (CASA) re-issued a pamphlet entitled "Our Badge of Infamy." First published by the New York headquarters of the ACPFB in 1959 as part of a petition to the United Nations protesting the "treatment of the Mexican immigrant in the United States," this rather extraordinary document was the product of long collaboration between immigrant rights organizers on the East and West Coasts. Its repurposing by CASA indicates the persistence of this collaboration across time as well as space. These two versions of "Our Badge of Infamy" connect political movements usually considered historically and geographically distinct. Only the cover changes between first and second version: the prose and analysis remains unchanged.

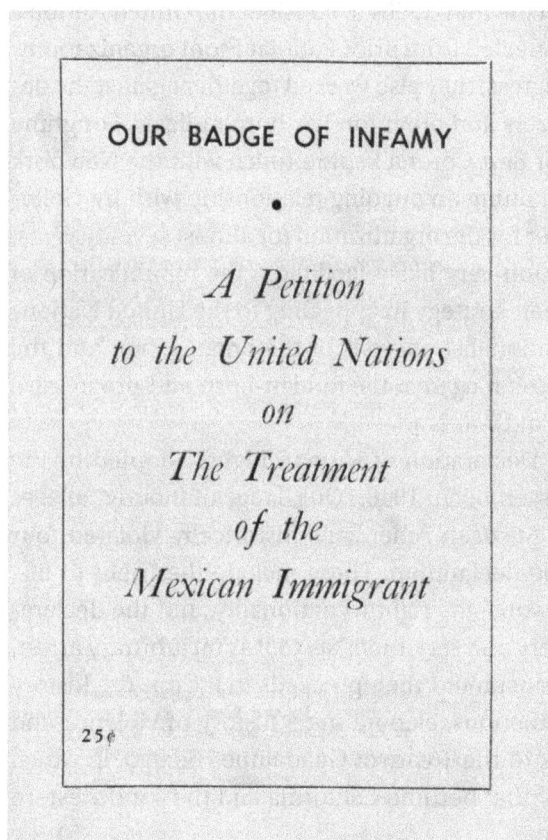

OUR BADGE OF INFAMY

•

A Petition

to the United Nations

on

The Treatment

of the

Mexican Immigrant

25¢

Original edition of *Our Badge of Infamy*, 1959. Courtesy of the American Left Ephemera Collection, 1875–2015. Archives Service Center, University of Pittsburgh.

The year the pamphlet was first issued (1959) saw the national office of the ACPFB engaged in ongoing organizing work against national origins quotas and the enhanced deportation provisions of the McCarran-Walter Act. At the same time, the New York office coordinated with the Los Angeles branch to organize within Mexican American communities contending with the ongoing depredations of Operation Wetback and border enforcement that increasingly crept north to Los Angeles.[8]

Sheltering under the umbrella of a national organization that was itself hit hard by federal repression of organizations suspected of Communist ties, immigrant rights advocates on both coasts worked together on fundraising, public relations, and legal defense for those in deportation proceedings. By collaborating on the creation of "Our Badge of Infamy," they simultaneously petitioned the United Nations to address the ongoing crisis of Mexican American rights. The New York and Los Angeles offices strategized together about how and where to petition for the rights of the foreign-born, and began in the mid-1950s to consider the United Nations. These organizers were connected from prior Popular Front organizations, such as the Civil Right Congress; they also worked together against the deportations of labor organizers and other foreign-born radicals. Longtime West Coast labor organizer Bert Corona kept in touch with the New York office of the ACPFB, maintaining an ongoing relationship with Ira Gollobin, who worked as a lawyer for the organization for almost seventy years. Corona's ongoing connection very likely facilitated the republication of "Our Badge of Infamy." Their strategy in appealing to the United Nations indicates both the internationalist analysis of the organization and the severity of domestic repression against the foreign-born and progressive activists during the early Cold War era.[9]

Invoking the Universal Declaration of Human Rights adopted by the United Nations General Assembly in 1948, "Our Badge of Infamy" alleges that the US treatment of Mexican Americans historically violated four of the central tenets of the declaration. These include the "right to life, liberty and security of person," the right to nationality, and the declaration's explicit ban on "slavery and servitude," as well as on arbitrary arrest, detention, and exile. The document then proceeds to lay out the history of these human rights infractions, elaborating a history of violence and repression that dates back to the Treaty of Guadalupe Hidalgo, in which Mexico ceded the territory that became California and the southwestern United States.

The narrative related by "Our Badge of Infamy" includes citizens, migrants, and contract laborers. Unlike the analysis prevalent in organizations such as the United Farm Workers in the early 1970s, the pamphlet connected the labor struggles of Mexican American workers to the importation of migrant contract workers implemented by the Bracero Program in 1946. Corona eventually worked with UFW leader Cesar Chavez to include undocumented workers in his organizing efforts, rather than excluding them as a threat to the wages of citizens and legal residents.[10]

In this telling, the deportation and denaturalization cases against Latinx labor organizers such as Nicaraguan-born Humberto Silex of the Union of Mine, Mill, and Smelter Workers in El Paso are part of the same history as the 1958 deaths of twelve braceros unable to escape a fire in a crowded truck. The land loss and terror suffered by Mexican Americans in the Southwest and Texas after 1848 appear as a component of ongoing struggles for labor and immigrant rights. The US-Mexico border arrives as a consequence of the Mexican-American War, but it does not determine the human rights of the people living on either side of it. The pamphlet describes the immiseration prevalent in border communities, as well as widespread police abuses of Mexican American citizens as part of the ongoing abrogation of Mexican American human rights. While condemning the treatment of migrant laborers and the raids characteristic of Operation Wetback, the document goes further, indicting epidemic police violence toward Mexican Americans.[11]

Preceding similar moves in key texts in Chicanx/Latinx history by more than a decade, the border-spanning prose of "Our Badge of Infamy" emanates from the multiracial solidarity of the Popular Front. Articulating a history that would have been familiar to California civil rights advocates such as the Asociación Nacional Mexicana-Americana, it draws heavily on what historian Michael Denning calls the "multi-ethnic internationalism" characteristic of California's Popular Front. Perceptible in the writings of lawyer-activist Carey McWilliams, this "multi-ethnic internationalism" also informs "Shame of a Nation: Police-State Terror against Mexican Americans in the U.S.A.," a 1954 indictment of Operation Wetback published by the Los Angeles Committee for the Protection of the Foreign Born that clearly influenced "Our Badge of Infamy."

Historian David Gutiérrez characterizes the Mexican American advocacy prose of this era as "emotionally charged rhetoric to deride campaigns such as Operation Wetback, describing them as manifestations of 'martial law' and 'pogroms' that smacked of the odious repatriation campaigns of the Great Depression, the wartime relocation of the Nisei, and even the Holocaust."[12] As Gutiérrez indicates, this prose emanated from multiracial struggles in California. It therefore contained appeals to the historical experiences of diverse migrant communities.

The Los Angeles CPFB emerged from coalitions made in the predominantly Jewish and Mexican American neighborhood of Boyle Heights. Early leaders included Russian Jewish labor leader Rose Chernin and Korean American architect and activist David Hyun. The organization fought deportation and denaturalization efforts against a wide range of foreign-born individuals. Their organizing work against Operation Wetback and its effects on Mexican American communities drew on this coalition work to mobilize a multiethnic and multiracial base. The LACPFB recognized that the raids, in the words of historian Natalia Molina, "undermined the rights of all, not just Mexicans."[13]

Through the multifaceted pipeline of the ACPFB, the "multi-ethnic internationalism" of California advocacy prose travelled between the West and East Coasts, accumulating additional meanings. The signers of "Our Badge of Infamy" were all ACPFB members, including Louise Pettibone Smith, who succeeded Abner Green as executive secretary after Green's untimely death in 1959. A Wellesley professor and the granddaughter of an abolitionist minister, Smith had been active in the defense of Julius and Ethel Rosenberg, as well as a member of the ACPFB; in 1971, she became executive secretary of the New York Committee to Free Angela Davis.[14] Other signatories belonged to organizations in Oregon, Utah, Michigan, and Connecticut. Their involvement with immigrant rights advocacy immersed these individuals in an internationalist critique of racial inequality and the broad human rights discourse surrounding the founding of the United Nations. Like California's advocacy prose, these discourses conceived of immigrant rights in broad, multiracial terms.[15]

Prior to "Our Badge of Infamy," the East Coast branch of the ACPFB tended to contextualize deportation and the repression of the foreign born in terms of white supremacy and what it called "anti-American" traditions of repression dating back to the Revolutionary Era. Its opposition to the repressive McCarran-Walter Act characterized the law as white supremacist, emanating from antiblack racism and anti-Asian immigration policy. Except where they specifically engaged in defense cases on behalf of Latinx like Humberto Silex, the prose of the national office referenced Mexican American history infrequently. This narrative took global white supremacy seriously, but tended to focus on the European, Asian, and West Indian cohorts who formed the organization on the East Coast. During the Cold War, the bulk of the work of the ACPFB consisted of defending leftist Euro-Americans against deportation. Bert Corona remembered that the Left, including the ACPFB, was much slower to defend Latinx deportees like Luisa Moreno and Humberto Silex than it was to defend "those of European descent."[16]

ACPFB rhetoric was antiracist, but not necessarily cognizant of the particular threats faced by Mexican American communities. For example, a memo featured at an ACPFB conference to repeal the McCarran-Walter Act in 1954 and likely penned by Executive Secretary Abner Green or Gollobin, both second-generation Jewish Americans, explained: "For the past 75 years we have taken an increasingly contemptuous and superior attitude toward two-thirds or three quarters of the world's population which is not white. This attitude developed despite the growing worldwide recognition and understanding of the contributions the colored peoples have made to civilization and are in a position to contribute to make. But with the passage of the Chinese Exclusion Act in 1882 we continued this anti-democratic development which culminated in the racist Walter-McCarran Law of 1952."[17]

The anti-American tradition of racism described in much ACPFB prose ran parallel to the abuses of Mexican Americans detailed in "Our Badge of Infamy." In a 1948 article published in *Jewish Life*, "Democracy and the Deportation Laws," Gollobin details the central role that nativism against the Chinese, as well as antiradical provisions, had in legitimating "limitations of the rights of aliens." Gollobin does not talk about the US-Mexico border or about police-community relations specifically, but in summarizing his account, he makes the stakes at play in unrestricted deportation powers clear: "Government would thereby cease to rest on the consent of the governed but on force and violence directed against the people." Because he maintained close contact with Corona, Gollobin was aware of the kinds of "violence and force" being mustered against Mexican American communities at the time. But "Our Badge of Infamy" nevertheless represented a new evolution for the national office.[18]

The original presentation of "Our Badge of Infamy" at the United Nations drew on the antiracist, internationalist discourse of the Popular Front. Brought together under the ACPFB umbrella, immigrant rights advocates shared a similar analysis of the deportation terror. Together they deployed a developing international human rights discourse to defend Mexican Americans against depredation by Webb's "sharp edge of sovereignty." Educated by advocates on the West Coast about the conditions in Mexican American communities in California and the Southwest, the national organization pressed its case to the United Nations. While Mexican Americans were the foil for Walter Prescott Webb's vision of American democracy, the experience of the border, or what he would have called the frontier, shaped the democratic appeal represented in "Our Badge of Infamy."

The repurposing of this pamphlet also evidences the historical trajectory of immigrant rights advocacy. Historians have tended to think about the "Old" and "New" Lefts separately; it is as if a historiographical ninety-eighth meridian divides class- and party-oriented internationalism from the race-, ethnicity-, and gender identity-based anticolonialism of the "New Social Movements." But the transmission of "Our Badge of Infamy" across this division suggests that the ACPFB defied this divide by straddling it. The ACPFB suffered repression during the height of the Cold War as a Popular Front-allied organization—Executive Secretary Abner Green spent six months in jail for refusing to turn over donation records; the organization was forced to register with the Subversive Activities Control Board between 1955 and 1965; and many regular members and supporters, including large numbers of Webb's university colleagues, defected for fear of being accused of crimes of association. However, it survived because diverse and ever-changing cohorts of migrants needed it to. Despite changing political contexts, the organization's critique of state power and its defense of the rights of the foreign-born remained imperative and generative. And because the ACPFB was grounded in migrant communities, it was able to change with the times.

The repurposing of "Our Badge of Infamy" evidences the adaptability of immigrant rights advocacy as well as the flexibility of emergent, identitarian groups. Initially, in the Chicano movement, local experiences of race and oppression took precedence over questions of immigration status. Brown Beret and lifetime activist Carlos Montes explained that initially immigrant rights were not part of what he called "the struggle of Chicanos for self-determination." The slogan of the Chicano Moratorium in 1970, for example, emphasized an anti-imperialist, antiwar Chicanx identity: "¡Raza Si, Guerra, No!" Unlike the "multi-ethnic internationalism" that informed LACPFB organizing against Operation Wetback, this nationalist interpretation of "self-determination" implicitly accepted the US-Mexico border as defining the Chicanx struggle. It explored international alliances, suggesting that the *Raza* should not invest in US imperialist wars. Like the notion of community control developed by Black Power organizations such as the Black Panthers, the idea of Chicanx communities as "internal colonies" drew parallels to global imperialism, but still accepted national geopolitical boundaries.[19]

CASA drew on Corona's deep roots in the labor left, including his connection to the "multi-ethnic internationalism" of the LACPFB, to create a space for the articulation of an immigrant rights discourse amid the flowering of Chicano organizations during this period. The reissue of "Our Badge of Infamy" was part of this work. Like many contemporary workers' centers, CASA combined migrant social services with community education and political organizing. It offered legal services, English classes, and classes on the history of Mexico and the United States. Politically, CASA was involved in multiple campaigns. In a history of the organization, Corona listed as priorities the freedom of political prisoners; the founding of the National Alliance Against Racism and Political Repression; solidarity work with Chile and Puerto Rico; and labor struggles, particularly those of teamsters, cannery workers, and shipyard, dock, construction, slaughterhouse, and steel workers. This internationalism brought to light parallels between the urban experiences of Chicanx and the violence of immigration enforcement.[20]

With the advocacy of CASA and other organizations, immigrant rights became a part of the West Coast Chicano movement. In 1970 Los Angeles police killed two undocumented movement activists, Guillardo Alcazar and Guillermo Beltran Sanchez. Ruben Salazar covered the story in the movement newspaper *La Raza*.[21] The case drew attention to the question of immigrant rights, and posed the particular situation of undocumented migrants as part of a broader constellation of repression. In 1975 CASA explained the political situation:

> [T]he immigrant workers with or without papers become the target of the massive propaganda and newsmedia. He [*sic*] is also the target of the police and other repressive law enforcement bodies, the racist court system, schools, hospitals and other institutions, creating the violation of the democratic rights of the immigrant— first the undocumented, then the "legal" resident. Not only is the

Latino the one to suffer the repression, but also the citizen, when his home has been violated and searched, his car has to pass the check points and in the case of the "legal" resident, he is forced to prove his right to legally reside in the United States. There are and have been numerous occasions of Latinos being deported because they forgot their documents at home.[22]

By 1975, then, immigrant rights had become part of some Chicanx movement discourses. Fighting INS intimidation and harassment paralleled other struggles for self-determination. In 1979 when Alberto Canedo, a four-year-old child, died at the San Ysidro Port of Entry, Congressman Edward Roybal called for hearings. A CASA flyer compared the cause of justice at the border to that of stopping the war in Vietnam: "The Migra's Vietnam-like actions have caused the death, beatings, sexual abuse and other countless acts of violations of La Raza's human, civil and constitutional rights."[23]

"St. Michael v. La Migra." David Avalos, 1974. Reprinted with permission of the artist.

CASA brought immigrant rights advocacy into the Chicanx Movement. Along with other emergent movements for racial justice, and with changing migrant cohorts after the 1965 Immigration and Nationality Act, work with Chicanx community organizations transformed the ACPFB. Beginning in 1968, members of this new generation of immigrant rights advocates engaged with issues of racism and police brutality, confronting the "sharp edge of sovereignty" in America's urban centers.

The "New" Immigration Reshapes the ACPFB

In December 1968, the New York office of the ACPFB issued another pamphlet, "What Is the American Committee for the Protection of the Foreign Born?" Likely intended for distribution at protests taking place around the city over the issue of community control in the predominantly African American Ocean Hill-Brownsville school district in Brooklyn, the text linked the presence of detention camps set up under the McCarran Walter Act, Nixon's "Law and Order" campaign, and the antidissent provisions of the Eastland Bill, then on the floor of the Senate. It explained that "the prime targets of these measures would be fighters for peace and freedom—militant Blacks, Indians, Mexican-Americans, Puerto Ricans, students, trade unionists and the foreign born."[24] By naming those subject to such repressive policies, this pamphlet connects various assaults against civil rights. It also links the constituencies of the "Old Left"—trade unionists and the foreign-born—with the emerging politics of Black, Red, and Brown Power.[25]

By 1968, the ACPFB was very much in transition. The Los Angeles Committee had closed its doors in 1965, becoming the Committee to Defend the Bill of Rights. Also in 1965, the same year that the Immigration and Nationality Act ended national origins quotas, the ACPFB was removed from Subversive Activities Control Board oversight. Much of the scholarly literature asserts that "not yet white" ethnics were by this time well on their way to segregated suburban whiteness, leaving behind them urban neighborhoods and national-origins-based advocacy work. Due as much to changes in their homelands as to changing US immigration policy, increased numbers of migrants from the Caribbean and Latin America came to the United States in this period. Haitians fled the ravages of successive Duvalier regimes, whereas Salvadorans, Guatemalans, Nicaraguans, and Chileans left the political volatility of their nations of origin.

Many other migrants from the Caribbean and the Americas sought work in a low-wage service sector economy that nevertheless offered more remuneration than was available to them at home.[26]

Through the ACPFB, these newer arrivals came into contact with activists from older cohorts who continued to organize against repression and for a more just immigration policy. Through labor unions and emergent nationality and Latinx community organizations in New York, Central American and Caribbean migrants encountered more settled European migrants who nonetheless continued to organize for immigrant rights. Many European Americans became eligible for historically restricted housing and work opportunities after World War II. But this comparatively new access to whiteness did not protect those targeted for deportation or denaturalization because the reforms of 1965 left undisturbed many of anti-immigrant provisions of McCarran-Walter-era legislation. Although the 1965 act's emphasis on family reunification stood to benefit the foreign-born who sought to bring their relatives over, many immigrant rights advocates continued to see the 1965 law as anti-immigrant. In 1967 Gollobin wrote in an ACPFB pamphlet entitled "The Foreign Born and the Bill of Rights," "[I]t soon became clear that the new law is the most restrictive in U.S. history. Instead of merely discriminating against certain people, the United States now bans immigrants from all nations unless they have close family ties or prove that their labor is needed."[27]

Like Gollobin, other ACPFB advocates questioned the direction of the 1965 reforms. Because of their long experience with federal repression, they were keenly aware of the survival of Cold War policies. The new law left Smith Act provisions for "alien" registration on the books, it kept legal provisions against the entry of suspected "subversives," and it maintained deportation as a technology of immigration enforcement. Immigrant rights activists had long campaigned for a statute of limitations on deportation and denaturalization, to avoid the widespread practice of deporting older immigrants on the basis of suspected political alliances decades in the past, but Congress declined to implement these much-needed reforms. Prior to 1965, despite being constrained in its lobbying because of its status as a suspected subversive organization, the ACPFB had worked for immigration reform that would have abolished the "distinctions between native and naturalized citizens to insure full protection of our laws to all." The 1965 act did not realize this radical vision.[28]

As a result, the ACPFB continued to represent European immigrants in their struggles with denaturalization and deportation. Both the New York and Los Angeles offices represented Greek American Gus Polites against deportation in the early 1960s. Polites, described in ACPFB publicity as a "trade unionist and leader in the Greek community," had been honored by Franklin Delano Roosevelt for his "anti-Fascist leadership" during World War II. He became a citizen in 1942, but was denaturalized in 1953 on grounds of prior membership in the Communist Party. This denaturalization rendered him deportable. The ACPFB lost the case, and Polites was deported in 1963. He left a native-born wife, children, and grandchildren. Polites's death in 1968 prompted the ACPFB to note that congressional failure to enact a statute of limitations on deportation had resulted in the "heartless destruction of an American family."[29]

Because they continued to be affected by "the deportation terror," many European American immigrants continued to support the ACPFB's fight against INS repression. Despite their increasing access to the benefits of whiteness, many European Americans recognized the threat to members of their communities posed by provisions allowing for continued repression against foreign-born activists, artists, and journalists. Many of these people were union members and progressive activists. Even without deportation, denaturalization alone meant the loss of the benefits of citizenship, including social security for retired or disabled individuals. The Committee worked to oppose denaturalization in cases like those of Elsie Leger and Beryl Davis, who had to stop working because of illness and lost their social security benefits in Pennsylvania. In New York, ACPFB events continued to bring sponsorship from Finnish, Italian, Estonian, Irish, Lithuanian, Polish, Russian, Hungarian, and Ukrainian organizations into the 1970s.[30]

Even if they were, by some measures, "becoming white," many foreign-born denizens, particularly those who were or had been progressive activists, experienced what the ACPFB called "second class citizenship," because they lived with the fears of deportation and loss. Advocates saluted the family reunification provisions of the 1965 Act while noting the irony that the law still allowed for the destruction of immigrant families already living in the country. In the words of a 1967 pamphlet: "[A] foreign-born person is never secure in his residence and citizenship. Even after a lifetime here, he can be denaturalized and deported. There is no time limit. In recent years, even grandfathers and grandmothers have been torn from their families, sent to countries completely strange to them, whose language they do not speak, and deprived of means of support since even their social security is cut off by law."[31]

Individuals subject to denaturalization and deportation, then, tended not to experience the benefits of "whiteness" as much as the ongoing depredations of being foreign born.

Consistent with its history as a Popular Front organization, the ACPFB had always maintained strong allies in the labor movement. Many of the progressive, foreign-born activists targeted for deportation had been involved in union organizing and labor politics. While many unions moved away from such progressive alliances because of the impact of anti-Communist measures like the Taft-Hartley Act (1948), other trade unionists recognized the ongoing importance of the immigrant rights struggle for labor organizing and workers' rights in general. The unions most likely to be engaged with immigrant rights in this period employed migrants from Latin America and the Caribbean: the Hotel Trades Council, Amalgamated Meat Cutters, the Ship Clerks' Association, the United Furniture Workers' Union, the Drug and Hospital Employees, and the Hotel, Restaurant, and Club Employees Union. Henry Foner represented the Joint Board of the Fur, Leather and Machine Workers Union in the ACPFB. Foner criticized the anti-immigrant politics of many unions, and the common practice in the period of calling on the INS to raid shops using undocumented labor. As a second-generation immigrant himself, Foner recognized the centrality of immigrants, and therefore of immigrant rights, to labor struggles: "[T]here is a new kind of foreign-born: the old type had declined. The new is younger with different ideas."[32]

As immigrant rights advocates surveyed the political terrain of the late 1960s and early 1970s, they observed similar kinds of repression being directed against activists, people of color, and the foreign-born. A discourse of community control, emanating from the struggles of black, Latinx, and native communities with urban policing, education, and housing, described this kind of repression in terms of police brutality. This discourse framed repression differently than the Cold War progressive rhetoric of Fascism and democracy. But it described similar things: detention and deportation without due process for the foreign-born; the threat to citizens of detention in camps authorized by the McCarran Act of 1950; and constant raids by police, the FBI, and the INS. An ACPFB "Statement on the Struggle Against a Police State" proclaimed in 1968: "Brutal repression has become reaction's reply to the powerful, broadening mass movements for human rights and human dignity that are sweeping across our country. To Black people, to Indians, to Mexican-Americans, to Puerto Ricans, to dissenting young people, to militant workers and to the foreign born—to all who seek their rightful place in the sun of freedom—the answer is being given: KEEP OUT!"[33]

For the ACPFB, repression against the foreign-born had a long history. The internationalism of the organization's 1969 holiday card invoked the long fetch of anti-imperialism in immigrant rights organizing, and at the same time managed to strike a contemporary note: "Immigration authorities have intensified their illegal harassment of Latin Americans (especially Dominicans), Greeks, Iranians and other national groups who are seeking the support of the American people in the fight against the dictatorships ruling their countries." This combination of anti-imperialism and immigrant rights advocacy would have been familiar to older cohorts of the foreign born; it also reached out to the new constituencies converging in New York City at the time.[34]

The ACPFB drew on its antiracist internationalism to critique changing immigration policies. At the same time, the organization brought to emergent social movements an understanding that many denizens of aggrieved, urban communities were also foreign-born. In its analysis, struggles for urban empowerment included ongoing work for immigrant rights. In the post-1965 period, coalitions for immigrant rights increasingly came to include leadership from newly arrived Haitian and Latin American cohorts.

In 1972 President Nixon's appointed INS Commissioner, Leonard Chapman, initiated "Area Control Operations." Like Joseph Swing, who had orchestrated Operation Wetback, Chapman was retired military; he had served in the Marine Corps in the Pacific Arena during World War II and was promoted to general by Johnson during the Vietnam War. Perhaps because both men had prior military experience, they tended to see issues of immigration in terms of counterinsurgency strategy. As ethnic studies scholar Eric Tang points out, by the late 1960s, military counterinsurgency strategies originating in the proxy wars of the Cold War era gained traction as a means of establishing "law and order" in urban policy circles.[35]

Like Swing's Operation Wetback, Area Control Operations took the form of urban dragnets against what ACPFB attorney Ira Gollobin described as "Latin-looking persons." They targeted immigrant neighborhoods and workplaces, often taking the form of workplace raids. As described in a joint letter from the ACPFB and the Coalition of Latin Americans/Friends of Latin America of Jackson Heights in 1972, "Immigration authorities have been conducting a series of dragnet raids—on a subway station, at a dance hall, on the street, anywhere. Thousands have already been victimized, if they were dark skinned and looked Latino."[36]

Typical of those caught in the Area Control Operations dragnets were three Ecuadorian migrants arrested in Queens in November 1975. At 7:30 a.m., a Mr. and Mrs. Miguel Marquez, also with Mrs. Marquez's sister, were on their way to work when they were stopped by the INS. The two women showed green cards, but they were still arrested and detained. INS District Director Maurice Killy described the reasons for their arrest: "their dress, what clothes appear to be foreign manufacture...work clothes, carrying their lunch; general facial structure; speaking in a foreign language; and the location.... There were large concentrations of illegal aliens." The ACPFB sued the INS for civil rights damages under a 1975 Supreme Court decision that ruled random arrests based on appearances illegal; the case was successful, even if recognition of it was limited.[37]

The INS continued to target Latinx and other racialized immigrants throughout the 1970s. This, in turn, transformed the coalition advocating for immigrant rights. For example, in 1973 the ACPFB participated in a New York City protest rally against the "immigration dragnet." The rally drew together a broad array of comparatively new Latin American and Caribbean national associations, such as the Circulo Social Salvadoreño and the Haitian American Citizens Society, along with some unions whose membership combined newer immigrants with European American workers.

Immigrant rights advocates collaborated nationally to respond to dragnets at the local level. They deployed geographic organizing as well as historical memory to respond to repression against the foreign-born. For example, as they considered the cases of Vietnamese students threatened with deportation because of their antiwar activism, ACPFB council members in New York recalled the ACPFB's defense of Korean American expatriates during the Cold War.[38]

On their separate coasts, but linked through their correspondence and political connections, Ira Gollobin, Rose Chernin, and Bert Corona collaborated to create charters asserting basic human rights for immigrants that responded to the depredations of dragnets and police brutality. In a 1974 pamphlet, "The Foreign Born and the Bill of Rights," Gollobin drew on California labor history to oppose an employer sanctions bill being considered in New York State: "[T]he experience of California demonstrated that such legislation results in a climate of fear, causing many employers to refuse to hire even [legal] residents; such laws lead to racial discrimination against Latin American workers and depress the wage standards of *all* workers; such laws permit unscrupulous employers to require foreign born employees to sign a statement that they are authorized to work, thereby keeping persons not authorized to work in a state of virtual peonage; such laws lead to unconstitutional raids by Immigration authorities."[39]

In the late 1960s and early 1970s the ACPFB drew on collaborative channels linking the now New York-based organization to struggles taking place in other locations and times. This ability to connect and repurpose allowed the organization to become useful to new cohorts of foreign-born coming into uncomfortable proximity with the "sharp edge of sovereignty." The frontier of these renewed struggles, in turn, transformed both the organization and immigrant rights advocacy in general.

Successive crises around the question of asylum for refugees from Haiti after the 1971 death of François "Papa Doc" Duvalier and the transition to the even more autocratic rule of his son, Jean Claude "Baby Doc" Duvalier, transformed immigration enforcement as well as popular and activist discourses. Advocacy for Haitians was central to the cause of immigrant rights during the 1970s. While the immigrant rights coalition saw those fleeing the repressive Duvalier regime as refugees deserving of asylum and shelter, federal policy perceived them as unauthorized economic migrants to be detained and deported. In the wake of World War II, both international and US policy recognized refugees as particular kinds of migrants whose plight made them eligible for asylum and aid. But the longstanding US alliance with the Duvaliers made the State Department unwilling to indict conditions in Haiti as instilling in migrants the "well-founded fear" stipulated in international refugee policy. As Haitians fled the Duvalier regime in the 1970s, many immigrant and civil rights advocates saw this division as based more on white supremacy and corrupt political alliances than the circumstances of migration.

Nevertheless, Haitians fled their country and took to the sea in large numbers. Many reached other Caribbean nations, such as Cuba, where they were welcomed, or the Bahamas, where they had few legal rights; others either made it to Florida or were rescued by the Coast Guard and detained there. These Haitian refugees arrived in a nation driven once again by a panic surrounding "illegal aliens" generated by the potent combination of economic downturn and the high-profile dragnet raids on immigrant communities generated by Area Control Operations. Without a broad national consensus on their refugee status, Haitians were received as undocumented, unwelcomed migrants.

In Miami, many refugees were housed at the Krome Avenue Detention Center. Ira Gollobin served as legal counsel for the National Council of Churches' District Court case to allow these Haitian detainees access to due process. Immigrant rights advocates blocked what they called a "sneak deportation" of Haitian refugees in Miami in 1975. In the same year, forty-seven Haitians were relocated from Miami to a detention facility in El Paso after their applications for political asylum were denied: they awaited deportation to Haiti. [40]

The statement of detainee Joseph Simann typified many of the stories of the El Paso Haitians. The Duvalierist secret police, the Tonton Macoute, asked him, his brother, and his father to guard returned refugees at the police station in their small town. Sympathizing with the situation of the returnees, they refused and were consequently detained and beaten. Simann's father died; Joseph escaped and fled to the Bahamas, where eventually his identity was revealed to the Haitian Embassy in Nassau. At that point, he fled to the United States.[41]

The ACPFB, practiced in identifying the white supremacy of immigration policy, worked in coalition with Haitian and other immigrant community groups on legal advocacy and political action. As leftists, they recognized the gap separating the federal welcome for Cuban "refugees" and the deportation of Haitians. Further, the organization had long criticized the racism of immigration enforcement. Promoting the treatment of Haitian refugees as "the most acute foreign born issue confronting the American people," they portrayed Haitian refugees as "the Pilgrims of Today!" They decried the violation of international protocol in the "preventive detention," en masse, of Haitians while their cases were being considered. Haitian refugees were given secret interviews, and had no opportunity to present witnesses or to provide documentation on their cases. When released from detention, they were not given temporary work permits to enable them to earn a living. As raids on New York Haitian

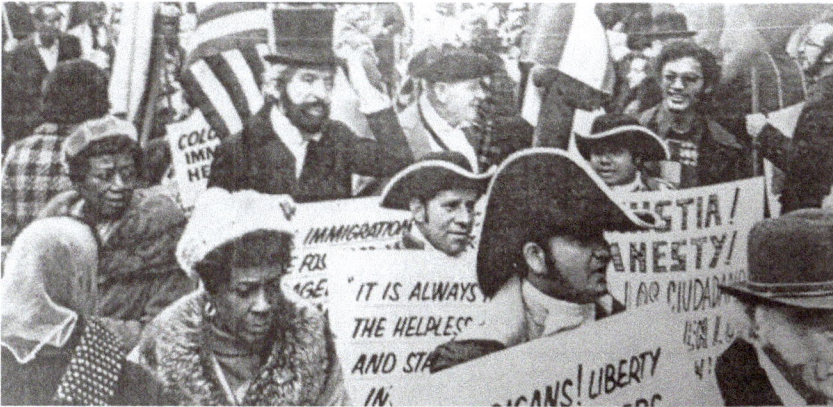

"The North American nation began with European immigrants who fled from religious and political persecution. Today, more than 200 years after its founding, Immigration authorities have begun a merciless pursuit of immigrants who come in search of a better standard of living." ACPFB, "In Defense of Foreign Born," *El Tiempo: El Diario de Todos Los Hispanos*, March 12, 1972. Image courtesy of the Tamiment Library and Robert F. Wagner Labor Archives, University of New York.

communities continued, the Ad Hoc Committee for the Defense of Haitian Refugees press release asserted that "organizers believe these raids represent an attempt to silence the growing protests" against the immigration dragnets. While it commented on the particular situation of Haitians, the press release reflected the familiarity of ACPFB advocates like Gollobin with the repression of immigrant rights advocacy.[42]

Immigrant rights advocates across the United States publicly mourned the suicide of Turenne Déville in immigration custody in 1974. After a fight with the Tonton Macoutes, Déville was jailed. Fearing death, he escaped to Nassau, in the Bahamas. Finding no asylum in Nassau, he found a boat to Miami, where he was taken into INS custody and jailed. Like many Haitians who arrived in Florida, Déville knew he had little hope of survival if he was returned into the hands of the Macoutes. The night before his scheduled deportation to Haiti, Déville hung himself in his cell. In his suicide note, he explained: "In Haiti there is no justice. The poor must die prematurely, often asphyxiated in jail. In Haiti's jail there is no food, no water.... I can't go back. If the regime falls today, I'm ready to go back; otherwise I'll not go back there. If the United States refuses to help me, send me to Africa."[43]

Déville's funeral was held at the Friendship Baptist Church in Miami. Those who attended received a flyer with his testimony about his experiences in Haiti and Nassau, and his request to be sent to Africa rather than being deported to Haiti. Added at the bottom was a statement, addressed to "Pallbearers, Fellow Haitian Brothers": "We the Black people of the Model City area and all concerned human beings of Dade County do hereby declare that our Black Haitian Brother Turenne Déville is now and forever as long as there are concerned citizens in Dade County...a citizen of Dade County and our community."[44]

Déville eluded deportation by killing himself. At his funeral, mourners asserted a radical vision of immigrant rights, in which foreign-born denizens could claim full citizenship as part of their human rights. This vision continued to inform the work of immigrant rights activists in the decades that followed. By the time the ACPFB closed its doors in 1982, many other immigrant rights organizations had formed. They continued the struggle, pressing for an amnesty partially realized in federal legislation in 1986, and inspiring new organizing in labor and civil rights communities into the early twenty-first century.

Conclusion: The "Long Fetch" of Struggles at the "Sharp Edge of Sovereignty"

Throughout the final thirteen years of the American Committee for the Protection of the Foreign Born, concerns about new migrant cohorts continued to influence the organization's work and its alliances on the ground. Shaped and guided by its coalitions with community groups, this Popular Front organization adapted to changing political contexts and survived well into the Reagan years.

Walter Prescott Webb envisioned a single frontier of Anglo-American settlement as having infused American life with its particular democratic institutions. In a neoliberal era in which national boundaries are continuously being challenged by the migration of capital as well as by coercive international trade agreements, there is no single frontier. Cultural, economic, and geographic boundaries are continually being reshaped; at the same time, successive waves of migration bring new groups of foreign-born arrivals to the United States. So the frontier does continually reinvigorate democracy, although in a different way than Webb envisioned. As frontiers change and the "sharp edge of sovereignty" cleaves new boundaries, immigrant rights advocates continually re-envision democratic citizenship.

Notes

1. Walter Prescott Webb, "Ended: 400 Year Boom: Reflections on the Age of the Frontier," *Harper's Magazine*, October 1951, 25–33.

2. Walter Prescott Webb, *The Texas Rangers: A Century of Frontier Defense* (Austin: University of Texas Press, 1965). For a revisionist take on agriculture and the West, see Frieda Knobloch, *The Culture of Wilderness: Agriculture as Colonization in the American West* (Chapel Hill: University of North Carolina, 1996); for struggles over settlement, see George Sanchez, *Becoming Mexican American: Ethnicity, Culture and Identity in Mexican American Los Angeles, 1900–1945* (New York: Oxford University Press, 1993), especially 38–39.

3. Walter Prescott Webb, *The Great Frontier* (Reno: University of Nevada Press, 2003), 2.

4. Webb, *The Great Frontier*, 3–4.

5. Daniel Kanstroom, *Deportation Nation: Outsiders in U.S. History* (Cambridge: Harvard University Press, 2007), 37.

6. George Lipsitz, *Footsteps in the Dark: The Hidden History of Popular Music* (Minneapolis: University of Minnesota Press, 2007), vii–viii.

7. United States v. Brignoni Ponce, 422 U.S. 873, 1974, https://supreme.justia.com/cases/federal/us/422/873/case.html (accessed February 18, 2016). On the history of urban raids, see Anna Pegler Gordon, *In Sight of America: Photography and the Development of U.S. Immigration Policy* (Berkeley: University of California Press, 2005), especially 67–103; Kelly Lytle Hernandez, *Migra!: A History of the U.S. Border Patrol* (Berkeley: University of California Press, 2010), especially 169–96.

8. On Operation Wetback, see Natalia Molina, *How Race Is Made in America: Immigration, Citizenship and the Historical Power of Racial Scripts* (Berkeley: University of California Press, 2014); David Gutiérrez, *Walls and Mirrors: Mexican Americans, Mexican Immigrants, and the Politics of Ethnicity* (Berkeley: University of California Press, 1995); Hernandez, *Migra!*; also Mai Ngai, *Impossible Subjects: Illegal Aliens and the Making of Modern America* (Princeton: Princeton University Press, 2004).

9. Letter from Josephine Yanez, LACPFB, to Abner Green, May 18, 1956, Folder 4, Box 1, LACPFB Papers, Southern California Research Library; Patricia Morgan, "Shame of a Nation: Police-State Terror Against Mexican-Americans in the U.S.A.," Los Angeles, L.A. Committee for the Protection of the Foreign Born, 1954, in Morris Fromkin Collection, University of Wisconsin-Milwaukee. On MacWilliams, see Michael Denning, *The Cultural Front* (New York: Verso, 1997). "Multi-ethnic internationalism" is Denning's phrase.

10. David Bacon, *The Right to Stay Home: How U.S. Policy Drives Mexican Migration* (Boston: Beacon Press, 2013).

11. "Synopsis of Proposed Petition to United Nations Commission on Human Rights Dealing with the Problems Facing Mexicans in the United States," Box 2, Folder 8; "Our Badge of Infamy: A Petition to the United States on the Treatment

of the Mexican Immigrant," published by the American Committee for the Protection of the Foreign Born, April 17, 1959, Box 1, Folder "1956–1959," both in ACPFB Papers, Tamiment Library, New York University (hereafter Tamiment). On the Silex case, see my *Against the Deportation Terror: Organizing for Immigrant Rights in the Twentieth Century* (Philadelphia: Temple University Press, 2017).

12. Gutiérrez, *Walls and Mirrors*, 173.

13. Molina, *How Race Is Made in America*, 117; George Sanchez, "'What's Good for Boyle Heights Is Good for the Jews': Creating a Multiracialism on the Eastside during the 1950s," *American Quarterly* 56, no. 3 (September 2004): 633–61; see also Jeffrey Garcilazo, "McCarthyism, Mexican Americans and the Los Angeles Committee for the Protection of the Foreign-Born, 1950–1954," *Western Historical Quarterly* 32, no. 3 (fall 2001): 273–93; Harry Carlisle (probable author), "Brief History of the Los Angeles Committee for the Protection of the Foreign Born," August 26, 1955, Box 1, Tamiment.

14. Bill of Rights Conference Highlights, 1971, in Folder "1969–1974," Box 1, Tamiment.

15. Typed manuscript, Louise Pettibone Smith biography, Box 1, Folder "Biographical Information: Louise Pettibone Smith," ACPFB Papers, Joseph A. Labadie Collection, University of Michigan, Ann Arbor (hereafter Labadie).

16. Mario Garcia, *Memories of Chicano History: The Life and Narrative of Bert Corona* (Berkeley: University of California Press, 2004), 119.

17. "The Racist Content of the Walter-McCarran Law (A Preliminary Memorandum), for New York Conference to Repeal the Walter-McCarran Law and Defend Its Victims," February 27, 1954, Yugoslav-American Hall, New York, NY, Box 1, Folder "1951–1954," Tamiment.

18. Ira Gollobin, "Democracy and the Deportation Laws," *Jewish Life*, June 1948, 16–19.

19. Carlos Montes, Interview with author, October 2013, Milwaukee.

20. CASA Bilingual Flyer, in Folder "Asociación Nacional Mexico-America, 1952," Box 29, Bert Corona Papers, (M248) 1923–1984, Stanford University Libraries, Special Collections (hereafter Corona Papers); also Garcia, *Memories of Chicano History*, 72–74; typed history of CASA in Corona Papers, Folder 8, Box 29.

21. Notes in Folder 11, "CASA Papers, Flyers and Misc. Notes, 1973–75," Corona Papers, Box 28. Carlos Montes advised me of the significance of this case, but could not recall the names of the murder victims when we spoke.

22. Pamphlet in Folder 7, CASA Documents, Box 29, Corona Papers.

23. Flyer, "Stop Border Killings," in Folder 11, Box 10, Corona Papers.

24. In Folder "Publicity/Activities/Events: 1968 Fight Back Rally, 12/15," Box 8, Labadie.

25. On Ocean Hill-Brownsville, see Jerold Podair, *The Strike That Changed New York: Blacks, Whites and the Ocean Hill-Brownsville Conflict* (New Haven: Yale University Press, 2002); Adina Back, "Blacks, Jews and the Struggle to Integrate Brooklyn's Junior High School 258: A Cold War Story," *Journal of Ethnic History* 20, no. 2 (winter 2001): 38–69.

26. See David Roediger, *Working toward Whiteness: How America's Immigrants*

Became White: The Strange Journey from Ellis Island to the Suburbs (New York: Basic Books, 2006); Matthew Frye Jacobson, *Whiteness of a Different Color: European Immigrants and the Alchemy of Race* (Cambridge: Harvard University Press, 1999); Thomas Sugrue, *The Origins of the Urban Crisis: Race and Inequality in Postwar Detroit* (Princeton: Princeton University Press, 2014).

27. In Folder "1960–1968," Box 2, Tamiment.

28. "Invitation to a National Meeting for the Rights of Foreign Born Americans, Jan. 14 & 15, 1961," in Folder "1960–1968," Box 2, Tamiment.

29. Press releases, April 3, 1967, and "Gus Polites (Greek) Dies in Exile," Folder "1960–1968," Box 2, Tamiment.

30. "Bill of Rights Conference Highlights," 1971, Folder "1960–1968," Box 2, Tamiment.

31. "Why? Exile and Second Class Citizenship," 1967, Folder "1960–1968," Box 2, Tamiment.

32. Minutes of Council Meeting, May 4, 1972, in Folder "Administration: Council Minutes, 1968–1972," Box 1, Labadie; also oral history interview with Henry Foner by Daniel Soyer, ILGWU Heritage Project, Kheel Center, Cornell University, http://ilgwu.ilr.cornell.edu/archives/oralHistories/HenryFoner.html. For unions engaged in immigrant rights, see Folder 3, "Ad Hoc Committee Against Repression in Haiti," Box 21, Ira Gollobin Haitian Refugees Collection, Schomburg Center for Research in Black Culture, New York (hereafter Schomburg); also "In Defense of Foreign Born," from *El Tiempo: El Diario de Todos Los Hispanos*, New York, March 12, 1972, in Folder "1969–1974," Box 2, Tamiment.

33. In Folder "1960–1968," Box 2, Tamiment.

34. In Folder "1969–1974," Box 2, Tamiment.

35. Eric Tang, *Unsettled: Cambodian Americans in the Hyperghetto* (Philadelphia: Temple University Press, 2015), 58–59.

36. "The Bill of Rights and the Foreign Born," speech given by Gollobin at Immigration Conference of New York Lawyers, February 22, 1975, in Folder 24, "The Bill of Rights of the Foreign Born, 1975," Box 9, Corona Papers; and "Letter," December 28, 1972, Folder "1969–1974," Box 2, Tamiment.

37. Press Release, "Important Disclosures in Damage Suit Against Immigration Dragnet Arrests," March 22, 1976, Folder 9, Box 21, Schomburg.

38. Minutes of Council Meeting, May 4, 1972, Folder "Administration: Council Minutes, 1968–1972," Box 1, Labadie.

39. "Will the Immigration Dragnet Reach You?"; "The Foreign Born and the Bill of Rights"; and Letter from Gollobin to Corona, August 12, 1974, all in Folder "1968–1974," Box 1, Tamiment; "Charter of Rights for Immigrant Workers," Folder 9, Box 10, Corona Papers.

40. Manny Ontiveros, "13 Haitians Face Deportation," from *El Paso Herald Post*, January 13, 1977, in Folder 15, "*Louis v. Nelson*, 1977," Box 4, Schomburg; "The Treatment of Haitian 'Boat People'—A National Scandal, 1979," "The Foreign Born and the Bill of Rights," and "Press Release: Alert Action Blocks Sneak Deportation of Haitian Refugees in Miami: Tragedy Averted," January 4, 1975, all in Folder 6, Box 2, Tamiment.

41. Statement of Joseph Simann, June 25, 1977, in Folder 15: "*Louis v. Nelson*, 1977," Box 4, Schomburg.

42. Press release, Grand Army Demonstration, 1974, Folder 4: "Grand Army Demo, 1974," Box 21, Schomburg.

43. Suicide note in "Flyer #5: Ad Hoc Committee for the Defense of Haitian Refugees Meeting Notes, Info on Haiti," Box 21, Schomburg.

44. Flyer from Déville's funeral, in Folder "1969–1974," Box 2, Tamiment.

About the Contributors

Rachel Ida Buff teaches history and comparative ethnic studies at the University of Wisconsin-Milwaukee. Her latest book is *Against the Deportation Terror: Organizing for Immigrant Rights in the Twentieth Century* (2017).

Donna R. Gabaccia is professor of history at the University of Toronto. She is the author of many books and articles on gender, class, and foodways among American immigrants; on Italian migration around the world; and on migration in global history. Her most recent book, *Gender and International Migration* (2015), won an honorable mention from the American Sociological Association's Thomas and Znaniecki Prize.

David C. LaFevor teaches Latin American history at the University of Texas at Arlington. His latest book is *The Third Century: A History of U.S.-Latin American Relations* (with Mark T. Gilderhus, 2017). His current book project is a history of prizefighting, masculinity, and national identity in Cuba and Mexico.

Natalia Molina's work lies at the intersections of race, gender, culture, and citizenship. She is the author of two award-winning books, *Fit to Be Citizens? Public Health and Race in Los Angeles, 1879–1939* (2006) and *How Race Is Made in America: Immigration, Citizenship, and the Historical Power of Racial Scripts* (2014). She is currently expanding her article, "The Importance of Place and Place-Makers in the Life of a Los Angeles Community: What Gentrification Erases from Echo Park," into a book.

Emily Pope-Obeda is a lecturer in the History and Literature program at Harvard University. Her work centers on migration, race and ethnicity, and labor and working-class history. She is currently working on a book manuscript on the growth of the deportation state in the 1920s.

Cristina Salinas is assistant professor of history at the University of Texas at Arlington and teaches courses in Mexican American history and ethnic studies. Her book, *Managed Migrations: Growers, Farmworkers, and U.S.-Mexico Border Enforcement in the Twentieth Century*, will be published in 2018.

Pablo Yankelevich is professor and researcher at the Centro de Estudios Históricos of El Colegio de México. He is editor of the journal *Historia Mexicana* and director of the book series Historias Mínimas (El Colegio de México). He conducts research in Mexican contemporary history, the history of Latin American exiles and political refugees, and the history of migration in Mexico. He is currently developing a project focused on social exclusion, discrimination, and racism in postrevolutionary Mexico. His latest books are *Ráfagas de un exilio: Argentinos en México* (2010); *¿Deseables o inconvenientes? Las fronteras de la extranjería en México posrevolucionario* (2011); *Exile and the Politics of Exclusion in the Americas* (coedited with Luis Roniger and James Green, 2012); *Migración y Racismo: Contribuciones a la historia de los extranjeros en México* (2015); and *Raza y política en Iberoamérica* (coedited with Tomás Pérez Vejo, 2017).

Elliot Young is professor of Latin American and borderlands history at Lewis & Clark College in Portland, Oregon. His most recent book is *Alien Nation: Chinese Migration in the Americas, the Coolie Era to WWII* (2014). Professor Young has published two other books on borderlands history: *Catarino Garza's Revolution on the Texas-Mexico Border* (2004) and *Continental Crossroads* (2004).

Kenyon Zimmer is associate professor of history at the University of Texas at Arlington and has written extensively on the intersection of migration and political radicalism. He is the author of *Immigrants against the State: Yiddish and Italian Anarchism in America* (2015) and coeditor of *Wobblies of the World: A Global History of the IWW* (2017).

Other Titles in the Walter Prescott Webb Memorial Lectures Series

Index

www.ingramcontent.com/pod-product-compliance
Lightning Source LLC
Chambersburg PA
CBHW072000260326
41914CB00004B/878